THE COMPLETE IDIOT'S GUIDE TO

DASH Diet Cooking

by Deirdre Rawlings, ND, PhD, MH

ALPHA

A member of Penguin Group (USA) Inc.

This book is dedicated to my mother, Jeanne, who inspired me with an understanding of nutrition and the healing powers of food.

ALPHA BOOKS

Published by the Penguin Group

Penguin Group (USA) Inc., 375 Hudson Street, New York, New York 10014, USA • Penguin Group (Canada), 90 Eglinton Avenue East, Suite 700, Toronto, Ontario M4P 2Y3, Canada (a division of Pearson Penguin Canada Inc.) • Penguin Books Ltd., 80 Strand, London WC2R 0RL, England • Penguin Ireland, 25 St. Stephen's Green, Dublin 2, Ireland (a division of Penguin Books Ltd.) • Penguin Group (Australia), 250 Camberwell Road, Camberwell, Victoria 3124, Australia (a division of Pearson Australia Group Pty. Ltd.) • Penguin Books India Pvt. Ltd., 11 Community Centre, Panchsheel Park, New Delhi—110 017, India • Penguin Group (NZ), 67 Apollo Drive, Rosedale, North Shore, Auckland 1311, New Zealand (a division of Pearson New Zealand Ltd.) • Penguin Books (South Africa) (Pty.) Ltd., 24 Sturdee Avenue, Rosebank, Johannesburg 2196, South Africa • Penguin Books Ltd., Registered Offices: 80 Strand, London WC2R 0RL, England

Copyright © 2012 by Deirdre Rawlings, ND, PhD, MH

International Standard Book Number: 978-1-61564-166-6
Library of Congress Catalog Card Number: 2011941054

14   13   12   8   7   6   5   4   3   2   1

Interpretation of the printing code: The rightmost number of the first series of numbers is the year of the book's printing; the rightmost number of the second series of numbers is the number of the book's printing. For example, a printing code of 12-1 shows that the first printing occurred in 2012.

Printed in the United States of America

Note: This publication contains the opinions and ideas of its author. It is intended to provide helpful and informative material on the subject matter covered. It is sold with the understanding that the author and publisher are not engaged in rendering professional services in the book. If the reader requires personal assistance or advice, a competent professional should be consulted.

The author and publisher specifically disclaim any responsibility for any liability, loss, or risk, personal or otherwise, which is incurred as a consequence, directly or indirectly, of the use and application of any of the contents of this book.

Most Alpha books are available at special quantity discounts for bulk purchases for sales promotions, premiums, fund-raising, or educational use. Special books, or book excerpts, can also be created to fit specific needs.

For details, write: Special Markets, Alpha Books, 375 Hudson Street, New York, NY 10014.

Publisher: *Marie Butler-Knight*

Associate Publisher: *Mike Sanders*

Executive Managing Editor: *Billy Fields*

Senior Acquisitions Editor: *Brook Farling*

Development Editor: *Nancy Lewis*

Senior Production Editor: *Janette Lynn*

Copy Editor: *Amy Borrelli*

Cover Designer: *Rebecca Batchelor*

Book Designers: *William Thomas, Rebecca Batchelor*

Indexer: *Tonya Heard*

Layout: *Ayanna Lacey*

Senior Proofreader: *Laura Caddell*

ALWAYS LEARNING   PEARSON

Contents

Part 2: Good-Start DASH Breakfasts 59

Introduction

If lowering your blood pressure is important, perhaps crucial, in order to improve the health of your heart and extend your quality of life, then this book will help you. The principles of DASH work because the diet contains key nutrients and balanced amounts of food servings to achieve the goal of lowered blood pressure. You'll not only find sound, scientific explanations for eating this way, but I've simplified and condensed the science behind it. I've broken it down into easy-to-understand chunks of information so that you can make it fit easily into your lifestyle and start working right away. The meal plans will make it simple to follow as you get started with your DASH diet. You'll find marked improvements in as little as 7 to 14 days.

The DASH diet focuses on nutrient-dense whole foods that contain a full array of minerals and vitamins as Mother Nature originally intended. Rather than focusing on how many milligrams of this mineral or that vitamin, you will simply be eating the whole foods from which they are derived. Eating the types of foods that you will find in the book's recipes will teach you the real basics of good nutrition and build a strong platform from which you can thrive. You'll witness the thrill of watching your blood pressure and cholesterol numbers go down, as your energy and vitality levels go up.

How This Book Is Organized

I've broken this book into five parts to help make it easier for you to implement your new DASH diet healthy-eating plan. Each part provides you with foundations from which to build on, including understanding the basics of how to put the DASH diet to work for you, meal planning, cooking, and implementation.

Part 1, What the DASH Diet's All About, navigates the scientific rationale behind the diet and discusses how and why it works. You'll discover the essential key nutrients your body needs daily that have numerous benefits to your health and controlling hypertension, as well as what foods they are abundantly found in. You'll discover exactly what a balanced diet really looks like and, with a few adjustments of your own, how to obtain it. We'll go into the proven principles of DASH and what makes them work, and then put them to the test on you personally with the 1-, 2-, and 3-week meal plans I've created. Finally, you'll get to see some nutrition principles that are effective and really works for you.

Part 2, Good-Start DASH Breakfasts, dives directly into food; it's all about starting your day off on the right foot with the right food. Whether you're a busy executive who drives through rush-hour traffic each day to get to the office and back, a mother of two toddlers, or a frequent traveler forced to dine out a lot, this diet can work for you. You'll find a selection of quick and easy weekday breakfasts that properly nourish and sustain you, as well as some satisfying leisurely weekend morning meals when you can give yourself the gift of more time to enjoy them. You may also enjoy some new-to-you ingredients that you can easily find at your local supermarket.

Part 3, Midday Meals and Anytime Snacks, introduces you to some scrumptious salads and delicious dressings that you will soon be enjoying on a regular basis as part of your daily dietary practice. You quite possibly may even find this to become a ritual that you really look forward to. You'll find many of your favorite dishes with some slight modifications to some of the ingredients. They taste delicious and will satisfy not only your appetite but also your waistline as your body gets leaner and stronger.

Part 4, On the Dinner Menu, brings us to dinner entrées, side dishes, and accompaniments such as breads. I've given you a wide range of offerings to suit most, if not all, of your dietary choices and preferences. As vegetables are very much a main fare in the DASH diet because of their high fiber and other essential nutrients, you'll find no shortage of vegetable selections to choose from. Seafood is also a great way to get our daily requirement of essential fatty acids, so I've included some fish choices among the heart-healthiest dishes. Some of your good old favorites are also included, except that they are enhanced in ways to sustain your health and vitality.

Part 5, Delectable Desserts, is where you'll find wonderful and delicious desserts and treats for those special occasions when your taste buds are invited to choose for you. It's perfectly within your heart-healthy diet to indulge yourself every so often with some sweets. It all boils down to the quality and nutrients within those dessert recipes. Fortunately, Mother Nature made sure that natural foods taste better than most, and there are lots of healthy foods to choose from.

The appendixes are an added bonus for you. You'll find some grocery shopping lists for the meal plans, as well as some helpful and enlightening nutritional information. I've included some fantastic resources for foods and other products, as well as further reading and other good-to-know stuff.

Extras

As you read through the book, you will notice bonus boxes that contain definitions, tips, warnings, and miscellaneous information to help in your understanding of the subject matter.

DEFINITION

These boxes provide you with the meaning of terms that are relevant to the topic at hand.

WARNING

These boxes provide you with things to watch out for regarding your heart and health.

GOOD TO KNOW

These boxes provide you with helpful information to maximize the results of your DASH diet.

HEART-HEALTHY TIP

These boxes provide you with helpful information concerning nutrients, latest studies, or advice that is good to know and increases your level of understanding.

Acknowledgments

First of all, thank you to the nutrition researchers, dietitians, medical doctors, research groups, steering committee, writers, members of the DASH Collaborate Research Group, and DASH team who did an outstanding job on bringing this information together and making it available to us.

Like many people involved in nutritional research, I'm very grateful for the scientific legacy of great innovators such as Weston Price, DDS; Francis Pottenger, MD; Emanuel Cheraskin, MD, DMD; Peter D'Adamo, ND; James D'Adamo, ND; Royal Lee, DDS; George Watson, PhD; Deepak Chopra, MD; David R. Hawkins, MD; and William G. Crook, MD, to name only a few.

Very special thanks go to Rudolph Ballentine, MD; Abram Hoffer, MD; Morton Walker, DPM; Bernard Jensen, DC; Carl C. Pfeiffer, MD, PhD; Samuel Epstein, MD; Candace B. Pert, PhD; Andrew Weil, MD; Gabriel Cousens, MD; Sherry Rogers, MD; Doris Rapp, MD; Anne Louise Gittleman, PhD; and Jeffrey Bland, PhD.

And, of course, much love and gratitude go to my husband, Jonathan, for his patience and understanding during the writing process; and to my family and friends for their continued support and encouragement.

Special thanks go to Marilyn Allen of the Allen O'Shea Literary Agency, for having faith and confidence in me to do this book justice. Also thanks to Brook Farling, the acquisitions editor at Alpha Books, for guiding the process from beginning to end with professionalism and expertise.

Special Thanks to the Technical Reviewer

The Complete Idiot's Guide to DASH Diet Cooking was reviewed by an expert who double-checked the accuracy of what you'll learn here, to help us ensure that this book gives you everything you need to know about cooking for the DASH diet. Special thanks are extended to Sophia Kamveris, MS, RD, LD.

Trademarks

All terms mentioned in this book that are known to be or are suspected of being trademarks or service marks have been appropriately capitalized. Alpha Books and Penguin Group (USA) Inc. cannot attest to the accuracy of this information. Use of a term in this book should not be regarded as affecting the validity of any trademark or service mark.

What the DASH Diet's All About

Part 1 discusses nutritious ways that the DASH diet principles can nourish and strengthen you and your heart. The DASH diet can help you achieve your goal of lowering blood pressure and increasing heart health. You'll soon see results and marked improvements as you begin applying these principles and follow the DASH diet meal suggestions.

Maintaining a healthy heart along with its accompanying optimum blood pressure and cholesterol levels is within your reach. With the information in this part, you will soon have all the necessary tools to guide you toward living healthier and longer.

What Is the DASH Diet?

In This Chapter

- Understanding DASH diet basics
- Lowering your blood pressure with healthy eating
- Learning how the DASH diet works
- Discovering the ease of weight loss with DASH

DASH stands for Dietary Approaches to Stop Hypertension. The DASH diet is recommended for those attempting to control and lower blood pressure, and it can accomplish this in as little as 14 days. DASH has numerous advantages and has been called a "diet for all diseases" because everyone can benefit from applying DASH diet principles. This chapter will discuss these principles and how simple it is to implement them.

One of the first changes you can make to reduce high blood pressure is through your diet. Reducing salt intake is a good place to start, but we'll also be discussing the specific foods known to be beneficial for controlling *blood pressure*. The factors that influence your success in following the DASH diet are pretty straightforward. The DASH diet encourages you to eat foods lower in sodium while consuming a variety of nutrient-dense foods rich in minerals such as potassium, calcium, and magnesium that help lower blood pressure.

Most people know that being overweight is a prime risk factor for developing *hypertension*. But did you know that the DASH diet can provide the perfect foundation for a healthy weight-loss plan? A side benefit of the DASH diet is its ability to help you lose weight relatively easily.

Blood pressure is the measurement of the force against the walls of your arteries as your heart pumps blood through your body. High blood pressure (hypertension) is when your blood pressure is 140/90 mmHg or above most of the time.

Hypertension is the term used to describe high blood pressure.

Getting to Know DASH

DASH is a healthy eating plan that's proven to help you prevent and control hypertension (the medical term for high blood pressure).

Established by the National Institutes of Health, the aim of the DASH diet is to reduce the amount of sodium in your diet and increase the amount of essential nutrients. The DASH diet focuses on nutrient-dense whole foods containing a blend of key nutrients your body needs for supporting health and longevity. Mineral-rich foods, such as fruits and vegetables, contain potassium, magnesium, and calcium—all beneficial because they help to reduce sodium and lower blood pressure. Rather than relying solely on individual nutritional supplements, DASH supports a balanced and doable way of eating. This makes DASH easy to follow and available to everyone. Simply put, everyone who follows the DASH-style eating plan sees benefits in their health, and so can you.

If you're one of the 50 to 60 million (or one in four) adults in the United States who have hypertension, the DASH diet can help you lower your blood pressure. High blood pressure affects about 60 percent of people over the age of 60. Another 55 million people in America have prehypertension, a condition that also increases the chance of heart disease and stroke. The DASH diet is effective in that it works rapidly—within 14 days—and it works for men and women, African Americans and Caucasians, and for people of all age groups.

HEART-HEALTHY TIP

The most reliable way to find out if you have high blood pressure is to have your blood pressure checked. Your qualified health professional should check your blood pressure at least once a year, or more often as necessary. If someone in your family has been diagnosed with high blood pressure you may want to get yours checked as a precautionary measure. Many pharmacies offer free machines for checking your blood pressure and this is a great way to keep an eye on yours. While a single elevated blood pressure reading doesn't mean you have high blood pressure, it's a sign that further observation is needed.

The DASH diet has been proven to successfully lower blood pressure levels as much as most prescription blood pressure medications. DASH has numerous other health benefits, including lowering your cholesterol levels, increasing "good" *HDL* cholesterol, and decreasing "bad" *LDL* cholesterol (which helps prevent heart disease). Eating the DASH way also offers protection against conditions such as diabetes, heart disease, stroke, cancer, and osteoporosis.

> **DEFINITION**
>
> **HDL** stands for high-density lipoprotein and is known as "the good cholesterol."
> **LDL** stands for low-density lipoprotein and is known as the "bad cholesterol."

Lowering Hypertension with DASH

Blood pressure tends to naturally go up as you age, starting as early as your teens. Your diet and lifestyle habits play a key role in all of this. Genetics are another major factor as to how likely you are to develop high blood pressure, especially if there is a family history of it. When you have high blood pressure, the heart must work harder to pump blood throughout your body. This can harm blood vessels and organs such as your heart, brain, kidney, and even your eyes. Left uncontrolled, it can lead to heart and kidney disease, stroke, and increased risk of blindness.

Blood pressure is measured by using a special device, called a sphygmomanometer or blood pressure meter, to read two numbers. The top number, known as the systolic number, is the pressure against the arteries when the heart beats. The bottom number, known as the diastolic number, is the force in the arteries when the heart is relaxed. A normal healthy blood pressure for an adult is 120/80. If the numbers go consistently beyond 140/90, it is considered high and classified as mild hypertension. Anything above these numbers is classified as high or chronic hypertension and must come down for optimum health.

High amounts of sodium in the diet can cause these numbers to go up and affects your blood pressure in a negative way. The excess sodium causes water to be retained in the bloodstream, which increases the overall volume of blood beyond what the vessels are naturally able to hold. This excess volume exerts pressure on the artery walls, causing nerve damage and blockages. This can cause nerve damage to delicate nerve endings and cell walls. Eventually this puts you at higher risk for a variety of serious conditions, such as heart and kidney disease, strokes, and even blindness.

Sodium is a mineral, or metallic element, and is considered an essential nutrient. However, like all things, moderation is key. Sodium can come from salt, which is sodium chloride, however many foods also contain lots of sodium. Processed foods, canned or frozen foods, and seafood all contain more than enough for our daily dietary allowance. It is important to keep sodium levels in check; you can do this by being aware of the factors that influence it. Many people eat far too much salt without even realizing it. It isn't only the amount of salt you sprinkle on your food at the dinner table; salt is added to packaged, frozen, or fast foods in excessive quantities, mainly to preserve it. If you are eating more packaged or fast foods than fresh, whole, unprocessed ones, you can easily consume two or three times the recommended daily amount of sodium without realizing it. Over time, this can cause a series of health risks and problems, such as weight gain or increased stress, as well as leading to kidney and heart troubles later on. Fortunately though, DASH can help you lower your sodium levels within just a few short weeks when you apply the principles in this book.

One of the main goals of DASH is reducing how much sodium you eat as a means to lower your blood pressure. The DASH diet encourages you to reduce the sodium in your diet through its use of health-supporting nutrients, such as plant phytochemicals, antioxidants, minerals, and fiber, to name a few. DASH also naturally increases the amounts of other important minerals in your diet, such as potassium, magnesium, and calcium. Increasing these minerals through better food choices improves your metabolism and provides a counterbalance effect on sodium levels in your blood.

The Importance of Potassium

Sodium works in conjunction with potassium, another major mineral in the body. Potassium is such an important nutrient for human health that some experts call it the *most* important nutrient. A lack of potassium can lead directly to heart disease, hypertension, kidney disease, diabetes, and weight gain. It is generally recognized that the average person may not get enough potassium in his or her diet, but gets far too much sodium.

Normal body functioning depends on the correct ratio and balance of these two important minerals, both inside and outside of cells. Our bodies require more potassium than sodium for proper functioning and health. Unfortunately, the standard American diet (SAD) contains about three to four times the necessary daily amount of sodium and far too little of the daily intake of potassium. Studies clearly show that the relative imbalance of this ratio is directly related to hypertension, heart and kidney disease, osteoporosis, diabetes, weight gain, and even cases of paralysis.

WARNING

Low potassium levels can lead to such symptoms as: muscle weakness, fatigue, irregular heart beat, mental confusion, and bowel changes. See your doctor about having your potassium levels checked or if you exhibit any of these symptoms.

The Sodium Factor

As mentioned, hypertension is influenced by many different factors, and the DASH diet addresses a variety of these. For instance, the high sodium diet that is typical of most Americans promotes higher blood pressure. The average American consumes 3,400 milligrams of sodium a day. The DASH diet aims to keep sodium levels at a modest level of under 2,300 milligrams a day. A lower sodium version of the diet reduces sodium consumption to 1,500 milligrams a day and is even more effective for those sensitive to salt.

Following a lower sodium diet may be challenging for people because they do not realize how much sodium they have been consuming. If you've ever had the experience of your rings being tight around your fingers from swelling the next morning after dining out the night before, this is caused from too much sodium. The DASH diet seeks to make this easier by encouraging people to look at labels and nutritional information to find products that are lower in sodium. In the DASH diet, you would consume a great deal of fruits and vegetables, which are typically very low in sodium. It also limits many of the high-fat, high-cholesterol, and high-calorie foods that are also often laden with salt.

Better Food Choices

The DASH diet promotes the consumption of healthy nutrients that have been scientifically shown to reduce blood pressure. These nutrients include potassium, magnesium, calcium, and different antioxidants. With its recommendation of plentiful fruits and vegetables such as bananas and dark greens, the DASH diet provides more of these nutrients.

The DASH diet is also effective because it reduces consumption of food items that can raise blood pressure. For instance, a diet high in fat and sugar increases your chances of hypertension. The DASH diet limits the amount of high-fat meat, keeps fats and oils to two to three servings a day, and includes sweets in strict moderation at less than five servings per week. Because alcohol has been shown to have a calamitous effect on blood pressure, due mainly to its high sugar content, men should limit themselves to two drinks a day, whereas women should restrict themselves to one. When you stop consuming foods and beverages that raise blood pressure, you may find yourself rewarded with more ideal numbers!

> **HEART-HEALTHY TIP**
>
> Studies have tested the DASH diet's efficacy in various groups and found that middle-aged and senior adults will find it especially effective in lowering their blood pressure. Even those who are 55 years of age and have normal blood pressure will still face a 90 percent risk of developing the condition. Following the DASH diet may stop it before it starts. Since many people have undiagnosed hypertension, it can even be effective in those without knowledge of their condition.

More Fiber

The DASH diet includes a great deal of fiber in the form of the many fruits and vegetables consumed. Studies have shown that a diet high in fiber can help individuals lower their blood pressure. In addition, foods with a great deal of fiber can counteract hunger and cause one to consume less food overall. This can lead to healthy weight loss with a lowering of blood pressure.

And finally, getting the recommended daily amount of fiber (six to nine servings for adults) helps you to detoxify your colon, promotes healthy digestion, and gives you a feeling of fullness. The DASH diet provides more than enough fiber each day.

Portion Control

The DASH diet promotes moderate portion sizes. The portions at today's mealtimes are often far greater than recommended. It is not unusual for a single restaurant meal to have a day's worth of calories, fat, and sodium. The DASH diet promotes healthy serving sizes that will fill you up but not add unattractive bulk on your body or raise points on the blood pressure monitor.

With its healthy eating choices and limit on high-fat food, the DASH diet also promotes weight loss. Because excess weight can raise blood pressure, this is another way it can be effective. Plus, as you get your portions under control, your appetite is curbed and your stomach will shrink making it easier to eat the DASH way.

The DASH diet can translate to a decrease of eight to fourteen points in systolic blood pressure. This significant decrease can reduce your risk of stroke, cardiovascular problems, and other serious medical issues. In studies, this diet has been shown to be more effective in lowering blood pressure than many other diets, including "fad" diets that promise drastic yet unrealistic results. The combination of healthy eating and lowered salt intake makes a formidable foe against hypertension. The DASH diet is a healthy and effective choice for everyone, and not only those suffering from high blood pressure.

Losing Weight with DASH

The DASH diet is indisputably effective in the fight against hypertension, yet many people do not realize its potential in the battle of the bulge. With 34 percent of adult Americans overweight and an additional 34 percent dangerously obese, it is vital that people choose healthier eating options. The DASH diet's emphasis on moderate portions and healthier, low-fat food can help those stubborn pounds melt away.

To lose weight using DASH, you must pay strict attention to the recommended foods. The DASH diet emphasizes foods that are relatively low in calories such as fruits and vegetables. You can enjoy a hearty meal without consuming 3 days' worth of calories. Follow the DASH guidelines (outlined in Chapter 2) and fill your plate with fruits and vegetables instead of burgers and fries.

GOOD TO KNOW

Simply put, energy density is the number of calories (energy) in a given amount (volume) of food. For weight control, your best bets are healthy foods that provide low energy but high volume. Foods such as fruits and vegetables tend to be low in energy density and calories. This means you can eat more and feel fuller on less calories.

In addition, the DASH diet dictates serving sizes that are far more reasonable than what you often see on today's plates. For example, a serving of grain would be one slice of bread, not two, and only half cup of cooked pasta or rice. A fat or oil can be 1 teaspoon of vegetable oil, which is much less than many people use in preparing foods. Learn the serving sizes of the food and make sure to adhere to them. This will ensure your success.

The DASH diet prompts you to spend a high proportion of your calories on nutrient-rich foods like fruits, vegetables, nuts, grains, and seeds. These foods do not tend to have as many calories as "fattier" foods such as meats and cheeses. If you like to snack, you can nosh on these healthier foods without significant damage to your calorie count. Although you may be eating all the time, you can still lose weight if you consume fewer calories. Many of the fruits and vegetables—such as spinach and broccoli, for example—are extremely low in calories; however, they can still fill you up so that you feel less hungry.

The fiber and other nutrients prevalent in the DASH diet are also conducive to weight loss. When you eat food that is high in fiber, you will not feel as hungry later. You can choose foods that digest slower and may not even notice that you are eating less. Without that gnawing emptiness in your stomach, you may find yourself snacking less. Your total caloric intake for the day will lessen, thus leading to weight loss. Because you are not feeling deprived, you may also be less likely to go on an eating binge that can sabotage your hard work in a matter of minutes.

The DASH diet limits sweets and other food items that can easily add pounds. The limit of five sweets per week does not leave you feeling completely deprived, but restricts the high-calorie items that can destroy any diet. Because sweets contain a great many calories for their size, you may consume far more than you should before you start to feel full. The diet also limits alcohol and other high-calorie drinks such as soda. These are shockingly high in sugar and calories, yet they do not tend to make you feel full. They furnish "empty" calories, with no nutritional benefit, leaving you poised to eat more to satisfy your hunger.

With the DASH diet, you learn to substitute unhealthy foods for more sensible choices. This does not mean you cannot get the same experience. If you have a sweet tooth, then do not despair—you can still eat sweet foods. However instead of eating a candy bar, the DASH diet would encourage healthier and yet still sweet options such as strawberries, bananas, and berries. The DASH diet is not telling you to never eat sweets again, just smaller portions of it, if necessary.

The DASH diet can be effective at promoting weight loss because it focuses on a sustainable diet that provides a variety of different foods. *Fad diets* that cut out entire food groups or are extremely strict may work for a short time while you can "handle it." However, most people will eventually rebel against diets that make them feel hungry all the time or crave forbidden foods. The weight may reappear as quickly as it disappeared. The DASH diet aims to be a reasonable plan that gives many different choices of good food to eat. You can still enjoy a variety of foods, and may even find new ones to enjoy.

DEFINITION

Fad diets refer to any style of eating plan that is not sustainable over the long term. Examples are all-liquid diets, high-protein diets, or fruit-only diets. These diets are popular in the media for a short time but then they fade away. The DASH diet is suitable for everyone.

When losing weight on the DASH diet, it is vital to stay informed of your nutritional choices. Many people are blissfully unaware of just how unhealthy many of their dietary decisions are, especially meals purchased outside of the home. It is important to read the nutrition labels of any prepared foods that you purchase (coming up in Chapter 3). Especially pay attention to portion size. One "large" candy bar may contain four portions or servings—that means you must multiply the number of calories by four. For example, a regular size candy bar may contain between 200 to 300 calories per serving and 140 milligrams of sodium, whereas a large size could contain up to double this amount. Or, an "individual size" bag of potato chips at 250 calories might be three servings (for an actual 750 calories total). Most eateries offer nutrition information for their foods on their websites or at the actual restaurants. Read through these and choose the options that contain food recommendations harmonious with the DASH diet.

With the DASH diet, you may find yourself fitting back into clothes you thought you may never wear again. Healthy weight loss can also lower blood pressure, adding further fuel to its hypertension-fighting power. Its health and weight-loss benefits make the DASH an ideal choice for everybody.

Eating the DASH way makes it easier to lose weight than ever. It guides you toward healthier meals and snack choices and draws from a variety of food groups that provide your daily requirements of nutrients and fiber.

The Least You Need to Know

- Eating the DASH way lowers your cholesterol levels and reduces the risk for stroke, heart disease, osteoporosis, cancer, and diabetes.
- Lowering dietary sodium and increasing key nutrients substantially lowers blood pressure. It's a key strategy of DASH.
- DASH guides you toward healthier choices that draw from a variety of food groups that provide your daily requirements of nutrients and fiber. Losing weight follows easily.

The Basics of DASH

In This Chapter

- Knowing the fundamentals of healthy DASH
- Finding DASH serving sizes and portions that work
- Making DASH doable for you

There are several core nutritional values and principles that make the DASH diet work successfully to lower blood pressure. Once you know these principles, it can make the world of difference between average versus extraordinary results. Applying these will make everything easier for you in the short and long term. I'll discuss these principles in this chapter.

Knowing how much to eat and exercising control over your food intake is central to your DASH diet success. Working out portions and serving sizes as well as controlling how much you eat is critical. Certain key nutrients and vitamins your body needs, and which are found in food, make all the difference. In this chapter I will discuss what foods contain the key nutrients that help balance your metabolism and control appetite.

Using DASH is what will prove to you that the principles are correct, and powerful. Making changes to your diet and eating is challenging at the best of times. However, the tools available in this chapter will aid you in your success, and then DASH will become an enjoyable part of your daily life.

Balancing Your Diet

Central to what makes the DASH diet work so well and consistently is through the use of whole foods and very little processed ones. Whole foods are foods that are unprocessed and unrefined, or processed minimally, before being consumed.

Fruits and vegetables are great examples of whole foods. They are unprocessed and unrefined, and can be eaten without any additives or modifications. For example, a serving of strawberries would be a whole food, while strawberry jam, which contains additives and preservatives, wouldn't be. Whole foods are the best source of nutrition as they provide us with maximum *nutrient density*. Examples are vegetables and fruits, particularly those grown organically; raw nuts and seeds; and whole grains, such as quinoa, brown rice, beans, and legumes.

DEFINITION

One of the best ways to assess a food's value is to determine whether it is a whole food and if it has nutrient density. Whole foods are foods that are unprocessed and unrefined, or refined as little as possible before being consumed. A food's **nutrient density** is the amount of vitamins, minerals, essential fatty acids, carbo-hydrate, and protein it has relative to its caloric content. The more nutrient-dense a food is, the more it supports good health.

Whole foods are common, everyday foods complete with all their rich natural endowment of nutrients. They typically are not genetically modified nor do they contain artificial or irradiated ingredients, as this tends to devitalize and diminish the food's nutritional value and affects our levels of energy and vitality along with it. In addition, whole foods are high in antioxidants, which possess anti-inflammatory properties helpful to people with hypertension or high cholesterol. They also contain fiber and essential fatty acids, and all together these function to increase immunity and improve overall health. You will find a wide selection of whole, unprocessed foods contained throughout the recipes in this book to support your health.

Most fruits and vegetables should be eaten in their entirety, because every part, including the skin, contains valuable nutrients. Eat at least eight to ten servings of colorful fruits and vegetables a day whenever possible. That may sound like a lot, but one serving is only half a cup, and this food source is crucial to reducing hyperten-sion, lowering cholesterol, and increasing your energy levels, as well as helping you shed a few excess pounds. These plant foods are the greatest source of the vitamins, minerals, antioxidants, and *phytonutrients* that help you create and preserve health. Everyone, from physicians and scientists to health experts, agrees that eating fruits and vegetables is paramount to enjoying longevity, energy, and lasting health, and you will find them in abundance in the recipes that follow starting in Part 2.

DEFINITION

Phyto originates from a Greek word meaning "plant," and **phytonutrients** (or phytochemicals) are the biologically active substances in plants responsible for giving them color, flavor, and natural disease resistance. In the last couple of decades, scientists have begun to see that they provide a vital biological function in humans as well. Fruits, vegetables, grains, legumes, nuts, and teas are the richest sources of phytonutrients.

Food, in its most basic form, is really a form of life energy that communicates with us on a cellular level, signaling all kinds of bodily functions and processes that keep us healthy. These can include anything from switching on important brain neurotransmitters that help you feel calm, focused, and satiated, to releasing fat-storing hormones such as glucagon that help you to lose weight and shed excess fat more easily.

Homeostasis, which is simply another word for balance, occurs naturally when your diet is properly balanced with the three main classes of foods, known as macronutrients. We derive most of our nutrition from macronutrients, which consist of protein, fat, and carbohydrates, and the right ratio of minerals, which they contain.

In addition to macronutrients are nutrients called micronutrients. These are the vitamins, minerals, and trace elements that are absorbed through the digestive tract from our foods and from supplements. Eating a variety of foods that contain the highest-quality nutrients in the right quantities of macro- and micronutrients helps you achieve your highest potential for health, vitality, and freedom from disease.

Here is a breakdown of macronutrients in greater detail and which foods they are typically found in.

The Power of Protein

Protein is the basic material of all living cells. It is found throughout the body in muscle, bone, skin, hair, and virtually every other body part and tissue. Some 22 basic building blocks, called amino acids, are pieced together in varying combinations to make different kinds of protein. Following genetic instructions, the body strings together amino acids to make you what you are and to keep you that way.

There are eight basic essential amino acids, without which the body cannot function. Most of the remaining 14 amino acids can be manufactured in the body when supplied with the right ingredients of protein-rich foods. Because the body doesn't store amino acids, as it does fats or carbohydrates, it needs a daily supply of them to make new protein. If a shortage of amino acids becomes chronic, which can occur if the diet is deficient in essential amino acids, the protein-building process stops, and the body suffers. There are numerous studies showing that increasing your daily intake of plant protein sources and fiber, which plants and grains contain plenty of, can cut the risk of hypertension by up to 50 percent. Since plant protein sources do not contain a full complement of all eight of the essential amino acids, it is important to get these into your daily diet somehow. You can do this either from combining certain grains (such as brown rice, beans, or quinoa) together, and adding in vegetables for added vitamins, minerals, fiber, and plant phytonutrients.

The best-quality protein foods, in terms of amino acid balance, are free-range organic eggs, quinoa, soybeans, lentils, fish, and meat. Dairy products such as cheeses also contain certain amounts of protein. Animal protein sources are not always the ultimate forms of protein, because they also contain a lot of undesirable fat. Also, unless the meat is organic and free range, it's likely to contain antibiotics and hormones, which the animal stores in its fat cells. There is a concern that these can get transferred to your metabolism and cells when you eat the meat and its fat.

HEART-HEALTHY TIP

You may not want to eliminate meat from your diet entirely, but there are ways to cut back on the fat it contains. Trim all the fat surrounding any meats before cooking them. Select the leanest cuts of meat possible, and choose cuts that are less marbled with fat. Consider other meats such as game, turkey, chicken, and fish.

Meat is also acid-forming for blood pH levels, which can lead to the loss of minerals, including more calcium than normal being excreted through the kidneys. This can increase the risk of osteoporosis among frequent meat eaters and lead to hardening of the arteries. Meats are also high in cholesterol, particularly the bad kind, LDL, so you may want to eat meat only in moderation, say two to three times a week, and certainly no more than one small serving of lean meats per day.

To consume a diet that contains enough—but not too much—protein, simply replace animal products with grains, vegetables, beans, peas, legumes (like lentils and chickpeas), nuts, seeds, and fruits. These foods contain plenty of fiber, and this will support you in lowering your blood pressure while enhancing your weight-loss efforts.

Watch Those Fats and Oils

Fats and oils (also referred to as fatty acids) in their natural state are necessary to promote health. Essential fatty acids (EFAs) are vital components of fats and oils that cannot be produced by the body naturally; therefore, it's essential that we get them from dietary sources. EFAs are necessary for many of the body's functions, such as a healthy nervous system, healthy skin, and production of hormones for the glands of the adrenals, thyroid, and sex glands. They insulate us, protect internal organs, and keep our body heat regulated.

Fats taste good and are important for good health; however, they must be balanced to include a variety of natural oils from varying plant and animal sources. Problems can arise as a result of eating too much of the wrong kinds of fat, particularly hydrogenated or partially hydrogenated fats, which are also known as trans fats. These fats are dangerous because they increase the LDL cholesterol levels while reducing the amount of beneficial HDL cholesterol in your body. This significantly increases your risk of a heart attack.

WARNING

Hydrogenated or partially hydrogenated fats (aka: trans fats) can disturb metabolism of fats in the body and lead to health problems, such as cancer and cardiovascular disease. Trans fats can also increase total cholesterol levels. They are found in margarine, high-fat baked goods (especially doughnuts, cookies, and cakes), potato chips, crackers, and bread. Read labels and avoid them as much as possible.

The kind of fat and the balance of various fats are critical in determining how fat contributes to disease. When we do not pay attention to proper fatty acid balance, we can develop serious health problems, most of which affect the brain and the central nervous system.

Because essential fatty acids play such an important role in forming the delicate structures that make up your brain and nervous system, they are vital to include in your daily diet. Often enough, the major problem with fats is not caused by eating too much fat so much as it is by eating too little, particularly too few essential fatty acids, such as omega-3s and omega-6s. As there are 9 calories per gram of fat compared with 4 calories per gram of carbohydrate and protein, you will want to limit the amount you eat. Essential fatty acids are found in fish, nuts, seeds, oils, and vegetables.

Alpha-linolenic acid is the principal omega-3 fatty acid, which a healthy human with good nutrition will convert into EPA and later into DHA (which stands for docosa-hexaenoic acid).

Omega-3s are found in foods such as flax seed oil, flax seed meal, Brazil nuts, sesame seeds, avocados, walnuts, dark-green leafy vegetables (kale, spinach, purslane, cabbage, collards, Swiss chard, mustard greens), wheat germ oil, and cold-water fish such as salmon, tuna, sardines, anchovies, and mackerel.

Linoleic acid is the primary omega-6 fatty acid. A healthy human with good nutrition will convert linoleic acid into gamma linolenic acid (GLA), which in turn is synthe-sized, with EPA from the omega-3 group, into eicosanoids.

Although most Americans get more than enough linoleic acid, it frequently fails to get converted to GLA due to metabolic problems caused by diets high in sugar, alco-hol, or trans fats, or by smoking, pollution, stress, aging, viral infections, and other illnesses such as diabetes and cardiovascular disease. It is therefore recommended that these factors be reduced or eliminated. The recipes in this book have been formulated especially with this in mind. In addition, supplementing with GLA-rich foods such as borage oil, evening primrose oil, and black currant seed oil would be beneficial.

Omega-6s are primarily found in flax seed oil, flax seeds, flax seed meal, olives, olive oil, hempseeds, hempseed oil, sunflower seeds, sunflower oil, sesame seeds, sesame oil, pistachio nuts, pine nuts, pumpkin seeds, evening primrose oil, black currant seed oil, and chicken. Coconut oil contains approximately 4 percent omega-6. Coconut oil is also helpful in several immune-deficiency conditions, because it contains high levels of a medium-chain fatty acid called lauric acid and another called caprylic acid, both of which have been helpful in inhibiting viruses. These fatty acids are readily absorbed by the body and used for energy. Lauric and caprylic acid compounds have also proven to be antiviral, antibacterial, and antifungal, mak-ing coconut oil an excellent supplement for intestinal disorders. Coconut oil is stable, even during long periods of storage. This makes it ideal for cooking and baking.

Carbohydrates: Simple and Complex

Carbohydrates are an important component of the DASH diet as they are often our main source of energy. Carbohydrates come in two forms: simple (also called fast releasing) and complex (also known as starch and considered slow releasing). Most sugars, sweets, refined foods, white flour, malts, and honey are fast releasing, because they tend to produce a sudden burst of energy followed by a slump. In addition, refined foods such as sugar and flour lack the essential vitamins and minerals (micro-nutrients) the body needs to use them properly, and so they are best avoided.

The rate at which how quickly or moderately your body breaks carbohydrates down into blood glucose (blood sugar) for energy is measured via the *glycemic index* (GI). This is based on a numerical scale from 0 to 100. This is important because the presence of glucose in the bloodstream usually triggers the release of insulin, a hormone that helps glucose get into cells where it can be used for energy but that also can help our body store excess sugar as fat. You will find a GI of the values of certain foods in Appendix B to help you become aware of the glycemic value of various carbohydrates. An awareness of a food's glycemic index can help you control blood sugar levels, and by doing so may help you improve cholesterol levels, reduce risk for cardiovascular disease or stroke, prevent certain cancers, lose weight, and prevent insulin resistance and type 2 diabetes.

DEFINITION

The **glycemic index** scores foods on a scale from 0 to 100. Foods considered to be low glycemic are those with a GI of less than 55. Foods with higher GI numbers stimulate higher blood sugar and insulin responses. Relying on low-glycemic foods can help people who are concerned about their blood sugar levels improve their health. To slow down the rate at which your blood sugar rises, add more fiber or include healthy amounts of fat and protein to each meal.

When you eat slow-releasing or complex carbohydrates, such as whole grains, vegetables, legumes, or simpler carbohydrates such as some fruits, the body does exactly what it is designed to do. It digests the foods and gradually releases their potential energy. What's more, all the nutrients that the body needs for digestion and metabolism are present in those whole foods. These foods also contain a less digestible type of carbohydrate called fiber, which helps keep the digestive system running smoothly. (More on fiber in the next section.)

Slow-releasing complex carbohydrate foods—some fresh fruits, vegetables, beans, and whole grains—provide the highest nutrient density and are an efficient form of fuel to keep your energy levels sustained for several hours. As a suggestion your goal each day should be to:

- Eat eight to ten servings of dark-green vegetables, such as broccoli, spinach, brussels sprouts, green beans, and green and red peppers—either raw or lightly cooked. Eat two to four servings daily of root vegetables, such as carrots, potatoes, onions, garlic, turnips, and parsnips.

- Eat one or two servings of fresh fruit, such as apples, pears, berries, melons, or citrus fruit.

- Eat three or four servings of whole grains, such as whole-grain brown rice, millet, rye, quinoa, beans, or whole wheat.

- Avoid any form of sugar, foods with added sugar, white flour, and refined foods.

Here's another way to look at fast-releasing and slow-releasing carbohydrates. Some carbohydrate-rich foods put more stress than others on the system that controls the body's blood sugar. Some foods cause the blood sugar level to rise rapidly, while others have almost less adverse effects on blood sugar control.

Beneficial Fiber

Fiber is a vitally important form of carbohydrate. Fiber includes cellulose, hemi-cellulose, pectin, and gums, and it is sometimes called bulk or roughage. There are two basic types of fiber: soluble fiber and insoluble fiber, both of which are undigested. They are not absorbed into the bloodstream but instead work to promote efficient waste from the colon and increase the bulk of feces. The bulk helps to push food along the gut, thereby reducing bowel transit time and constipation. Soluble fiber forms a gel when mixed with liquid, while insoluble fiber does not. Insoluble fiber passes through our intestines largely intact.

Sources of soluble fiber include vegetables; fruits; grains; beans and legumes; barley; rice; oat bran; nuts and seeds; and psyllium husk. Sources of insoluble fiber include vegetables such as green beans and those with dark-green leaves, fruit skins and root vegetable skins, whole-wheat products, corn and wheat bran, and nuts and seeds.

Fiber has several important health benefits. It retains water, resulting in softer and bulkier stools, which prevents constipation. Numerous studies show this also helps with weight loss. A high-fiber diet also reduces the risk of colon cancer by keeping the digestive tract clean.

In addition, soluble fiber binds with certain substances that would normally result in the production of cholesterol and eliminates these substances from the body. In this way, a high-fiber diet helps lower blood cholesterol levels and reduces the risk of hypertension and heart disease. Aim to eat at least 35 grams a day; 50 to 65 grams per day is even better.

As you can see, there is plenty of evidence to support that eating a diet containing the right balance of macronutrients for your particular metabolism, together with an abundance of vitamins, minerals, and essential fatty acids, is the best diet to lower blood pressure. Overall, it creates better health, increases longevity, and helps you

maintain an ideal weight. The DASH recipes in this book have been created especially with this in mind to help support you in making the right choices.

HEART-HEALTHY TIP

Elevated cholesterol levels are known to be one of the major risk factors in heart
disease and hypertension. A number of studies have linked high-fiber intake
with low levels of cholesterol. Fiber has been proven to alter fat or cholesterol
absorption in the large bowel. Some studies suggest that soluble fiber produces
a reduction in LDL ("bad") cholesterol levels without decreasing HDL ("good")
cholesterol levels.

Diet and Food Matters

A good deal of energy is consumed and wasted by the body's attempts to disarm or
rid the body of toxic chemicals from our food sources. The toxins that cannot be
eliminated accumulate in the body tissue and blood vessels and contribute to hypertension and heart disease. Unfortunately, it is virtually impossible to avoid all these
substances completely, because there is nowhere on our planet that is not somehow
contaminated by the products of our modern chemical age. Being diligent in making
the wisest choices carries its own rewards.

Many people consume far too many of their daily calories from processed foods.
Most of these processed foods not only have huge amounts of salt added, but in a
great many cases, large amounts of potassium have been depleted. Most processed
foods are far too high in sodium. This is often because higher sodium content is
added during the canning or processing of that food in order to preserve it for shelf
life. This upsets the delicate balance between potassium and sodium levels in the
human body. If you take any unprocessed vegetable or fruit in its natural state, you
will find that in 99 percent of all cases, such foods will have 20 to 100 times as much
potassium as sodium. Keeping your ratio of sodium to potassium balanced is a key
factor to what makes the DASH diet successful. Aim to eat generous amounts of fresh
vegetables and fruits each day as these are higher in potassium than sodium. This is
not hard to do if you are consuming plenty of fresh seasonal foods.

Choose organically grown whole foods as much as possible. This will ensure a supe-
rior quality of food with higher nutritional value than those grown conventionally.
Genuine organic soil is not only rich in trace elements not available to commercially
grown plants, but also in microorganisms, which support immune system function.
Foods grown organically are nourished by natural light, clean water, and have other
intangible benefits that support our health and longevity. Let's face it, when we

put inferior foods into our body, we end up paying for it with our health sometime later, by way of high cholesterol and high blood pressure, digestive upsets, or lack of energy, for example.

The recipes in this book are loaded with whole foods that contain key nutrients that contribute to your success. Minerals such as calcium, potassium, and magnesium, for example, have been proven beneficial for helping with lowering blood pressure, stroke, and heart attack risk.

Dishing Up DASH: Target Calories and Serving Sizes

Putting DASH principles into action and making it work for you can be broken down into a few fundamentals and easy steps. To help you get maximum results from your DASH diet eating plan and to put it into the real world, I have based it around cooking for the family. This includes finding the calorie and serving sizes needed by the whole family or those participating in the plan. This will simplify your meal planning. If you are doing the DASH diet on your own, simply ignore the references to family calculations.

Apply these three easy steps to help you create your own best DASH eating system:

1. Learn how to pick your target weight for you and your family members.

2. Calculate you and your family's daily calorie needs.

3. Find out how many daily servings from each food group you'll need for you and your family.

Weighing In

Most people have an idea of their ideal weight, and it is often not the weight they are at currently. Being overweight is a significant risk factor for high blood pressure; therefore, establishing what is a healthy weight is a good starting point for DASH.

A simple method to estimate your "ideal weight" is to use the following steps:

1. For women, start with 100 pounds for your first 5 feet of height, then add 5 pounds for each additional inch of height. For men, start with 106 pounds for your first 5 feet of height, then add 6 pounds for each additional inch of height.

2. Add or subtract 10 percent for heavy or light frame body types.

For example: A 5'6" woman should "ideally" be between 117 pounds (light frame) and 143 pounds (heavy frame), as an average guideline. A 5'9" man should be between 144 pounds (light frame) and 176 pounds (heavy frame).

Another way you can refine what your recommended standard weight should be is by use of the *body mass index (BMI)*. This is a measure of body fat based on height and weight that applies to adult men and women. It gives a generalized guideline as to your weight but does not go into detail for body types and shapes; for instance, an athlete could weigh more for his height due to his exceptional muscle mass. When you use the BMI, consider making adjustments for your body type and your activity level. You will find the BMI table in Appendix C.

> **DEFINITION**
>
> The **body mass index** (BMI) is a tool that is often used to determine whether a person's health is at risk due to his or her weight. It is a ratio of your weight to your height. See Appendix C to calculate your BMI. A BMI of 18.5 to 24.9 is considered healthy; 25 to 29.9 is considered overweight; and 30 or more is considered obese.

Your Ideal Weight

In Chapter 1 we discussed losing weight, which entails burning more calories than you consume to support your current weight. Using your "ideal weight" as your "target weight" over time will bring you your desired results. However, by choosing a target weight that is less than your intended ideal weight is one strategy for reaching your ideal weight more rapidly.

The following table helps you understand how many calories per pound/kilogram of body weight you need per day to maintain a weight without loss or accumulation.

Calculate Calories to Maintain Weight

	Sedentary	Moderate	Active
Calories per lb.			
Women	11.8	14.7	16.7
Men	13.1	16.4	18.5
Calories per kg			
Women	25.9	32.4	36.7
Men	28.8	36.0	40.8

By finding yourself on the table, you will see the amount of calories used for your activity level by gender per pound or kilogram. Simply multiplying your current weight by the appropriate factor shown on the table will show you what your current average calorie consumption per day should be.

By plugging in what you believe to be your ideal weight, you will see the amount of calories that you need to consume in order to maintain that ideal weight when you reach it. If you choose to become more aggressive in your weight loss, then you will want to choose a target weight that's lower than your intended ideal weight, unless you are planning to raise your activity level. Increased activity means your body needs more calories to sustain the weight you have.

Be realistic on selecting your target weight to make it easier to adjust to. As a rule of thumb it may be wise to start the program using your ideal weight as your target. Then, when you become accustomed to this daily calorie intake, you can reset your target weight to an even lower level to achieve faster results. You may want to consult with your health practitioner on this.

> Example calculation:
>
> For a moderately active female
>
> Your current weight: 160 lb. × 14.7 = 2,352 calories per day
>
> Your ideal weight: 140 lb. × 14.7 = 2,058 calories per day

Food Groups and Servings

The following table helps you understand what a standard serving size looks like. Several examples are given in each food group of what a serving would be.

Food Group Serving Sizes

Food Group	Serving Size
Vegetables	1/2 cup cooked or raw vegetables
	1 cup raw leafy vegetables
	6 fluid oz. vegetable juice
Fruits	1/4 cup dried fruit
	1/2 cup fresh, frozen, or light canned fruit
	1 medium fruit
	6 fluid oz. fruit juice

Food Group	Serving Size
Grains, Starch	1 slice bread
	$\frac{1}{2}$ cup dry cereal
	$\frac{1}{2}$ cup cooked cereal, rice, pasta, corn
Beans	$\frac{1}{2}$ cup cooked beans
Nuts & Seeds	2 TB. seeds
	$1\frac{1}{2}$ oz. or $\frac{1}{3}$ cup nuts
	2 TB. nut butter (almond, peanut, sesame)
Dairy	8 fluid oz. milk
	$1\frac{1}{2}$ oz. cheese
	1 cup plain yogurt
	$\frac{1}{2}$ cup cottage cheese
Meats & Fish	$2\frac{1}{2}$–$3\frac{1}{2}$ oz. cooked meats, poultry, or fish
	1 egg or 2 egg whites
Fats & Oils	1 tsp. vegetable oil, coconut oil, butter
	1 TB. low-fat mayonnaise or regular salad dressing
	2 TB. light salad dressing
Sweets	1 TB. maple syrup or honey
	1 TB. sugar
	1 TB. jelly or jam
	$\frac{1}{2}$ cup low-fat or nonfat frozen yogurt
	2–3 pieces hard candy
	8 fluid oz.
	1 popsicle

To maintain proper health and to make the DASH diet sustainable, you have to eat from all of the recommended food groups as indicated in the following table. This table helps you find out how many servings from each food group you'll need for your and your family's daily needs.

Food Groups with Daily Serving Recommendations

| | Individual Calorie Intake Ranges | | | |
Food Group	1,400–1,800 # of Daily Servings	1,800–2,200	2,200–2,600	2,600–3,000
Vegetables	4–6	4–6	5–7	7–9
Fruits	3–4	3–4	4–5	5–6
Grains, starch	6	7	9	11
Beans	$\frac{1}{4}$	$\frac{1}{2}$	$\frac{1}{2}$	$\frac{1}{2}$
Nuts & Seeds	2-3 per week	3-4 per week	3-4 per week	4-5 per week
Dairy	2-3	3	3	3-4
Meats & Fish	$1\frac{1}{2}$	$1\frac{1}{2}$	2	$2\frac{1}{2}$
Fats & Oils	1	2	3	4
Sweets	$\frac{1}{2}$	$\frac{1}{2}$	1	2

Choosing recipes and foods that provide servings from all of the necessary food groups is key to your success. As I mentioned earlier in this chapter, balancing your food intake to help you get all the macronutrients your body needs daily is essential. Monitoring servings and portions is a good habit to establish—once you learn this, it will set you up for success.

The human body thrives on a diet which contains all of the essential key nutrients that sustain good health and optimum well-being. This includes finding a comfortable weight as well as functioning in a body that's energized and full of vitality. As you get further into applying the principles found in the DASH diet and sampling the recipes in this book, the easier, more simple, and fun it will become.

Making DASH Simple, Easy, and Fun!

Like any new dietary or lifestyle improvement, mastering new habits and behaviors is a process that takes time and becomes easier the more you practice. With each meal you prepare and cook, learning to implement DASH diet principles will become second nature. Your blood pressure numbers will go down, and so, too, will your cholesterol numbers. As your health improves, you'll have more energy and a renewed sense of vitality. This leads to greater overall happiness.

This is an opportunity to change and to have some fun experimenting with new foods and cooking methods. Try different ethnic menus or theme menus such as Indian, Mediterranean, or Asian cuisine. Stretch yourself while being realistic, set achievable goals, clarify your expectations, and you will ensure success.

Keep your DASH diet cooking simple, easy, and fun and don't take it all too seriously. If you falter and don't achieve the degree of success you wanted as you begin, or are disappointed to have days when you are not able to follow your DASH diet cooking plan, don't worry, that is life. If your goals were too aggressive, dial them back; this is not about doing without—it is embracing effective change.

It is okay to have, and even schedule, break-out days once in a while; remember, it is what you do most of the time that matters!

The Least You Need to Know

- Whole foods contain more potassium, calcium, magnesium, vitamins, fiber, and essential minerals that help lower blood pressure.
- Choose nutrient-dense foods as these contain more "bang for the bite." This includes more whole foods and less processed ones.
- Balancing your macronutrients is important. Choose foods high in fiber, complex carbohydrates, and healthy omega-3 essential fatty acids, and include plant as well as low-fat animal sources of protein each day.
- Get clear on your target calorie needs for you and your family.
- Make DASH easier and more fun by setting realistic goals.

Preparing for DASH

In This Chapter

- Reducing sodium is easier than you may think
- Understanding label guidelines
- Knowing which additives and foods to avoid
- DASH pantry building blocks
- Cooking the DASH-healthy way

One of the most successful results of the DASH diet study comes about from eating a little less salt than the typical standard American diet (SAD) meal you may have eaten previously. I'll show you some healthy choices that are satisfying as well as tasty.

Understanding food labels and nutritional recommendations will guide you toward making empowering decisions that help lower your blood pressure. Armed with a little extra knowledge that I'll share with you in this chapter, along with a keen desire to kick hypertension to the curb, you'll be poised for success.

Did you know that food additives such as monosodium glutamate (MSG) and sodium nitrate are often disguised in our foods and can contribute to high blood pressure? Knowledge is power when you know which foods are best avoided because they can ruin your good efforts at reducing hypertension. We'll cover that in more detail here plus I'll show you how to do a pantry makeover that's healthy and blood pressure friendly, too. Speaking of success in the kitchen, there's a whole world of useful gadgets and small appliances designed to help us eat more healthfully. Although some of these items are not essential to eating the DASH way, they can make the process easier and more fun. You'll soon learn how stocking your healthy DASH pantry is crucial to your success when you know what to keep and what to toss.

Another critical element of maintaining a healthy and DASH-friendly eating regimen is looking at both food storage and the methods you use to cook your food. I'll show you which ones are the best when it comes to eating DASH meals.

Healthy Sodium Solutions

Salt is a stealthy foe. When cooked, its taste can practically disappear. You may have a clear understanding of the fat and calories in the food you consume, and yet no idea of how much sodium you actually eat. It is a dangerous omission, for as you are probably well aware by now, an excess of sodium can raise blood pressure and leads to hypertension, a.k.a. the "silent killer." The 3,400 milligrams of sodium that the average American eats is far too much; however, there are many healthy options that allow you to enjoy your food with much less salt.

When cooking food, look for lower-salt recipes. The recipes in this book have been carefully prepared and selected so as to offer you many options to ensure your DASH diet success. You can also alter many recipes from other sources; lower the salt content by swapping it out with fresh herbs and spices. You may be astonished to learn just how much salt is in food that doesn't taste salty. For instance, prepared soups are often outrageously salty, containing half of the daily recommended allotment of sodium (or more), and yet many people add more salt to them. You may not notice that much of a difference in your meal if you lower the amount of salt you put in.

You should limit the salt you add after food is cooked as well. Do not automatically reach for the salt shaker; taste your food instead. When you add salt to a meal, do not give a hearty shake, but place a little on your hand and add in the smallest amount that would work. You can slowly wean yourself off of it.

There are many foods that are naturally low in sodium, such as fruits and vegetables. Fruits and vegetables are highly favored in the DASH diet and are very conducive to weight loss. Fill your plate and meals with these to add bulk without the added sodium. You will also gain heartier meals without calories and give yourself vital nutrients and minerals that help reduce high blood pressure.

HEART-HEALTHY TIP

Know how much sodium is in each serving. If the label says 150 milligrams sodium per ¼ cup and you eat ½ cup, you've consumed twice as much, or 300 milligrams. Keep in mind that 1 teaspoon salt contains 2,300 milligrams of sodium.

You will find a rainbow of flavors to use in your food instead of salt. Common and exotic spices add sparkle to any meal without the cost of blood pressure points. Consider pepper, oregano, parsley, garlic, or one of the many spice mixtures you can make yourself or purchase in stores. Of course, make sure that there is not hidden sodium in these and always read the labels. One of my favorites is ginger, turmeric, celery salt, and allspice mixed together. As an added bonus, many spices such as cinnamon and turmeric have positive health benefits. Be sure to check all labels for their sodium content.

You must be very careful with processed or prepared foods because many are perilously high in sodium. Even processed foods that characterize themselves as the ultimate representation of healthy living with low calories and fat typically still load in the sodium. Read the labels and do not just blindly accept a food just because it claims to be "low sodium." Some are lower than the regular version of a food—but still extremely high. For instance, a brand of canned soup may boast 30 percent lower sodium than the regular product. However, if the regular product had 1,000 milligrams of sodium (as many do), then this would still lead to an outrageous amount of 700 milligrams of sodium—hardly a low-sodium food. Look at the actual sodium content and choose those that are consistent with your sodium intake goal.

When it comes to prepared foods, do not despair if you crave a food that is scandalously high in sodium. You may be able to enjoy it with less sodium by diluting it. For instance, perhaps there is a prepared pasta dish whose sauce is bursting with sodium. You can also simply add water to the sauce or mix it with a salt-free version of a sauce to make it less salty. You would eat only a portion and save the rest for another meal.

Of course, you could simply eat less of the food that is higher in sodium. Find creative ways to do so. For instance, if you like a prepared soup that is very salty, then instead of eating it as a soup, use it as a dip with some vegetables. You will have much less sodium than if you had eaten an entire bowl, but you can still enjoy the taste.

You can also lower your sodium intake by eating salty items in moderation. Many sauces and even salad dressings are very high in sodium (again, read labels). Instead of pouring these over your meals, dip your fork in before every spoonful to get the taste without drowning your food in a sea of salt. And speaking of a sea of salt, I recommend using either of these two healthier salts: Celtic sea salt or Himalayan crystal salt. Both can be purchased either online or from a health-food store. These contain microminerals that are better for your health.

Snack foods are often bursting with sodium. Instead of snacking on chips or other items with a lot of sodium, munch on vegetables or fruits like carrot sticks or apple slices. Look for low-salt or salt-free chips, preferably made with whole grains. Try baked chips instead of deep fried, as these are lower in saturated fat, which is known to clog arteries and thereby increase your risk for high blood pressure.

There are many other ways to flavor foods without salt. Try different combinations of foods. You may add something tart or sweet to a meal. As the famous proverb states, think outside of the box—or at least the salt shaker. Instead of adding salt to your soup, try some flavorful dill.

HEART-HEALTHY TIP

Experiment a little. Try fresh garlic or garlic powder, lemon juice, cumin, nutmeg, cinnamon, fresh ground pepper, tarragon, and oregano. These flavorful herbs and spices will help add more flavor and zest to your meals.

It is very important to be aware of the sodium in the foods you eat. Read nutrition labels on both food purchased for the home and while you are eating out. Remember that food does not have to taste salty to be full of salt. Even sweet foods such as ice cream may contain salt. Many cereals are relatively high in salt. Sodium can also be present in varying amounts in bread. Look for lower-salt versions of all of these. Also pay close attention to serving size. A can of soup may not seem so bad until you realize that most cans contain two (or more) servings and people will generally eat the whole can in a single meal. Either stick to the smaller servings or choose a different food if you know that you will not be able to stop yourself from eating more than the recommended serving.

Many raw foods are naturally low in sodium. These include dried beans, some yogurts, and lentils. Alternatively, processed meats and other foods are much higher in salt. For healthy low-sodium meals, choose a base that is low in sodium. Use dry beans and cook them instead of baked beans that are already very salty. You can combine beans, vegetables, and spices in a delicious low-sodium stew or chili. Make pasta and create a sodium-free tomato sauce from fresh tomatoes and spices.

It is not difficult to create healthier versions of many sodium-rich foods. Pizza is extremely high in sodium and can sabotage any diet that seeks to keep sodium at a reasonable level. Make your own pizza with a low-fat flatbread (or homemade low-salt pizza dough). Use a no-salt-added tomato sauce or tomato purée and go very easy on the cheese, which tends to be high in fat and sodium. You can enjoy a delicious pizza with a fraction of the sodium of take-out pizza.

You may think that you will yearn for the sodium once it is gone; however, studies have shown that people tend to adjust to the taste of less salty foods very quickly. Reduce the amount that you use, and after a short period of time you will not miss it. You will experience the myriad of natural flavors present in the food instead. With a low-salt diet you can and will lower your risk of developing hypertension, and be able to keep it under control if you already have it.

Nutrition Facts and Reading Food Labels

Food labels can be especially important in helping you to keep sodium to a minimum and to lower your blood pressure. Sodium in a number of forms is often added during food processing. Monitoring food labels is one of the best ways to become familiar with which foods have sodium added and in what amounts.

Understanding the nutritional information on the food you buy will help guide you toward planning healthier meals and snacks. For someone on the DASH diet, reading food labels is a good habit to get into. You will come to understand that labels contain important information, such as sodium, sugar, fat, and calorie content, which will help you to make healthy food choices. Knowing how to read a food label and understanding the benefits and risks of the ingredients listed on it will enable you to decide if the product is a nutritious and essential food, an occasional treat, or something to be avoided altogether.

WARNING

Just because the label classifies a serving size as "recommended or suggested" does not mean it's the amount you consume. For example, the label of a 15-ounce can of soup shows two servings, but many of us will eat the entire can in one sitting.

Here's the scoop on food labels. The fact is that they can be misleading. The USDA guidelines say that the total daily value acceptable for sodium intake is no more than 2,300 to 2,500 milligrams per day. This amount can be quite easy to surpass, however, especially if you have a taste for salty foods or add salt to your meals. Restaurant foods and fast foods are often high in this most common flavor enhancer, too, so pay particular attention as to where your daily intake is coming from.

The DASH diet study determined that it is better for your blood pressure if you eat less sodium than the USDA recommends—preferably between 1,500 and 2,000 milligrams a day. The American Heart Association recommends that everyone consume less than 1,500 milligrams of sodium per day. I would recommend that you eat the lowest possible amount and try not to go above 1,500 milligrams per day wherever possible.

Every food label is required to list the serving size and how many servings are in a package. You'll also find the amount of sodium per serving in milligrams, plus the percent of daily value, which is based on a 2,000-calorie diet. If you eat more or less than 2,000 calories each day, you'll need to adjust the percent of daily value accordingly to suit your calorie requirements.

When reading a label, the "% Daily Value" column of numbers on the right-hand side of the Nutrition Facts panel is the one that you will want to focus on. Ideally, you will want to ensure that the percent daily value for sodium is 5 or less, which is considered low in sodium. Any number higher than 20 percent is considered high in that nutrient.

HEART-HEALTHY TIP

On a food package, "reduced sodium" indicates 25 percent less sodium content than the "normal" version of that food; "light in sodium" means the sodium has been reduced by at least 50 percent; "low sodium" means the food has 140 milligrams or less per serving; "very low sodium," 35 milligrams or less; and "sodium-free" means the food has less than 5 milligrams per serving.

Here are some more tips to help you reduce your sodium intake and lower your blood pressure:

- Cook without salt; use herbs and spices instead. Try using herbs and natural plant–based flavorings such as ginger, garlic, cilantro, cumin, allspice, fresh lemon juice, and a splash of wine.

- Avoid using salty flavorings such as bouillon, seasoning packets, soy sauce, and meat tenderizers, as these contain large amounts of sodium, along with artificial flavorings that are bad for your health.

- If you are using canned vegetables and beans, rinse them under purified water and drain them well before using. You would be surprised at how much sodium is added to canned goods.

- Remove the salt shaker from the dinner table. Use celery salt, which has minerals such as potassium. Or try using powdered sea vegetables such as dulse or wakame, which contain natural sodium and are nutrient rich with minerals.

- When dining out, learn to recognize the terms on the menu that indicate a preparation might be high in sodium. These include the following terms: pickled, smoked, teriyaki, soy sauce, and in broth.

- Check your medication labels, as these can also be a source of sodium. Ask the pharmacist if you are unsure.

High blood pressure tends to be more common in overweight people, those with high cholesterol levels, and those who consume excessive fats in their diet. Therefore, anyone with hypertension or a tendency towards high blood pressure should watch calorie and fat intake as well as sodium; food labels clearly list this information.

As you begin eating with less sodium, your taste buds will be rejuvenated and you will find that your enjoyment for eating increases. Your blood pressure levels will go down and your energy levels will go up. The benefits far outweigh any challenges you may have and are well worth it.

Food Processing and Additives

Avoiding toxins in your diet is a key component to enhancing your health and lowering your risk factor for disease, including hypertension. Food additives are included in all processed foods; these can often be harmful and undermine your health. Food manufacturers add them to increase the shelf life of the product as well as enhance its flavor (if only artificially) to attract more buyers of their products.

Some of the immediate effects caused from food additives may include headaches, extreme fatigue, dehydration, or reduced ability to focus. Those with long-term effects could increase your risk of cardiovascular disease, and even lead to cancer. Make a decision to either cut down on those food additives or cut them out altogether. It may seem difficult to change habits and find substitutes for the foods you enjoy, but the rewards are well worth it. Remind yourself that you will be adding wholesome new flavors and foods to your diet that you may come to like as much or even more. Plus, the effects from eating in this way will increase your energy, help you maintain the best weight for your height, and add more energy and vitality to your life.

GOOD TO KNOW

According to Webster's Online Dictionary, an additive is "a substance added to another in relatively small amounts to effect a desired change in properties."

Here is a brief list of some key additives to avoid (or eat only occasionally):

- Hydrogenated fats (trans fats)—Lead to atherosclerosis and obesity, and increase the risk for cardiovascular disease.

- MSG (monosodium glutamate)—High in sodium and leads to a variety of symptoms such as allergic reactions, dizziness, chest pains, headaches; MSG is a neurotoxin.

- Preservatives (BHA, BHT, EDTA, etc.)—Known to cause allergic reactions, possibly cause cancer, and may be toxic to the nervous system and the liver.

- Sodium sulfites—Known neurotoxins which can cause allergic reactions and possibly cancer.

- Sodium nitrates/nitrites—Cause blockages in the body and possibly cancer.

- Artificial sweeteners—One of the newest sugar substitutes, sucralose (Splenda), is a sugar molecule with three chlorine atoms hanging onto it. Chlorine is a known toxin.

- High-fructose corn syrup—A sweetener derived from corn, generally those varieties that are genetically modified. Due to its low cost to manufacture, it is often used instead of cane sugar, however, it is controversial due to the increasing risks of obesity and diabetes from its use.

- Artificial sweeteners—Specifically aspartame (more popularly known as NutraSweet and Equal). Aspartame is a known neurotoxin and cancer-causing agent. The components of this toxic sweetener may lead to a variety of symptoms, including hyperactivity and behavioral problems, allergies, chronic fatigue, fibromyalgia, hypoglycemia, weight gain, and increased triglycerides (blood fats), which ultimately leads to hypertension. It is best avoided at all costs.

Reduce or avoid completely any regular use of foods containing these additives. Some people are more sensitive than others and the best way to prevent harm from these poisons is to avoid them entirely. Your body will thank you and your blood pressure numbers will improve.

Stocking Your Healthy DASH Pantry

Set the stage for success by stocking the pantry and refrigerator with DASH-healthy ingredients. The contents of the pantry may vary with the seasons, but the need to keep healthy ingredients on hand for preparing DASH-friendly meals never changes. The first step, before filling the pantry with healthy foods and ingredients, is to toss out any items that are detrimental to building health.

Products containing hydrogenated vegetable oil, vegetable shortening, or partially hydrogenated vegetable oils are first to go. Check for them in margarine, cookies, crackers, cereals, frozen foods, breads, pastries, muffins, donuts, snack foods, salad dressings, mayonnaise, peanut butter, potato chips, candy bars, and other packaged foods.

While you are cleaning out your pantry, discard the following foods, because they are devoid of nutrients: highly processed foods, including white flour products and enriched products; foods with high-sugar content; foods filled with preservatives and colorings; foods with a long shelf life; and foods past their expiration dates. Once this is done, congratulate yourself. You've taken an important step on your road to reducing high blood pressure and increasing energy and vitality.

Next, it is time to restock your pantry and refrigerator with staples. You will want to carry enough supplies to make a variety of DASH-healthy meals for at least several days. At first, it may be a whole new way of looking at "stocking up" because you'll be making more regular trips to the grocery store and you'll need to plan your meals, but it's worth it because you'll be eating healthier foods. You'll also have more energy from eating this way, too, as your health improves.

In stocking up with vegetables, variety is the key word to remember. I recommend that you make 50 percent of them green leafy ones because these are loaded with magnesium, calcium, and potassium, all of which are heart-healthy minerals. The other staple vegetables to have on hand include green beans, cabbage, sweet potatoes, peas, cauliflower, onions, winter squash, and peppers.

WARNING

Make a point to avoid all cured meats, such as bacon, ham, luncheon meats, sausage, and hot dogs, because of their high sodium, fat, and cancer-causing nitrites and nitrates.

Choose foods that are low in saturated fats as these are heart healthiest. Eating fish is one of the smartest and simplest things you can do for your heart. Seafood contains important heart-protective vitamins and minerals and very little artery-clogging saturated fat. Go for wild-caught, deep-sea cold water fish, such as salmon, halibut, herring, mackerel, tuna, and trout.

Meats and poultry are other common sources of saturated fats. Turkey and chicken breast are lower in saturated fat than beef, pork, and lamb. Make sure to take the skin off poultry, and try to avoid having it with a gravy, which may be high in sodium. I recommend allocating one day a week where you "go vegetarian," as giving up meat just one day a week can help cut saturated fat intake by 15 percent.

In the dairy department, switch to nonfat (skim) milk. Notice how nonfat milk has no saturated fat, contains less calories, and still has protein and calcium. If you are lactose intolerant, you can find lactose-free milk or take lactose-digesting enzymes to ease digestion. I recommend using more nut and rice milks, as these contain plenty of calcium, taste great in smoothies and over cereals, and are healthy choices overall.

When choosing cheeses and yogurts, try to buy reduced fat or nonfat whenever possible. The daily maximum of saturated fat for someone on a 2,000-calorie diet is 20 grams. Aim to never consume more than 15 grams per day, except on special occasions and halve this amount if your cholesterol is high. This is not a hard goal to achieve on a daily basis once you become more aware and read labels.

I recommend shopping at local farmers' markets or co-ops, where you can learn precisely how the food was grown and assure quality. Let's face it, when we buy cheap foods we pay for it later with our health. The food sold at these markets tends to be fresher, less expensive, and less chemically treated than that available in some super-markets. Your patronage helps support small or family farms.

Buy fresh products a few days before they ripen fully. There's no point in buying fresh vegetables and fruits if they turn brown and mushy a day or two after you bring them home. Unless you plan to eat it within a day or two, buy fruits and vegetables that are still firm to the touch, check expiration dates on bagged produce, and stay away from green potatoes or onions that have started to sprout.

GOOD TO KNOW

If you can't find the produce in the state of ripeness you want, ask to speak to the produce manager, to see if there's more in the back waiting to be put on the shelves.

Choose organically grown foods whenever possible. Organic foods are grown without chemical fertilizers and pesticides and are therefore less toxic to your body. Animals raised on organic farms are not fed dangerous hormones and antibiotics, which means there's no added risk that they'll be passed on to us through the food we eat.

In Appendix D you will find a shopping list of food items that serve as the foundation for a DASH diet pantry. These items supply many of the ingredients you'll need to prepare the recipes in this book.

Equipping Your DASH Kitchen

Setting up your kitchen so that it helps you work efficiently will set the stage for your DASH diet success. The kitchen is an environment that prominently displays how we nourish ourselves and our family, so you will want to consider important tools and cooking techniques as much as anything.

I am basically a creature of habit when it comes to cooking, so I like to have things positioned around me where I can grab them easily. I have arranged my kitchen so I can turn from the stove to the fridge and back again on a mere pivot of a foot. I keep spices close to the stove, a vegetable scrub brush at hand, a cutting board in easy reach of both stove and sink, and baskets filled with onions, garlic, and squash.

It's not necessary to have high-tech, state-of-the-art equipment to deliver DASH-healthy meals. There are, however, some important tools and implements to have on hand that will make your life easier, whether you are a novice or experienced cook.

For preparing vegetables, chopping, cleaning, trimming, or slicing, having several knives of different sizes are useful. Since browning vegetables is also an integral part of nutrient-rich DASH dishes, a well-seasoned cast-iron skillet is a must.

A food processor makes quick work of chopping and grating, which is great when you are short on time but still want to eat healthy, homemade foods. Preparing large amounts of food is a breeze when you use a food processor. It reduces the seemingly endless preparation times for dishes such as vegetables, soups, and casseroles, and can reduce your chopping, blending, and mixing time by as much as 90 percent. It can also process nuts and seeds into various consistencies. Look for a model with a minimum capacity of 8 to 10 cups and that comes with both sharp- and soft-edged S-blades, as well as shredding and slicing wheels.

An electric high-speed blender is useful for mixing, blending, and grinding. Use it for blending smoothies and shakes, making soups, and achieving the desired degree of smoothness when blending nuts, making pâtés, or liquefying vegetables.

A handheld blender is a low-cost useful appliance that's great for blending soup while it's still in the pot, as well as whipping cream and beating eggs.

A juice extractor is one of the most convenient ways to get maximum nutrients and important blood pressure–lowering minerals from fresh fruits and vegetables. The juices extracted from fresh, raw vegetables and fruits furnish all the cells and tissues of the body with minerals, vitamins, and nutritional enzymes in a form that's readily digested and assimilated.

GOOD TO KNOW

Some juice extractors have additional blades that enable you to chop and grind food, allowing you to prepare dishes such as nut butters and milks and fruit sorbets. One of the best brands to look for: Green Star, which is capable of juicing all types of produce, including green leafy vegetables, and can homogenize nuts and seeds for spreads.

A wok is one of the most useful cooking devices you can own. The wok has the special ability to cook food quickly, so that it retains almost all its nutritional elements. Vegetables most commonly cooked in a wok are carrots, beans (including snap or green beans and soybeans), bamboo sprouts, broccoli, onions, garlic, cabbage, and mushrooms. Using a wok, you can sauté, stew, deep-fry, steam, or stir-fry a meal in just a few minutes. Woks are unbeatable for cooking a bunch of ingredients in a single pan.

Cooking Methods and Food Storage

The cooking methods most commonly used in the recipes in this book involve either dry or moist heat. Here are some descriptions for your reference:

- Sautéing is cooking foods uncovered in a skillet, with a small amount of oil at very high temperature. It is a relatively quick way to cook food and allows the flavors to be released along with the nutrients.

- Baking and roasting are simple methods of food preparation that use dry heat in a ventilated space to cook foods thoroughly. Baking, of course, is done in the oven and helps to tenderize vegetables and meats that require long cooking times.

- Pressure cooking tenderizes grains, such as rice, and beans and legumes. It also helps bring out the flavor and nutrients of meats and it greatly reduces their cooking time.

- Broiling and grilling entail cooking foods one side at a time on very high heat so the juices are locked inside. Grilled foods are often soaked in advance in home prepared or low-sodium marinades.

- Braising means browning, then boiling or simmering foods in a skillet or saucepan. Combining oil and water in the skillet or saucepan allows you to use less oil, thereby reducing any additional fat.

- Boiling generally refers to cooking foods submerged in water that has come to a rolling boil.

- Steaming is cooking foods with the steam that comes from boiling. You can place a small steaming basket inside a saucepan and place your food inside this, then cover with a lid.

- Stir-frying is cooking foods in a wok or skillet on high heat with a moderate amount of oil. Foods are kept moving in the pan so they are coated and cooked on all sides.

It is important to cook foods so as to keep their vital, wholesome, and health-giving properties as well as their nutrition. We want our food to retain its flavor, color, and vitality as much as possible.

The Least You Need to Know

- To reduce high blood pressure, you will want to lower the amount of sodium and fat in your diet, as well as consuming zero hydrogenated or trans fats. Increase your fiber consumption by eating six to nine servings of vegetables per day.

- Sharpen your awareness about what you're currently eating. Then you can take steps to make the changes you desire for a healthier future.

- When it comes to filling your DASH pantry, a little planning goes a long way. With a well-stocked pantry, more of your energy will be free to cook and create meals that nourish you and your family.

- Having the right equipment will make your life easier, whether you like to cook or don't want to spend your time cooking.
- The key is to keep your food and kitchen clean and organized, and to use the food you buy in a timely manner.

DASH Diet Menu Plans

In This Chapter

- Using the recommended plan
- Eating properly the first 3 weeks
- Knowing what's best to eat when you're out

To get you started quickly, here are some sample meal plans for 3 weeks. You can substitute any of the meals and snacks listed here for any of the meals and snacks recipes listed throughout the book.

The protein portions here may need to be increased, depending on your size and level of activity. As a guideline, and in keeping with a 2,000-calorie diet, the safest bet is to stick with between 4 to 6 ounces of protein per day, depending again on your size and level of activity.

If you're uncertain about your calorie range intake, check yourself against the body mass index to gain further clarity (refer to the BMI chart in Appendix C). We are not going for perfection, because that simply doesn't exist. What we are going for is reversing or preventing hypertension and cardiovascular disease as well as lowering your sodium intake.

Keeping it simple is really the way to go, and there are a few keys to ensuring a successful outcome. Start by drinking lots of pure filtered water throughout the day—at least one 8-ounce glass of water every waking hour. This not only keeps your kidneys happy and flushes out toxins, but it also balances your sodium levels and keeps your metabolism humming along.

I recommend having at least one scoop of a high-quality protein powder mixed in cold, filtered water for ultimate energy each day. Remember to toss in some mixed berries or other favorite fresh seasonal fruits for antioxidants, DASH-healthy minerals, and even more energy.

> **GOOD TO KNOW**
>
> Once a week, you can substitute one of these meals with a "cheat meal." You will enjoy this new DASH eating plan and have lower sodium as well. Remember, you can "cheat" once a week only!

Week 1 Eating Plan

Your first week will be easier than you think—remember to embrace the new you.

Monday

Breakfast

Berry Buzz Protein Smoothie (Chapter 5) or DASH'n'Berry Heart-Felt Smoothie (Chapter 20)

Lunch

Broccoli with Walnuts and Avocado Salad (Chapter 7), slice of sweet or savory bread (Chapter 18)

Snack

¼ cup raw almonds (or raw nuts of any kind)

Snack #2 (optional)

1 cup nonfat or low-fat cottage cheese mixed in a bowl with ½ cup chopped berries and ¼ cup raw pine nuts

Dinner

4–6 ounces of chicken, beef, or fish with 2 cups stir-fried or steamed fresh seasonal vegetables

Tuesday

Breakfast

Banana Quinoa Porridge or DASH-ing Cheese and Herb Omelet (Chapter 5), slice of sweet or savory bread (Chapter 18), and green tea

Lunch

Swiss Chard and Apple Salad (Chapter 7) or a Turkey or Chicken Salad Sandwich (Chapter 9), and green tea

Snack

Protein shake with fresh or frozen berries or Berry Buzz Protein Smoothie (Chapter 5)

Snack #2 (optional)

¼ cup unsalted raw mixed nuts

Dinner

Choose from Part 4 recipes under vegetarian, beef, poultry, or seafood dishes, add your choice of veggie sides (Chapter 17), and green tea

Wednesday

Breakfast

Stabilizing Salmon Omelet with Fresh Chives or Flourless Chicken Pancakes (Chapter 6), and green tea

Lunch

Asparagus, Romaine, and Orange Salad (Chapter 7), and green tea

Snack

Protein shake with fresh berries or banana

Snack #2 (optional)

Tofu and Sesame Butter–Stuffed Celery or Crispy Nuts Trail Mix (Chapter 11)

Dinner

Choose from Part 4 recipes under vegetarian, beef, poultry, or seafood dishes, add your choice of veggie sides (Chapter 17), and green tea

Thursday

Breakfast

Marvelous Muesli with Delicious Nut Milk (Chapter 5), slice of sweet or savory bread, and green tea

Lunch

Greek Salad DASH Style (Chapter 7) and green tea

Snack

Protein shake with fresh seasonal fruits

Snack #2 (optional)

1 TB. raw tahini or nut butter spread on apple slices or slice sweet or savory bread

Dinner

Choose from Part 4 recipes under vegetarian, beef, poultry, or seafood dishes, add your choice of veggie sides (Chapter 17), and green tea

Friday

Breakfast

Baked Granola with Delicious Nut Milk (Chapter 5), slice of sweet or savory bread, and green tea

Lunch

Select a recipe from "Scrumptious Salads" (Chapter 7) and green tea

Snack

Protein shake with fresh seasonal fruits

Snack #2 (optional)

¼ cup raw unsalted nuts or apple with nut butter

Dinner

Choose from Part 4 recipes under vegetarian, beef, poultry, or seafood dishes, add your choice of veggie sides (Chapter 17), and green tea

Saturday

Breakfast

Nourishing Hot Rice Cereal Indian Style or Stabilizing Salmon Omelet with Fresh Chives (Chapter 6), slice of sweet or savory bread, and green tea

Lunch

Select a recipe from "Scrumptious Salads" (Chapter 7) and green tea

Snack

Slice of sweet or savory bread and an apple

Snack #2 (optional)

Protein shake with fresh seasonal fruits

Dinner

Choose from Part 4 recipes under vegetarian, beef, poultry, or seafood dishes, add your choice of veggie sides (Chapter 17), and green tea

Sunday

Breakfast

Spicy Spinach and Asparagus Pancakes with Herbed Chevre (Chapter 6), slice of sweet or savory bread, and green tea

Lunch

Select a recipe from "Scrumptious Salads" (Chapter 7) and green tea

Snack

Protein shake with fresh seasonal fruits

Snack #2 (optional)

Nutrient-Dense Hummus (Chapter 11) with Kale Curry Crackers (Chapter 11) or Love-Your-Heart Lentil Pâté (Chapter 11)

Dinner

Choose from Part 4 recipes under vegetarian, beef, poultry, or seafood dishes, add your choice of veggie sides (Chapter 17), and green tea

Week 2 Eating Plan

The second week is easier than the first, and it's okay to reward yourself with dessert every now and again.

Monday

Breakfast

Baked Granola or Marvelous Muesli, with Delicious Nut Milk (all from Chapter 5), slice of sweet or savory bread, and green tea

Lunch

Select a recipe from "Scrumptious Salads" (Chapter 7) and green tea

Snack

Protein shake with fresh seasonal fruits

Snack #2 (optional)

Turkey Avocado Roll-Ups or Love-Your-Heart Lentil Pâté (Chapter 11)

Dinner

Choose from Part 4 recipes under vegetarian, beef, poultry, or seafood dishes, add your choice of veggie sides (Chapter 17), and green tea

Tuesday

Breakfast

Berry Date Oatmeal Porridge or Banana Quinoa Porridge (Chapter 5) with fresh fruits, or Marvelous Muesli with Delicious Nut Milk (Chapter 5), and green tea

Lunch

Select a recipe from "Scrumptious Salads" (Chapter 7) and green tea

Snack

Protein shake with fresh seasonal fruits

Snack #2 (optional)

1 slice Tuna Radicchio Mozzarella Pizza (Chapter 11) or $\frac{1}{4}$ cup raw unsalted nuts

Dinner

Choose from Part 4 recipes under vegetarian, beef, poultry, or seafood dishes, add your choice of veggie sides (Chapter 17), and green tea

Wednesday

Breakfast

Hi-Fiber Blueberry Muffin, Baked Granola with Delicious Nut Milk (Chapter 5), and green tea

Lunch

Select a recipe from "Scrumptious Salads" (Chapter 7) and green tea

Snack

Protein shake with fresh seasonal fruits

Snack #2 (optional)

Lemon Tahini Sauce (Chapter 11) with celery or carrot sticks

Dinner

Choose from Part 4 recipes under vegetarian, beef, poultry, or seafood dishes, add your choice of veggie sides (Chapter 17), and green tea

Thursday

Breakfast

DASH-ing Cheese and Herb Omelet (Chapter 5), slice of sweet or savory bread, and green tea

Lunch

Select a recipe from "Scrumptious Salads" (Chapter 7) and green tea

Snack

Protein shake with fresh seasonal fruits

Snack #2 (optional)

$\frac{1}{2}$ cup nonfat cottage cheese mixed with $\frac{1}{2}$ fresh berries and $\frac{1}{4}$ cup pine nuts

Dinner

Choose from Part 4 recipes under vegetarian, beef, poultry, or seafood dishes, add your choice of veggie sides (Chapter 17), and green tea

Friday

Breakfast

Scrambled tofu or eggs with jalapeño, slice of sweet or savory bread, and green tea

Lunch

Select a recipe from "Scrumptious Salads" (Chapter 7) and green tea

Snack

Protein shake with fresh seasonal fruits

Snack #2 (optional)

Turkey Avocado Roll-Ups (Chapter 11) with carrot sticks or celery

Dinner

Choose from Part 4 recipes under vegetarian, beef, poultry, or seafood dishes, add your choice of veggie sides (Chapter 17), and green tea

Saturday

Breakfast

Energizing Feta Frittata (Chapter 6), slice of sweet or savory bread, and green tea

Lunch

Select a recipe from "Scrumptious Salads" (Chapter 7) and green tea

Snack

Protein shake with fresh seasonal fruits

Snack #2 (optional)

Nutrient-Dense Hummus (Chapter 11) with Kale Curry Crackers (Chapter 11), or ¼ cup Crispy Nuts Trail Mix (Chapter 11)

Dinner

Choose from Part 4 recipes under vegetarian, beef, poultry, or seafood dishes, add your choice of veggie sides (Chapter 17), and green tea

Sunday

Breakfast

Cottage Cheese Pancake with Banana (Chapter 6), sweet or savory bread, and green tea

Lunch

Select a recipe from "Scrumptious Salads" (Chapter 7) and green tea

Snack

Protein shake with fresh seasonal fruits

Snack #2 (optional)

Apple with nut butter or slice of savory bread with nut butter

Dinner

Choose from Part 4 recipes under vegetarian, beef, poultry, or seafood dishes, add your choice of veggie sides (Chapter 17), and green tea

Week 3 Eating Plan

In the third week you are feeling lighter and have more energy because you made it through the first 2 weeks and are doing well.

Monday

Breakfast

DASH-ing Cheese and Herb Omelet (Chapter 5) or Marvelous Muesli with Delicious Nut Milk (Chapter 5), slice of sweet or savory bread, and green tea

Lunch

Select a recipe from "Scrumptious Salads" (Chapter 7) and green tea

Snack

Protein shake with fresh seasonal fruits

Snack #2 (optional)

Nutrient-Dense Hummus (Chapter 11) with Kale Curry Crackers (Chapter 11), or 1 slice Gluten-Free Veggie Pizza (Chapter 9)

Dinner

Choose from Part 4 recipes under vegetarian, beef, poultry, or seafood dishes, add your choice of veggie sides (Chapter 17), and green tea

Tuesday

Breakfast

Marvelous Muesli with Delicious Nut Milk or Banana Quinoa Porridge (Chapter 5), slice of sweet or savory bread, and green tea

Lunch

Select a recipe from "Scrumptious Salads" (Chapter 7) and green tea

Snack

Protein shake with fresh seasonal fruits

Snack #2 (optional)

¼ cup raw unsalted nuts or celery stick with nut butter

Dinner

Choose from Part 4 recipes under vegetarian, beef, poultry, or seafood dishes, add your choice of veggie sides (Chapter 17), and green tea

Wednesday

Breakfast

DASH-ing Cheese and Herb Omelet (Chapter 5), slice of sweet or savory bread with avocado or nut butter, and green tea

Lunch

Select a recipe from "Scrumptious Salads" (Chapter 7) and green tea

Snack

Protein shake with fresh seasonal fruits

Snack #2 (optional)

$\frac{1}{2}$ Nut Butter and Raisin Sandwich (Chapter 9)

Dinner

Choose from Part 4 recipes under vegetarian, beef, poultry, or seafood dishes, add your choice of veggie sides (Chapter 17), and green tea

Thursday

Breakfast

Hi-Fiber Blueberry Muffins, Berry Buzz Protein Smoothie (Chapter 5), and green tea

Lunch

Select a recipe from "Scrumptious Salads" (Chapter 7) and green tea

Snack

Marvelous Muesli or Baked Granola with Delicious Nut Milk (Chapter 5)

Snack #2 (optional)

Slice of sweet or savory bread with avocado or nut butter

Dinner

Choose from Part 4 recipes under vegetarian, beef, poultry, or seafood dishes, add your choice of veggie sides (Chapter 17), and green tea

Friday

Breakfast

Banana Quinoa Porridge (Chapter 5), sweet or savory bread or muffin (Chapter 18), and green tea

Lunch

Select a recipe from "Scrumptious Salads" (Chapter 7) and green tea

Snack

Protein shake with fresh seasonal fruits

Snack #2 (optional)

Nutrient-Dense Hummus (Chapter 11) with Kale Curry Crackers (Chapter 11), or ¼ cup Crispy Nuts Trail Mix (Chapter 11)

Dinner

Choose from Part 4 recipes under vegetarian, beef, poultry, or seafood dishes, add your choice of veggie sides (Chapter 17), and green tea

Saturday

Breakfast

Flourless Chicken Pancakes or Cottage Cheese Pancake with Banana (Chapter 6), slice of sweet or savory bread, and green tea

Lunch

Select a recipe from "Scrumptious Salads" (Chapter 7) and green tea

Snack

Protein shake with fresh seasonal fruits

Snack #2 (optional)

Select 1 cup of any of the recipes in "Sumptuous Soups" (Chapter 10), slice of sweet or savory bread

Dinner

Choose from Part 4 recipes under vegetarian, beef, poultry, or seafood dishes, add your choice of veggie sides (Chapter 17), and green tea

Sunday

Breakfast

Stabilizing Salmon Omelet with Fresh Chives or Nourishing Hot Rice Cereal Indian Style (Chapter 6), slice of sweet or savory bread, and green tea

Lunch

Select a recipe from "Scrumptious Salads" (Chapter 7) and green tea

Snack

Protein shake with fresh seasonal fruits

Snack #2 (optional)

1 slice Gluten-Free Veggie Pizza (Chapter 9) or ¼ cup raw unsalted nuts

Dinner

Choose from Part 4 recipes under vegetarian, beef, poultry, or seafood dishes, add your choice of veggie sides (Chapter 17), and green tea

DASH Meals Away from Home

In the comfort of your own home, it is simple to create delicious and healthy meals consistent with the DASH diet. But when you find yourself dining at a local restaurant, friend's house, work, or on vacation, you might need some extra help. With the proper knowledge and effort, you can follow the DASH diet anywhere and everywhere.

DASH meals consist of a great deal of fruits and vegetables, thus it is vital to include these in your diet. When going to a restaurant, look for meals that have these heavily incorporated into the recipe. If you are at an Italian restaurant, for instance, choose a low-fat pasta dish with marinara sauce and vegetables. At a Mexican restaurant you can order a vegetable-filled burrito. Add a fresh, raw salad with your meal, as this will aid in digestion as well as supply important minerals and fiber. Avoid cheese, which contains extra sodium, and high-fat ingredients.

Do not forget about the sides. Substitute healthy accompaniments such as vegetables for otherwise unhealthy choices. Choose steamed (and butter-free) mixed vegetables instead of french fries. Most restaurants will allow you to substitute sides for healthier choices. Even fast-food eateries have started to offer healthier sides such as apple slices and carrot sticks.

Since you will not be preparing the meals yourself, you will need to ascertain exactly what is in the food you are served. This includes calories, fat, and sodium. Because taste does not always accurately reflect food items that are high in unhealthy ingredients, you will need to find out in a more definitive fashion. Most restaurants offer nutrition guidelines for foods they serve. This information may be on a website, on the menu, or in a pamphlet. You may be shocked and dismayed by the numbers, but it can lead you to better choices. If you are at a relative's or a close friend's house, ask about the ingredients or just watch as they cook. Make wise choices.

It is important to learn about the foods that are typically high in fat and sodium so that you will know to stay away from them. For instance, hamburgers, pizza, and soup usually have higher-than-normal levels of sodium. If you cannot find out how much fat and salt is in the meal, stay away from these as a practice. On the internet and in books you can find general guidelines on the average nutritional information of different foods.

GOOD TO KNOW

If you carry an iPhone or Android, you can find apps that contain a comprehensive database of over 1,258,000 foods and restaurant items. Check out MyFitnessPal app to help make life easier when it comes to calories and your health.

Learn what meals are typically low in fat and sodium so that you will automatically know the better choices. Of course, you already know that fruits and vegetables are fine. Remember that different versions of the same meal (for example, fried items versus baked) can be drastically different in nutritional information. Think about each and every ingredient as well as preparation methods.

Do not forget about drinks. Alcohol should be limited at restaurants. Remember that sugary drinks count as sweets, of which you only have five per week in the DASH diet. Limit desserts while dining out. Instead of ordering an ice-cream sundae at a fast-food restaurant, look for some healthier alternatives. Many fast-food restaurants have started to offer fruit and yogurt parfaits. Although parfaits may not be a "health food" when served at a restaurant since they can be high in sugar, they are far better than saturated fat–laden ice cream.

You will need to learn to say "Hold the …" often. It is okay to ask others to modify meals to decrease the fat and sodium and be more consistent with the DASH diet. For instance, ask your server to not add butter and salt to your vegetables and other foods. If you get a sandwich, tell him or her not to butter the bread or add mayonnaise. Request that sauces and dressings be served on the side.

Consider this example. If you are at an Italian restaurant, you might choose a marinara sauce instead of a cream-based sauce since it is far healthier. However, even that can be full of salt and calories. Ask for a light sauce or have them put it on the side so you can add just enough to satisfy you. Of course, the extent to which they can comply will range by restaurant and dish. Look for eateries and meals that are more flexible.

It can be a little more challenging when you are at someone else's house. If you are, consider offering to cook a meal so that you can create dishes consistent with your diet. Explain your situation so as not to insult your host, if necessary.

HEART-HEALTHY TIP

At parties, look for the vegetable plate and fruit platter and avoid chips, pretzels, and salted nuts.

Another way to follow the DASH diet while away from home is to bring your own food to the table. If you are staying with someone else, then buy your own groceries. These can be fruits and vegetables to supplement family meals. Buy healthy snacks that are suitable for the DASH diet, such as low-sodium popcorn and carrot sticks.

When eating on the job, you can also bring your own food. Make a brown bag lunch or buy a healthy premade meal. Try to find meals that are less processed because those tend to be lower in fat and sodium.

Do not be afraid to bring your own food, even to a restaurant. Of course, you are not going to walk in with an entire buffet for one; however, you may be able to bring in something small. For instance, if you have a fat- and sodium-free salad dressing that you like, bring it to put on your salad. You can also eat healthy before you go so that you are not too hungry at the restaurant.

Most restaurants focus more on taste than on healthy eating choices, and thus it is much more of a challenge to follow a healthy eating plan while eating out. If you can minimize eating out, then do so. You can still go to the grocery store while on vacation. Choose a hotel room that has a small kitchenette so you do not have to eat every meal out while on a personal vacation or business trip.

Consider all aspects of the DASH diet when eating your meals outside of the home. The DASH diet emphasizes whole grains. When eating at a sandwich shop, ask for multigrain bread. Ask for whole wheat or even spinach pasta at an Italian shop. Do not choose a lot of heavy and fatty meat, and remember that even lean meats still contain a certain amount of fat.

It is imperative to be aware of serving size when eating out. If you are at someone else's house, then ask to serve yourself. If your host serves you too much (as many do), you might feel compelled to finish every morsel. Restaurant meals in particular often have enough for two, three, or more servings. Because some feel that they have to "clean their plate," ask for half of it to be packaged right away to keep yourself from overeating.

Even though you may not be within the safe confines of your home, you can still adhere to the DASH diet. Keep track of what you eat in a small food diary. You can use a piece of paper, a PDA, or even a smartphone with the correct application. With the knowledge and discipline you can successfully continue with the DASH diet while on the go. Your weight and blood pressure will thank you.

The Least You Need to Know

- You can substitute any of the meals or snacks listed in each of the meal plans for any of the meals and snacks recipes listed throughout the book.
- It's okay to be creative at restaurants by choosing your own healthy food selections for your meal. You pay for it with your health as well as your wallet.
- Remember to count sweet drinks as part of your DASH eating plan.
- Sticking to your DASH eating plan is easy with a little bit of planning beforehand.

Good-Start DASH Breakfasts

You've probably heard it said that breakfast is the most important meal of the day ... and it's true. Breakfast switches on your metabolism and provides your body with the most nourishment when you feed yourself with essential nutrients.

The recipes in this part are both nourishing and balancing for your entire body. It's okay to eat a light breakfast, as long as it contains some healthy proteins, fats, and carbohydrates. Eating a healthy breakfast, such as the ones outlined in these recipes, will actually provide you with more energy. You will also find that your energy is more stable for longer periods of time (as your blood sugar levels become balanced) and your cravings will decrease.

Quick Weekday Breakfasts

In This Chapter

- Eight quick and easy breakfasts for busy days
- A selection of nourishing meals with all the right stuff

Breakfast is the most important meal of the day because it sets the pace for your metabolism, making it either more or less efficient. In addition, eating breakfast allows you to restock the energy stores that have been depleted overnight and begin the day with a tank full of the right fuel.

All of the breakfast recipes in this and the next chapter have been specially formulated with heart-healthy ingredients that include healthy proteins, healthy fats, and low-on-the-glycemic-index carbohydrates. You will find them easy to prepare and quick to make, even for the most novice cook. Whatever your excuses, eating a good breakfast is essential for improving your cardiovascular system and reducing hypertension. You may even lose a few inches around your waistline, too.

Baked Granola

If you're a cereal eater who loves the crunch, texture, and flavor of delicious granola, then look no further than this delicious treat. It's not only heart healthy, but the flavors will melt in your mouth.

Yield:	Serving size:	Prep time:	Cook time:
1 gallon	1½ cups	15 minutes	50 minutes

6 cups rolled oats	¾ cup barley malt powder
3½ cups rye flakes	⅔ cup grape seed oil
2 cups shredded coconut	½ cup pure maple syrup
2 cups sunflower seeds	1 TB. pure vanilla extract
1 cup sesame seeds	1 TB. pure almond extract
1 cup walnuts, chopped	¼ tsp. pure maple extract
1 cup pecans, chopped	1 cup raisins, optional
1 cup almonds, chopped	

1. Preheat the oven to 375°F.

2. In a large bowl, combine oats, rye flakes, coconut, sunflower seeds, sesame seeds, walnuts, pecans, and almonds. Set aside.

3. In a separate bowl, stir together barley malt, oil, syrup, vanilla extract, almond extract, and maple extract.

4. Add wet mixture to dry mixture and mix together well. (For granola that sticks together more, use a food processor to combine the wet and dry mixtures.)

5. Spread the combined mixture onto a large baking sheet and bake for 50 minutes, or until mixture is lightly browned.

6. Let cool for 30 minutes.

7. Mix in raisins and serve immediately or store in an airtight, sealable container for future breakfasts.

HEART-HEALTHY TIP

Barley malt powder is sometimes called flour. It is made from grain that is fermented, then dried and ground. This process turns the grain's starches into sugars. It is super healthy, since the sugars are largely maltose, which does not cause a sharp spike in insulin and keeps energy stable for hours.

Marvelous Muesli

Loaded with fiber, this sublimely tasty muesli is nutrient rich, crunchy, and flavorful. It will satisfy your appetite for hours and keep your system working like a well-oiled machine.

Yield:	Serving size:	Prep time:	Cook time:
6 cups	1 cup	10 minutes	Soak overnight

2 cups rolled oats

1 cup rye flakes

1 cup dried dates, chopped

1 cup raisins

1 cup almonds, chopped loosely

$\frac{1}{2}$ cup walnuts, chopped loosely

$\frac{1}{2}$ cup pecans, chopped loosely

$\frac{1}{2}$ cup sunflower seeds

$\frac{1}{3}$ cup shredded coconut

1 tsp. pure vanilla extract

$\frac{1}{4}$ tsp. ground nutmeg

$\frac{1}{2}$ tsp. ground cinnamon

4 cups apple cider

1 banana

1. In a large bowl, combine oats, rye flakes, dates, raisins, almonds, walnuts, pecans, sunflower seeds, coconut, vanilla extract, nutmeg, and cinnamon. Mix well.

2. Place mixture in an airtight, sealable container and stir in apple cider.

3. Refrigerate overnight and serve in the morning with chopped banana.

HEART-HEALTHY TIP

For added fiber and to increase antioxidants, add your favorite seasonal fresh fruits to this delicious muesli just prior to serving. This cereal can be stored in the refrigerator for several days.

Delicious Nut Milk

Enjoy this enzyme-packed, nutrient-rich alternative to cow's milk. It's a good source of protein and heart-healthy fats. Enjoy your fresh milk over granola, muesli, with dessert, or on its own.

Yield:	Serving size:	Prep time:	Cook time:
2 cups	2 cups	10 minutes	None

1 cup nuts (almonds, pecans, macadamia, or hazelnut) or 1 cup sesame seeds

2 cups spring or filtered water

$\frac{1}{2}$ cup dried fruit such as figs, dates, or raisins

Dash cinnamon

Piece of cheesecloth or nut milk bag (mesh)

1. Place the nuts or sesame seeds in an electric blender and pulverize. Add 1 cup water gradually, while continuing to blend on high.

2. Combine dried fruit and cinnamon in a separate bowl, and add additional 1 cup water.

3. Strain through a piece of cheesecloth or nut milk bag.

4. Serve or refrigerate for later.

GOOD TO KNOW

You can dehydrate the pulp that remains after straining. Simply spread it onto a flat oven tray and place in the oven at 110°F for a couple of hours, or until totally dry and flakey. Sprinkle pulp on top of desserts, or use as "flour" in bread recipes.

Hi-Fiber Blueberry Muffins

These simple to make fiber-full blueberry muffins are loaded with heart-healthy minerals such as calcium and potassium. The addition of ricotta cheese and eggs makes them nourishing and helps to satisfy your appetite for hours. Great for breakfast or a snack.

Yield:	Serving size:	Prep time:	Cook time:
12 muffins	1 muffin	12 minutes	20 minutes

1 cup whole-grain wheat flour

1 cup rolled oats

$1\frac{1}{2}$ tsp. cinnamon

$\frac{1}{2}$ tsp. gluten-free baking powder

$\frac{1}{4}$ tsp. baking soda

10 oz. ricotta cheese

6 TB. or 1 scoop whey protein powder

$\frac{1}{4}$ cup macadamia nut oil

2 eggs

3 tsp. stevia powder

$\frac{1}{2}$ cup rice milk or nut milk

$1\frac{1}{2}$ cups fresh or frozen blueberries

$\frac{1}{2}$ cup walnuts, chopped

2 cups fresh berries

1. Preheat the oven to 400°F. Grease muffin tins.

2. In a large mixing bowl, combine flour, rolled oats, cinnamon, baking powder, and baking soda.

3. In a food processor or blender, blend ricotta cheese, protein powder, macadamia nut oil, eggs, stevia extract, and rice milk or nut milk until smooth.

4. Stir into dry mixture.

5. Gently fold in blueberries and walnuts.

6. Fill muffin tins to top and bake 18 to 20 minutes.

7. Serve each muffin with $\frac{1}{3}$ cup fresh berries.

HEART-HEALTHY TIP

Stevia extract, which comes from a small plant native to Paraguay and Brazil, is 250 times sweeter than table sugar. It promotes healthy blood sugar levels and is available in most health-food stores and many supermarkets.

Banana Quinoa Porridge

If you've never tried quinoa for breakfast, you're in for a treat. Quinoa is great with the sweet taste of fruit or served with more savory items such as vegetables. It is a dieter's dream because it is satisfying and will fill you up, is low in cholesterol, rich in fiber, digests slowly, and has a low glycemic index, helping you keep your blood sugar levels stable for hours.

Yield:	Serving size:	Prep time:	Cook time:
6 cups	1 cup	10 minutes	None

4 cups quinoa

10 cups filtered water

1 cup dates, without pits

1 banana, peeled and sliced

1 tsp. cinnamon

1 tsp. nutmeg

1. Soak quinoa overnight in 8 cups filtered water and drain the next morning.

2. Soak dates overnight in 2 cups filtered water. Retain $1\frac{1}{2}$ cups soak water.

3. Blend quinoa, dates, date soak water, banana, cinnamon, and nutmeg in an electric blender until smooth.

4. Serve cold or at room temperature.

GOOD TO KNOW

Quinoa is a flavorful source of plant-derived calcium, so it helps regulate contraction of the heart, and facilitates nerve and muscle function. It's a DASH-friendly grain that also contains impressive amounts of potassium, magnesium, and zinc.

Berry Date Oatmeal Porridge

High in soluble fiber and protein, oats have been proven to lower cholesterol, prevent heart disease, and boost serotonin (which improves mood). Porridge is digested slowly and helps keep you full for longer. The addition of nuts, dates, and berries packs this porridge full of antioxidants and heart-healthy minerals. It tastes darn delicious, too!

Yield:	Serving size:	Prep time:	Cook time:
6 cups	1 cup	10 minutes	None

3 cups steel cut oats, soaked

8 cups filtered water

1 cup dates, soaked

1 TB. cinnamon

1 tsp. nutmeg

$\frac{1}{2}$ cup walnuts, chopped

$\frac{1}{2}$ cup almonds, chopped

2-3 cups berries

1. Soak steel cut oats overnight in 6 cups filtered water and drain the next morning.

2. Soak dates overnight in 2 cups filtered water. Retain $1\frac{1}{2}$ cups soak water.

3. Blend steel cut oats, dates, date soak water, cinnamon, and nutmeg in an electric blender until smooth.

4. Add the almonds and walnuts to the mixture.

5. Serve with fresh berries.

HEART-HEALTHY TIP

Simply serve this porridge with nut milk and you will increase your calcium and magnesium levels as well as add more flavor to this delicious dish.

Berry Buzz Protein Smoothie

Power up your metabolism with protein from the milk and whey powder. Then supercharge it with a shot of antioxidants from the delicious, nutrient-rich, and heart-healthy berries and fiber. This one's a great grab-'n'-go breakfast or anytime snack.

Yield:	Serving size:	Prep time:	Cook time:
2 cups	2 cups	5 minutes	None

1 cup milk (almond, cow, or goat)

¼ cup almonds or macadamia nuts

1 cup fresh or frozen berries

1 cup filtered water

1 scoop or 6 TB. whey protein powder

1 TB. flax seed oil

1 tsp. cinnamon

½ cup ice cubes (optional)

1. Blend milk and nuts for 3 minutes.

2. Add berries, water, whey protein powder, flax seed oil, cinnamon, and ice cubes.

3. Blend for 2 to 3 minutes.

HEART-HEALTHY TIP

Whey protein powder is a pure protein with little to no fat. It is a perfect complement to your DASH diet as it is low in carbohydrates and low on the glycemic index. It helps you burn more calories and lose weight easier and quicker.

DASH-ing Cheese and Herb Omelet

Make breakfast special with this simple but wholesome cottage cheese and herb omelet. Feel free to add sliced fresh mushrooms to vary the flavors and serve with fresh herbs and salad greens. It's simple, delicious, and DASH healthy.

Yield:	Serving size:	Prep time:	Cook time:
1 omelet	$\frac{1}{2}$ omelet	8 minutes	10 minutes

$\frac{1}{2}$ tsp. onion powder

$\frac{1}{3}$ cup low-fat cottage cheese

3 medium eggs

Pinch oregano

Pinch basil

Pinch thyme

1 TB. parsley, chopped

Pinch ground black pepper, or to taste

1. In a medium bowl, mix together onion powder and cottage cheese. Set aside.

2. In a small bowl, beat eggs, oregano, basil, thyme, parsley, and pepper, with a fork.

3. In a nonstick skillet, over medium heat, add 1 tablespoon grape seed oil, and when hot, add egg mixture. Fry egg mixture on one side until set and not runny. Turn and fry on other side until cooked through.

4. Quickly spread cottage cheese mixture on $\frac{1}{2}$ of omelet, fold omelet over.

5. Fry on both sides until cottage cheese is warm and begins to melt.

6. Serve immediately.

HEART-HEALTHY TIP

You can use a special omelet pan or a small nonstick frying pan to make an omelet. The main thing to remember when choosing a pan is that it should have a thick base to distribute heat evenly and have shallow, gently sloping sides.

Leisurely Weekend Breakfasts

In This Chapter

- Seven nourishing weekend-style breakfasts
- DASH-healthy ingredients and a variety of choices

The breakfast recipes in this chapter have been created specifically with guidelines and recommendations that follow DASH-healthy ingredients. Plenty of thought has gone into ensuring these recipes provide you with the necessary vitamins and minerals essential for energy production as well as keeping you nourished and grounded.

It's always a welcome treat to spend some extra time on the weekend to make sure you start your day with a nourishing and balanced breakfast. You'll find a combination of choices and flavors to suit any taste sensation or desire.

Variety is the spice of life, and you will thrive when you start the day out with a hearty, healthy breakfast. I think you will enjoy the variety included here.

Nourishing Hot Rice Cereal Indian Style

This rice dish is delicious and full of surprises. Raisins, bell peppers, peas, and potatoes make their appearance, as well as lots of aromatic spices from cumin to coriander.

Yield:	Serving size:	Prep time:	Cook time:
4 cups	1 cup	15 minutes	20 minutes

1 cup farina

1/3 cup potatoes, diced

1/4 cup carrots, diced

1/4 cup fresh or frozen peas

2 TB. unsalted butter or ghee (clarified butter)

1 tsp. black mustard seeds

1/2 tsp. cumin seeds

1/2 tsp. ground turmeric

1/2 tsp. coriander

Pinch cayenne pepper

1 clove garlic, chopped fine

1 2/3 cups hot water

1 tsp. salt, Celtic or Himalayan

1/3 cup green bell pepper, diced

1/4 cup raisins

1/4 cup whole cashews, unsalted

1 tsp. fresh lemon juice

1 TB. fresh cilantro, chopped

1. In a large saucepan, melt 3 tablespoons butter over medium heat.

2. Add *farina* to the pan and sauté, stirring constantly, until the farina becomes fragrant and begins to brown. Keep warm.

3. In a medium-size covered saucepan with a steamer basket, lightly steam potatoes, carrots, and peas over medium heat for 5 to 7 minutes.

4. In a small saucepan, make a *vagar* by melting butter over medium heat and adding mustard and cumin seeds.

5. When seeds start to pop, stir in turmeric, coriander, cayenne pepper, and garlic. Turn off heat.

6. Add vagar mixture to farina mixture and stir well.

7. Add hot water and salt, whisking to break up any lumps.

8. Add steamed vegetables, bell pepper, raisins, cashews, lemon juice, and cilantro.

9. Stir until fluffy. Serve immediately.

DEFINITION

Farina is a milled cereal grain that's made from wheat germ and the inner parts of wheat kernels. It has a high protein content and is adaptable for numerous dishes when it is prepared as a hot cereal. A **vagar** is a "ghee" based sauce in which hot spices are sautéed then added into the cereal. Ghee is clarified butter, which is often used in Indian or Asian dishes. It is a nutrient dense food and is considered one of the best oils for baking, sautéing, and deep fat frying. It is stable at high temperatures.

Spicy Spinach and Asparagus Pancakes with Herbed Chevre

Asparagus and spinach are a must for any heart-healthy diet as they are known for reducing inflammation and arthritis. Enjoy these delicious pancakes!

Yield:	Serving size:	Prep time:	Cook time:
8–10 small pancakes	2 pancakes	10 minutes	10 minutes

1 cup onion or scallion, finely chopped

1 cup asparagus, diced

4 cups spinach, washed, finely chopped

½ cup whole-wheat flour

2 large eggs, beaten

¼ tsp. Celtic or Himalayan salt

¼ tsp. freshly ground black pepper

Dash cayenne pepper

¼ cup chevre (goat cheese)

1 tsp. olive oil

1 TB. filtered water

Pinch black pepper

1 TB. parsley, chopped

1. In a large skillet, heat 1 tablespoon grape seed oil over medium heat. Add onion and sauté 1 to 2 minutes.

2. Add asparagus and sauté 2 more minutes.

3. Add spinach and cook about 1 more minute until asparagus is tender and spinach reduced.

4. Transfer the mixture to a medium bowl. Mix in flour, eggs, salt, black pepper, and cayenne pepper.

5. Heat 1 tablespoon grape seed oil in the skillet over medium heat.

6. Place ¼ cup of mixture into the skillet at a time. Cook over medium heat until crisp and golden, 2 to 3 minutes. Flip and cook 2 more minutes on other side. Add more oil between batches if needed.

7. In a small bowl, add chevre and stir in olive oil and water till texture is firm. Add pepper to taste.

8. Add fresh parsley. Serve each pancake with a dollop of the chevre on top.

GOOD TO KNOW

Goat cheese is lower in calories and fat than cow's milk cheeses. It is also higher in calcium, which assists the body's ability to burn fat, and it also plays a vital role in body functions such as blood clotting and blood pressure regulation, to name only a few.

Flourless Chicken Pancakes

These nutrient-rich flourless chicken pancakes are perfect when you are trying to live a low-carb lifestyle and keep your blood sugar balanced. They are high in protein and healthy fat, and will keep you energized for hours. Great for snacking on, too.

Yield:	Serving size:	Prep time:	Cook time:
4–5 pancakes	1–2 pancakes	10 minutes	10 minutes

1 chicken breast, medium size and precooked

Dash cayenne pepper (optional)

2 TB. parsley, chopped

3 large eggs, beaten

2 cups spinach or salad greens

½ avocado, peeled and sliced

2 TB. fresh lemon or lime juice

1. Blend chicken, cayenne pepper, parsley, and eggs in a food processor until completely smooth. Mixture will look like thick pancake batter.

2. Heat 1 tablespoon grape seed oil in a skillet. Add ¼ cup batter to skillet. Batter may need to be spread out so it's not too thick. Watch closely, flip pancake, and remove when cooked. Continue until all pancakes are cooked.

3. Serve over a bed of fresh spinach or salad greens and top with fresh avocado. Sprinkle with fresh lemon or lime juice.

GOOD TO KNOW

Gluten is a protein found in grains such as wheat, barley, rye, spelt, and triticale, and is restricted in the diets of people with celiac disease. Many people who take gluten products out of their diet have benefited in their health and energy levels.

Energizing Feta Frittata

Perfectly balanced with fiber and vitamins to sustain your energy levels for hours, this dish is delicious. It's high in protein to boost mood and topped with good oils and fats to round out the tastes, textures, and nutritional benefits. Your blood pressure will go down with this nutritious breakfast.

Yield:	Serving size:	Prep time:	Cook time:
2–3 frittatas	1 frittata	10 minutes	8–10 minutes

½ cup red or brown onion, chopped

1 cup kale, washed and chopped

½ cup zucchini, chopped

2 tsp. unsalted butter, or olive oil

3 large eggs, beaten

¼ cup parsley, chopped

Dash cayenne pepper (optional)

2 TB. sheep's milk feta, crumbled

1. Sauté onion and zucchini in a small ovenproof skillet. Then add the kale.

2. Add eggs, parsley, cayenne pepper, and feta, and cook without stirring, tilting the skillet while lifting the edge of the cooked egg with a spatula, allowing uncooked egg to flow underneath.

3. When no more uncooked egg will flow, put under a broiler and broil until top begins to brown, 1 to 2 minutes.

HEART-HEALTHY TIP

To reduce the amount of sodium in feta cheese, soak it in water for a few minutes then rinse thoroughly. This will reduce sodium content significantly without affecting the flavor too much.

Stabilizing Salmon Omelet with Fresh Chives

Salmon is brain food and high in omega-3 essential fatty acids. It contains important heart-healthy minerals such as calcium and potassium, as well as numerous vitamins. With the eggs and spinach in this dish, you will be more than satisfied for hours.

Yield:	Serving size:	Prep time:	Cook time:
2 omelets	1 omelet	10 minutes	10 minutes

1 can (7.5-oz.) salmon, packed in spring water	Dash freshly ground black pepper
2 tsp. lemon or lime juice	2 large eggs
2 TB. fresh chives or shallots, chopped	$\frac{1}{4}$ cup skim milk
Dash cayenne pepper (optional)	2 cups spinach or mixed salad greens
	$\frac{1}{2}$ avocado, peeled and sliced

1. Drain the juice out of the can of salmon and place the rest of the contents in a mixing bowl. Using a fork, mash the salmon well to break up all the pieces, skin and bones included.

2. Add the lemon or lime juice, chives or shallots, and cayenne pepper, and grind in the black pepper.

3. Break the eggs into the salmon mixture and mix in thoroughly. Add in the skim milk.

4. In a large saucepan, over medium heat, heat 1 tablespoon unsalted butter or grape seed oil and pour in the salmon-egg mixture, then smooth out with a spatula. Cook over a low heat for 5 to 6 minutes, or until set. Turn it over and cook a further 3 minutes, or finish under the broiler.

5. Serve immediately over spinach or salad greens and place avocado on top.

GOOD TO KNOW

Studies continue to prove that fish oils, especially omega-3, have a significantly positive effect on lowering hypertension.

Cottage Cheese Pancake with Banana

Enjoy the nutrient-dense richness of this balanced breakfast that's been naturally sweetened with apple juice. The inclusion of fresh banana adds potassium to help lower blood pressure and creates a calming effect.

Yield:	Serving size:	Prep time:	Cook time:
1 pancake	1 pancake	5 minutes	8–10 minutes

⅓ cup low-fat, low-sodium cottage cheese

1 large egg

2 TB. whole-wheat flour

¼ tsp. cinnamon

1 tsp. plus 1 TB. concentrated apple juice

1 banana, chopped

Sprinkle of cinnamon

1. In a medium bowl, beat together cottage cheese, egg, whole-wheat flour, cinnamon, and 1 teaspoon apple juice with fork until combined.

2. Heat 1 tablespoon grape seed oil or unsalted butter in a nonstick skillet over medium heat. Pour egg and cottage cheese mixture into the skillet when heated.

3. Cook until set and brown on one side. Flip over and spread 1 tablespoon apple juice on top.

4. Cook until puffed and brown on other side.

5. Serve with banana and sprinkle of cinnamon.

HEART-HEALTHY TIP

Low-sodium and fat-free versions of cottage cheese are available in most grocery stores. Be sure to read the nutrition label on the package of cheese to ensure you don't overdo your recommended intakes.

Scrambled Tofu Jalapeño

Soy-bean based products, such as tofu in this delicious dish, are a good alternative to meat because it contains all of the essential amino acids your body needs to make a complete protein, just like meat. It's high in fiber and flavor and helps to lower your blood pressure.

Yield:	Serving size:	Prep time:	Cook time:
4 cups	¼ pound	10 minutes	15 minutes

1 lb. firm tofu

½ small green bell pepper, chopped

½ small red bell pepper, chopped

½ medium jalapeño, chopped

2 small tomatoes, chopped coarsely

2 TB. parsley, chopped

2 small green onions, chopped

1 tsp. onion powder

Dash cayenne pepper (optional)

⅛ tsp. ground black pepper

¼ tsp. turmeric

2–3 cups spinach or mixed salad greens

1. Rinse tofu well and dry. In a medium bowl, mash tofu with fork into the consistency of scrambled eggs.

2. Stir in green bell pepper, red bell pepper, jalapeño, tomatoes, parsley, green onions, onion powder, cayenne pepper, black pepper, and turmeric.

3. Heat 1 tablespoon grape seed oil or unsalted butter in a nonstick frying pan. Transfer the tofu mixture to the pan and slowly simmer, covered, for 10 minutes over a medium heat.

4. Simmer uncovered for approximately 5 more minutes.

5. Serve immediately over a bed of spinach or mixed salad greens.

GOOD TO KNOW

Eating soy protein foods such as tofu and tempeh have been proven to directly lower LDL cholesterol levels. Soy is low in saturated fat and contains naturally occurring omega-3 essential fatty acids, which have known heart health benefits.

Midday Meals and Anytime Snacks

Taking just a few minutes more to prepare healthy meals and snacks gives you greater control over what you and your family are eating. This will provide you with the most energy for longer periods as you go about your day.

It's a good idea to seek out variety when it comes to healthy eating. I have made sure to include an array of sumptuous dishes that I am certain you will love once you get started eating and cooking the DASH-healthy way. Flavors, textures, and aromas—there's no shortage of pleasurable moments ahead of you as you dig into these delicious selections.

Scrumptious Salads

In This Chapter

- Twenty fresh and lively salads
- A multitude of antioxidant-rich vegetables

It's vital to your heart-healthy DASH diet to include plenty of antioxidants and vitamin C–rich foods such as fresh leafy greens and lively salads. These recipes contain foods for fighting stress, which also can help ward off the tendency to reach for sugary, high-glycemic carbohydrates. You'll find plenty of heart-strengthening DASH diet minerals such as magnesium, calcium, and potassium within recipes that contain very little sodium.

All of the recipes in this chapter contain ample amounts of vitamins A, C, and E, along with B-complex and numerous minerals to strengthen your blood vessels and arteries, and lower cholesterol. You'll also find lots of fiber sources to keep your metabolism efficient. I recommend eating at least one raw salad every day. You'll soon notice greater energy and improved metabolism.

Gradually you will learn how to eat to protect your heart and overall health. Experiment with these recipes until you find the right balance of foods that makes you feel best, as no two people are identical. Your taste buds will also enjoy the journey.

Swiss Chard and Apple Salad

Swiss chard, also called spinach chard, is high in magnesium and calcium, which helps keep all the nerves in a relaxed state. The addition of onions and red cabbage provide numerous antioxidants to help lower high blood pressure. This salad is full of fiber and also contains ample protein. Indulge yourself in this dish.

Yield:	Serving size:	Prep time:	Cook time:
3 quarts	2 cups	10 minutes	None

½ lb. Swiss chard, washed

½ lb. red cabbage

1 small red apple, chopped, not peeled

1 small Granny Smith apple, chopped

1 TB. pineapple juice or lemon juice

¼ cup red onion, diced

½ cup golden raisins

⅔ cup almonds, sliced

3 TB. apple cider vinegar

Zest and juice of 1 orange

1 TB. honey

1. Remove ribs of Swiss chard. Chop Swiss chard and cabbage into bite-size pieces and place in large bowl.

2. In a medium bowl, add apples and toss with pineapple or lemon juice to prevent browning.

3. Add onion, raisins, and almonds to greens.

4. Add vinegar, orange juice and zest, and honey. Toss thoroughly.

5. Serve immediately.

GOOD TO KNOW

The young leaves of Swiss chard are best used for preparing salads and the mature leaves are used for cooking. It is one of the most nutrient beneficial vegetables you can eat.

Waldorf Chicken Salad

The famous Waldorf Chicken Salad, full of apples, celery, walnuts, and raisins, gets full marks when it comes to being heart healthy. Try this dish using heart-healthy fish instead of chicken and enjoy every tasty morsel. This dish is great for reducing hypertension.

Yield:	Serving size:	Prep time:	Cook time:
2 quarts	1–2 cups	15 minutes	None

6 tart red apples

4 cups mixed lettuce greens, or spinach

6 stalks celery, chopped

½ cup lemon or lime juice

2 TB. walnuts, chopped

2 TB. mayonnaise, light, low sodium

1 lb. cooked chicken (or fish), diced

1. Wash apples, lettuce or spinach, and celery.

2. Core and dice apples (do not peel) and place in large bowl.

3. Pour lemon or lime juice over apples to prevent browning.

4. Combine celery, walnuts, and chicken (or fish). Toss in mayonnaise.

5. Gently mix in apples.

6. Place tossed salad in a large serving bowl.

GOOD TO KNOW

Walnuts not only taste scrumptious, they contain amazing health benefits for both your heart and your brain. High in omega-3 essential fatty acids, they boost moods and sharpen thinking. They are high in fiber, too. Enjoy them raw in salads or snack on them anytime.

Tomato and Hearts of Palm Salad with Roasted Pepitas

Enjoy all the heart-healthy benefits with heart of palms blended in fresh herbs and tomatoes. This recipe is high in magnesium and higher in lycopene, a powerful antioxidant that protects against heart disease and reduces the risk of prostate cancer. There are so many benefits in this tasty dish that you simply must try it.

Yield:	Serving size:	Prep time:	Cook time:
4 cups	1–2 cups	10 minutes	None

4 medium tomatoes, organic, diced

1 (8-oz.) can hearts of palm, drained and chopped

1 TB. pepitas

Juice of 3 limes, with pulp

1 TB. extra virgin olive oil, cold pressed

1 TB. flax seed oil, cold pressed

2 large garlic cloves, crushed

1 bunch cilantro, chopped

1 TB. mint, chopped

2 TB. roasted pepitas (pumpkin seeds)

Dash of cayenne pepper (optional)

1. In a medium bowl, blend tomato with hearts of palm.

2. Heat small skillet over medium heat and add pepitas. Remove from heat after 1 minute.

3. In a small bowl, mix the lime juice, extra virgin olive oil, flax seed oil, and garlic.

4. Add the chopped cilantro, mint, cayenne, and lime juice mixture to the diced tomato and hearts of palm. Toss well.

5. Serve with roasted cheddar-stuffed turkey burgers (Chapter 9).

GOOD TO KNOW

Pumpkin seeds are high in zinc, which is protective for bones as well as beneficial for men's prostate glands. It also contains anti-inflammatory properties. The mineral zinc is also essential for bone mineral density and preventing osteoporosis.

Broccoli with Walnuts and Avocado Salad

All of the DASH-friendly nutrients in this delicious salad are too numerous to mention, but know that it tastes like a slice of heaven. The sweet potatoes mixed with several fresh herbs and spices gives this nutrient-rich salad the full gamut of flavors. Definitely put this high on your list and enjoy often.

Yield:	Serving size:	Prep time:	Cook time:
4 cups	1–2 cups	10 minutes	None

½ cup sweet potatoes, diced, skin on

2 cups broccoli, finely chopped

1 ripe avocado, peeled and diced

¾ cup tomatoes, organic, diced

½ cup walnuts, chopped

2 TB. shredded coconut

2 cloves garlic, chopped

½ TB. fresh lemon or lime juice

Dash cayenne pepper (optional)

1 TB. fresh cilantro, chopped

1 TB. fresh basil, chopped

½ tsp. ground turmeric

½ tsp. black mustard seeds

½ tsp. cumin seeds

1. In a small, covered saucepan with a steamer basket, steam sweet potatoes in water for approximately 10 minutes, or until soft. Set aside and let cool.

2. In a blender or food processor, process 1 cup chopped broccoli until smooth.

3. In a medium-size bowl, combine sweet potatoes, broccoli, avocado, tomatoes, walnuts, coconut, lemon or lime juice, cayenne pepper, cilantro, and basil.

4. In a small saucepan or skillet, heat 2¼ teaspoons olive oil over medium heat and add turmeric, mustard, and cumin seeds, stirring constantly for 30 seconds.

5. Pour liquid mixture over vegetables and gently mix together. Serve immediately.

HEART-HEALTHY TIP

Broccoli is loaded with powerful antioxidants, in particular C, K, A, and folate, which remove plaque buildup from arteries. It's full of fiber to keep cholesterol at healthy levels, and is high in DASH-friendly minerals magnesium, calcium, and potassium. Enough good cannot be stated about how beneficial it is.

Cucumber and Tomato Salad with Citrus and Mint

The bell peppers in this salad give it a wonderful combination of textures and flavors as well as many DASH-healthy nutrients, such as fiber. Give the cayenne pepper a try in this recipe; it is a key spice to include in your heart-healthy meals, especially if you enjoy the flavor and zing that it brings.

Yield:	Serving size:	Prep time:	Cook time:
1 quart	1–2 cups	15 minutes	None

½ large cucumber, peeled, diced

½ medium green bell pepper, diced

2 whole tomatoes, organic, wedged or large diced

1 cup Swiss chard or spinach, chopped coarsely (optional)

1 tsp. black mustard seed

2 tsp. grated ginger

1 clove garlic, chopped

Pinch cayenne pepper (optional)

¼ cup mint, chopped

Pinch Celtic or Himalayan salt (optional)

2 TB. lemon or lime juice

1. Combine cucumber, green pepper, tomatoes, and Swiss chard or spinach in a bowl.

2. In a sauté pan, heat 2 tablespoons olive oil over medium heat and add mustard seed, ginger, garlic, and cayenne pepper. Stir until mustard seed starts to pop, less than 1 minute.

3. Allow oil to cool and toss with vegetables, adding the mint, salt, and lemon or lime juice.

4. Serve with grains, poultry, or meat dish.

HEART-HEALTHY TIP

Hot and spicy, cayenne pepper has been used in many cultures back through the ages as a weapon to prevent and even stop heart attacks as they are happening. Cayenne contains very many heart-healthy benefits. It can reduce blood cholesterol levels and dissolve fibrin, which helps prevent blood clots. I highly recommend adding this spice to your daily salad or entrée.

Wild Rice Salad with Apples, Walnuts, and Fresh, Wild Basil

This wild rice salad is not only tasty and delicious but contains antioxidants and dietary fiber and is loaded with plenty of heart-friendly minerals. You simply can't eat too much of this dish.

Yield:	Serving size:	Prep time:	Cook time:
1 quart	1 cup	10 minutes	50 minutes

1 cup wild rice

2 cups filtered water

$\frac{1}{3}$ cup olive oil plus 1 TB.

$\frac{1}{2}$ tsp. Celtic or Himalayan salt (optional)

1 cup walnuts, coarsely chopped

2 small celery stalks, sliced

1 cup collard greens, chopped (or use Swiss chard)

4 scallions, thinly sliced

1 cup raisins

1 medium red apple, organic, cored and diced

2 TB. fresh basil, chopped

2 TB. fresh parsley, chopped

Grated rind and juice of 1 lemon or lime

2 garlic cloves, pressed or finely chopped

Freshly ground black pepper

Dash cayenne pepper (optional)

1. Place rice in a strainer and rinse under cold water.

2. Put washed rice in a medium saucepan with water, 1 tablespoon oil, and salt. Cover, bring to a boil over medium-high heat, and reduce heat to simmer. Add a pinch of salt and tablespoon olive oil.

3. Cook 50 minutes, or until rice is tender and all water is absorbed.

4. Meanwhile, in a large bowl, combine walnuts, celery, collard greens or Swiss chard, scallions, raisins, apple, basil, parsley, and lemon rind.

5. In a jar with a tight-fitting lid, combine lemon juice, garlic, black pepper, cayenne pepper, and $\frac{1}{3}$ cup olive oil. Shake vigorously.

6. Pour half of dressing over apple mixture and toss well.

7. When rice is done, let it cool until just warm.

8. Combine with fruit mixture and pour remaining dressing over mixture.

9. Let sit at least 1 hour before serving at room temperature, on bed of mixed lettuce greens if desired.

HEART-HEALTHY TIP

Sulfur-containing garlic has numerous cardio-protective benefits, including its ability to help regulate the number of fat cells that get formed in our bodies. It contains the potent compound allicin, in addition to being an excellent source of DASH minerals like magnesium and the antioxidant selenium.

Quinoa Kale Tabouli

Enjoy the amino acid–rich protein of this nutrient-dense seed, quinoa, that was once considered "the gold of the Incas." It is a relative of Swiss chard, which together with kale in this antioxidant-rich tabouli salad is about as heart healthy as it gets. It's very high in fiber and tastes amazing. It's wonderful on the waistline also, so feel free to have two helpings.

Yield:	Serving size:	Prep time:	Cook time:
5 cups	1–2 cups	10 minutes	15 minutes

1 TB. light miso or Bragg Liquid Aminos

1–2 TB. extra virgin olive oil

1 cup quinoa, cooked

1 small bunch kale, washed and chopped

3 ripe tomatoes, organic, chopped

$\frac{1}{3}$ cup parsley, chopped

2 TB. fresh basil, chopped

1 clove garlic, chopped

Juice of 1 lemon or lime

Dash cayenne pepper (optional)

1. In a large bowl, mix miso or liquid amino acids with oil.

2. Mix in quinoa, kale, tomatoes, parsley, basil, garlic, cayenne, and lemon or lime juice.

3. Serve immediately.

GOOD TO KNOW

Bragg Liquid Aminos are a healthy alternative to soy and tamari because there is no table salt or preservatives added. Their natural salty flavor comes from the soybeans that are used to make Bragg Liquid Aminos, making them perfect for anyone on a low-sodium diet or following the DASH diet.

Lively Mixed Greens and Sprouts Salad

The crispy Romaine lettuce leaves in this recipe combine with the wondrous flavors of organic tomatoes and fresh herbs. This salad is extremely high in fiber to improve your digestion and loaded with cardio-compatible antioxidants. Indulge often in this healthy dish.

Yield:	Serving size:	Prep time:	Cook time:
4 cups	2 cups	15 minutes	None

1 cup Romaine lettuce, chopped

2 cups mixed salad greens

1 tomato, organic, chopped

1 cup sprouts, mixed (alfalfa, sunflower, buckwheat, and clover)

$\frac{1}{2}$ cup parsley, chopped

1 TB. basil, chopped

$\frac{1}{3}$ cup salad dressing of your choice (Chapter 8)

1 avocado, peeled, sliced

1. Place washed lettuce and salad greens in a large bowl.

2. Add tomato, sprouts, parsley, and basil, and toss with dressing.

3. Garnish with sliced avocado and a sprig of parsley.

4. Refrigerate and serve cold.

HEART-HEALTHY TIP

Alfalfa sprouts are known to deliver numerous health benefits, due mostly to their high saponins content. Saponins are plant molecules which act only within the intestinal tract to reduce inflammation that may be caused from ingesting bacteria from foods. Lowering inflammation is most beneficial for heart health, and can result in lowering high blood pressure in particular.

Greek Salad DASH Style

Enzymes—proteins that work in our digestive tract and help us break down fats, proteins, and carbohydrates—come from raw foods such as the ingredients found in this delicious, heart-healthy Greek salad. It's high in fiber and laden with DASH-healthy nutrients such as antioxidants to support your health.

Yield:	Serving size:	Prep time:	Cook time:
1 pint	12 cups	20 minutes	None

6 cups fresh romaine lettuce, chopped (1–2 medium heads)

¾ cup fresh cherry tomatoes, halved

½ cup red onions, thinly sliced

½ cup cucumbers, sliced

1 cup feta cheese (sheep or goat), crumbled

½ cup whole black olives, pitted

2 TB. scallions, chopped

¾ cup olive oil

2 TB. red wine vinegar

½ TB. dried basil

1 TB. garlic, finely chopped or minced

1 tsp. dried thyme

1 tsp. Bragg Liquid Aminos

¼ tsp. ground black pepper

Dash cayenne pepper (optional)

1. In a large bowl, combine lettuce, tomatoes, onions, cucumbers, feta cheese, olives, and scallions.

2. In a small bowl, whisk together olive oil, red wine vinegar, basil, garlic, thyme, amino acids, black pepper, and cayenne pepper.

3. Serve immediately.

HEART-HEALTHY TIP

Eating fibrous foods—such as dark-green leafy vegetables, fruits, and root vegetables—remains one of the most potent actions you can take to improve digestive and heart health.

Cardio Carrots and Walnut Salad

Enjoy the sunny flavors of carrots, herbs, and walnuts in this perfectly balanced, high-fiber dish. The beta-carotene in carrots is an antioxidant that converts to vitamin A, which helps strengthen blood vessels and improves eyesight. Walnuts provide essential fatty acids that feed the brain and increase focus. You can't go wrong eating this delicious salad every day.

Yield:	Serving size:	Prep time:	Cook time:
1 quart	1 cup	15 minutes	None

1 lb. carrots, cut into 3-inch-long sticks

½ cup walnuts, chopped

1 tsp. fresh basil, chopped

1 TB. fresh parsley, chopped

⅓ cup raisins (optional)

2 TB. red wine vinegar

2 TB. extra virgin olive oil

2 TB. fresh lemon or lime juice

2 garlic cloves, minced fine or pressed

Pinch Celtic or Himalayan salt (optional)

Pinch ground black pepper to taste

1. In a large bowl, combine carrot sticks, walnuts, basil, parsley, and raisins.

2. In a small bowl, whisk together red wine vinegar, olive oil, lemon juice, garlic, salt, and black pepper.

3. Place in a sealable container. Seal container and toss carrots and dressing together.

4. Store in refrigerator until serving time (at least 1 hour, preferably overnight).

HEART-HEALTHY TIP

A 10-year study conducted in the Netherlands on the risk of cardiovascular disease showed that participants who ate at least half a cup or more of carrots per day had a significantly lower risk for heart disease.

Asparagus, Romaine, and Orange Salad

Asparagus is loaded with potassium and folic acid, which are great for lowering blood pressure. The combination of flavors, from the orange and the Romaine, tastes deliciously cleansing on your palate. The high fiber from all ingredients, makes this dish a DASH-ing success.

Yield:	Serving size:	Prep time:	Cook time:
3 cups	1 cup	15 minutes	4 minutes

1 cup (8-oz.) asparagus, trimmed and cut into 2-inch pieces

2 large oranges

2 tomatoes, organic, cut into eighths

1 cup Romaine lettuce leaves, shredded

2 TB. extra virgin olive oil

$\frac{1}{2}$ tsp. red wine vinegar

Dash of cayenne pepper (optional)

Pinch Celtic or Himalayan salt (optional)

Freshly ground black pepper

1. In a medium saucepan with a steamer basket, steam asparagus over medium-high heat for 3 to 4 minutes until just tender. Drain and refresh under cold filtered water.

2. Grate rind from half an orange and reserve. Peel both oranges and cut into segments. Squeeze juice from the remaining membrane and reserve.

3. In a salad bowl, place asparagus, orange segments, tomatoes, and lettuce.

4. In a small bowl, mix together oil and vinegar, adding 1 tablespoon of reserved orange juice and 1 teaspoon of grated rind. Season with cayenne pepper, salt, and black pepper.

5. Just before serving, pour dressing over salad and mix gently to coat.

HEART-HEALTHY TIP

Asparagus has numerous medicinal benefits. The seeds and succulent shoots contain the potent antioxidants, carotene, selenium, and vitamin C, all of which strengthen the heart, kidneys, brain, and lungs.

DASH Nicoise Salad

This delicious salad is a perfectly balanced, nutrient-rich meal. It's loaded with DASH-friendly nutrients such as potassium, magnesium, calcium, zinc, folic acid, vitamin C, and high in fiber. You get protein from the tuna, eggs, and anchovies, along with heart- and brain-healthy omega-3 essential fatty acids—tons of enzymes for improving digestion, too!

Yield:	Serving size:	Prep time:	Cook time:
1 quart	2 cups	15 minutes	3–4 minutes

2 Romaine lettuce hearts

½ cucumber

3 hard-boiled eggs

4 firm ripe tomatoes, organic

½ cup tuna, packed with spring water

12 black olives, whole

2 TB. capers

½ cup green beans, lightly steamed for 3–4 minutes

1 red bell pepper

1 clove garlic, crushed

Pinch tarragon

1 cup French dressing

1. Cut lettuce hearts, cucumber, eggs, and tomatoes into quarters and arrange in a salad bowl.

2. Add tuna, olives, capers, and beans.

3. Remove the stalk and seeds from red bell pepper, chop into small pieces, and add to salad bowl.

4. In a small bowl, mix garlic and tarragon with French dressing, pour over salad, and serve.

HEART-HEALTHY TIP

Tuna is a great source of vitamin B_6, which lowers levels of homocysteine. High homocysteine levels are directly damaging to blood vessel walls, which is associated with atherosclerosis.

DASH-ing Coleslaw

Cabbage can provide you with some special blood pressure– and cholesterol-lowering benefits. It is high in fiber, vitamin C, and DASH minerals. The additional ingredients in this coleslaw make it an excellent enzyme-laden choice for your health. It tastes great, too!

Yield:	Serving size:	Prep time:	Cook time:
6 cups	12 cups	15 minutes	None

4 cups white cabbage, finely shredded

1 carrot, shredded

$\frac{1}{2}$ cup red apple, diced, unpeeled

$\frac{1}{2}$ cup raisins

$\frac{1}{4}$ cup toasted almonds, sliced

$\frac{1}{2}$ cup sour cream, low sodium, organic

$\frac{1}{2}$ cup mayonnaise, low sodium

1 tsp. Celtic or Himalayan salt (optional)

Dash cayenne pepper (optional)

Dash ground black pepper

2 TB. lemon or lime juice

$\frac{1}{2}$ tsp. prepared French mustard

1 tsp. grated orange rind

1. In a large bowl, lightly toss cabbage, carrot, apple, raisins, and almonds.

2. In a small bowl, mix sour cream, mayonnaise, salt, cayenne pepper, black pepper, lemon juice, and mustard. Combine with cabbage mixture.

3. Toss lightly and serve sprinkled with orange rind.

HEART-HEALTHY TIP

A certain compound found in cabbage called AITC has shown unique cancer-preventive properties—colon, prostate, and bladder cancer in particular. Researchers suggest regularly consuming the different types of cabbage (red, green, and Savoy) to experience its many health benefits.

Light Lentil, Tomato, and Feta Salad

High in fiber and plant protein, lentils readily absorb the variety of herbs and flavors around them. The addition of feta cheese and pine nuts gives this wonderful salad a distinctly enjoyable texture. It's loaded with fiber, minerals, and antioxidants.

Yield:	Serving size:	Prep time:	Cook time:
4 cups	1 cup	10 minutes	30 minutes

1 cup lentils, soaked for approximately 3 hours in cold water	4 TB. extra virgin olive oil
3 cups filtered water, cold	3 TB. fresh parsley, chopped
1 red onion, chopped	2 TB. fresh oregano, chopped
1 bay leaf	15 cherry tomatoes, halved
Pinch Celtic or Himalayan salt	$\frac{1}{3}$ cup feta cheese or goat cheese, crumbled, low sodium
Dash, freshly ground black pepper	3 TB. pine nuts, lightly toasted
Dash cayenne pepper (optional)	1 TB. sunflower seeds (optional)

1. Drain lentils after soaking and place in large saucepan. Pour in water and add onion and bay leaf.

2. Bring to a boil over medium-high heat. Boil for 10 minutes.

3. Lower heat to low and simmer for 15 to 20 minutes.

4. Drain lentils, discarding bay leaf, and pour into a serving bowl.

5. Add salt, black pepper, and cayenne pepper to taste.

6. Toss with olive oil. Set aside to cool.

7. Stir in parsley, oregano, and cherry tomatoes.

8. Add cheese and scatter pine nuts, and sunflower seeds, over salad.

9. Serve immediately.

HEART-HEALTHY TIP

Lentils are proven winners when it comes to heart health. They contain significant amounts of magnesium and folate, as well as vitamin B$_6$. A 19-year study showed a 15 percent risk reduction for cardiovascular disease from eating fiber found in lentils.

Sumptuous Sauerkraut Salad

One of the numerous benefits from eating this delicious raw cabbage salad is the high amounts of fiber coupled with the large number of probiotics that improves digestion. The added herbs and vegetables combine to make this dish flavorful as well as healing.

Yield:	Serving size:	Prep time:	Cook time:
6 cups	1 cup	15 minutes	None

1 lb. sauerkraut, low sodium, glass jar

½ cup onion, chopped

2 oz. pimiento, sliced

½ cup celery, sliced

1 cup carrot, shredded

1 green bell pepper, chopped

¼ cup apple cider vinegar

½ tsp. Celtic or Himalayan salt

Pinch ground black pepper

Dash cayenne pepper (optional)

½ tsp. caraway seeds

2 TB. parsley, chopped

1. Drain sauerkraut and combine with onion, pimiento, celery, carrot, and bell pepper in a large bowl. Toss gently.

2. In a small bowl, mix vinegar, salt, black pepper, cayenne pepper, and caraway seeds.

3. Pour dressing over sauerkraut mixture, toss lightly, and chill for 1 hour.

4. Sprinkle with chopped parsley before serving.

HEART-HEALTHY TIP

Sauerkraut contains healthy bacteria, or probiotics, which confer many health benefits on your gastrointestinal tract. Probiotics help regulate your immune system, as well as reduce allergies and skin problems such as eczema.

Red Salmon Salad with Avocado

With so many heart-healthy nutrients in this DASH dish, you simply can't go wrong. The combination of flavors together with the high fiber and antioxidants makes this an all-star meal for lowering hypertension.

Yield:	Serving size:	Prep time:	Cook time:
4–5 cups	1 cup	10 minutes	None

2 cups tinned red salmon, canned

½ cup celery, chopped

⅓ cup mayonnaise, no or low sodium

Dash of cayenne pepper (optional)

6–8 Romaine lettuce leaves

1 avocado, sliced

6 black olives, whole, pitted

Juice of 1 lemon or lime

1. Drain salmon and flake with a fork.

2. In a medium bowl, mix salmon with celery. Stir in mayonnaise and cayenne pepper.

3. Wash and drain lettuce leaves and place salmon mixture inside each leaf. Place sliced avocado on top.

4. Garnish with olives and serve with a sprinkle of lemon juice.

 HEART-HEALTHY TIP

Wild-caught Alaskan salmon poses the lowest health risk for contamination from mercury and other pollutants. It also contains the highest concentration of omega-3 essential fatty acids, which are known for their cholesterol-lowering anti-inflammatory benefits.

Curried Quinoa Salad

This creamy quinoa salad contains balanced amounts of plant protein to energize you for hours. It's high in antioxidants and a delicious combination of herbs and spices. Simply DASH-ing!

Yield:	Serving size:	Prep time:	Cook time:
1 quart	1 cup	15 minutes	20 minutes

¼ cup fresh lemon juice	2 cups cooked quinoa
2½ tsp. curry powder	12 green onions, diced
½ tsp. allspice	1 medium red pepper, diced
½ tsp. Celtic or Himalayan salt	1 cup raisins
1 clove garlic, chopped finely	½ cup canned or cooked chickpeas
½ tsp. ground black pepper	Dash cayenne pepper (optional)
¾ cup extra virgin olive oil	

1. In a small bowl, whisk together lemon juice, curry powder, allspice, salt, garlic, and black pepper. Gradually add oil to dressing mixture, whisking until all is blended. Set aside.

2. In a medium bowl, fluff quinoa with a fork. Add green onions, red pepper, raisins, chickpeas, and cayenne. Mix well.

3. Add dressing to quinoa mixture, toss, and chill for at least 2 hours or overnight.

HEART-HEALTHY TIP

Quinoa is an excellent source of magnesium, a mineral that relaxes blood vessels, preventing constriction of blood flow. It is also high in other important minerals such as manganese, iron, and copper. Quinoa is great for fighting atherosclerosis and heart disease.

Radish, Mango, and Apple Salad

Radishes not only taste delicious but have many digestive enzymes that help prevent excessive stomach acid and are especially good for repairing mucous membranes. Both mango and radishes are loaded in antioxidants and minerals such as calcium and magnesium. Together, they make a perfect DASH meal.

Yield:	Serving size:	Prep time:	Cook time:
1 quart	1 cup	15 minutes	None

½ cup sour cream, low fat, low sodium

2 tsp. creamed horseradish

1 TB. fresh parsley, chopped

Dash cayenne pepper (optional)

1 tsp. fresh ginger, finely chopped

1 TB. fresh dill

Pinch Celtic or Himalayan salt

Freshly ground black pepper

10–15 radishes, or 2 cups

1 dessert apple, peeled, cored, and thinly sliced

2 celery sticks, thinly sliced

1 small ripe mango

1 TB. fresh lemon or lime juice

1. In a small bowl, blend together sour cream, horseradish, parsley, cayenne pepper, ginger, dill, and fresh lemon or lime juice, and season with salt and black pepper to taste.

2. Remove tops and tails from radishes, then slice thinly. Place in a medium bowl and add apple and celery. Mix together.

3. Cut through mango lengthwise on either side of seed. Make even criss-cross cuts through each side section, then bend the peel back to separate the cubes. Add to bowl.

4. Pour dressing over vegetables and fruit and stir gently to coat.

5. Garnish with dill twigs before serving.

GOOD TO KNOW

Himalayan crystal salt is a high-quality natural rock salt that contains 84 elements found in the body. It has numerous health benefits, including the healthy regulation of your blood pressure. It is unlike regular table salt, and once you try it you won't want anything else.

Strawberry, Spinach, and Walnut Salad

Just as Popeye made himself strong by eating spinach, you can, too, with the anti-inflammatory compounds in this delicious spinach salad. The addition of fresh strawberries gives it added antioxidant power and essential DASH minerals such as magnesium, calcium, and potassium. This salad is bursting with flavor and heart-healthy omega-3 essential fatty acids with the addition of walnuts.

Yield:	Serving size:	Prep time:	Cook time:
1 quart	1–2 cups	10 minutes	None

2 TB. sesame seeds

½ cup extra virgin olive oil

¼ cup red wine vinegar

¼ tsp. paprika

¼ tsp. mustard

1 TB. dried minced onion

3 cups fresh spinach leaves, chopped, washed, and dried

2 cups strawberries, organic, sliced

¼ cup walnuts, chopped

1. In a small bowl, whisk together sesame seeds, olive oil, vinegar, paprika, mustard, and onion. Set aside.

2. In a large bowl, combine spinach, strawberries, and walnuts.

3. Pour dressing over salad, toss, and refrigerate 10 to 15 minutes before serving.

GOOD TO KNOW

When selecting spinach, always choose bright, vibrant-looking spinach leaves as they contain higher amounts of vitamin C and phytonutrients.

Broccoli, Spinach, and Avocado Salad

This salad provides a delightful blend of textures, colors, and flavors. It is nutrient rich, with antioxidants galore and extremely high quantities of fiber to help lower cholesterol and blood pressure levels. Serve with or without the spinach.

Yield:	Serving size:	Prep time:	Cook time:
4–5 cups	1–2 cups	15 minutes	None

½ cup extra virgin olive oil

2 TB. flax seed oil

2–3 TB. fresh lemon or lime juice

½ tsp. ground turmeric

½ tsp. minced onion

1 clove fresh garlic, chopped finely

Dash of cayenne pepper (optional)

2 cups broccoli, chopped

1 cup spinach, chopped, washed, and dried

1 ripe avocado, peeled and diced

½ cup tomatoes, organic, chopped

½ cup walnuts, chopped

2 TB. coconut, shredded

1 TB. fresh cilantro, chopped

1. In a small bowl, whisk together olive oil, flax seed oil, lemon or lime juice, turmeric, onion, and cayenne pepper. Taste test and set aside.

2. In a large bowl, combine broccoli, spinach, avocado, tomatoes, walnuts, coconut, and cilantro.

3. Pour dressing over salad, toss, and refrigerate 10 to 15 minutes before serving.

HEART-HEALTHY TIP

Avocados deliver almost 20 vitamins, minerals, and beneficial phytonutrients, making them a nutrient-dense, heart-healthy, and power-packed food.

Delicious Dressings

In This Chapter

- Dressing that makes salads come alive
- Using highly nutritious and delicious ingredients

In this chapter, you'll find simple dressings that perfectly complement any salad, blended naturally together with herbs, spices, and goodness for your heart-healthy DASH diet.

These simple dressings contain no dairy products and can be refrigerated for up to 3 days. They are blended with fresh vegetables and herbs because they deliver great taste with lots of nutrients and few calories.

These dressings are balancing for your digestive system and heart health; there is no salad that will not be enhanced by their goodness and flavor.

Cilantro Mint Chutney

Enjoy the luscious flavors of these herbs and spices that will delight your taste buds and soothe your digestion. The addition of fresh ginger and mint gives this dressing a nutritious punch, along with the zing of the jalapeño and garlic.

Yield:	Serving size:	Prep time:	Cook time:
1½ cups	2 tablespoons	10 minutes	None

1 bunch cilantro, well rinsed	2 TB. red onion, minced
½ bunch mint, well rinsed	3 TB. lemon or lime juice
2 TB. ginger, grated	2 TB. raw honey
¼ cup extra virgin olive oil	1–2 cloves garlic, chopped finely
1 tsp. whole coriander	Dash cayenne pepper (optional)
1–3 tsp. minced jalapeño, to taste	Pinch of Celtic or Himalayan salt

1. Combine cilantro, mint, ginger, oil, coriander, jalapeño, onion, lemon or lime juice, honey, garlic, cayenne pepper, and salt in a food processor or blender.

2. Blend until smooth.

3. Serve immediately or refrigerate until ready to use.

GOOD TO KNOW

Ginger is an all-star when it comes to healing. It contains powerful anti-inflammatory compounds that have been proven to relieve arthritis and muscular-related symptoms, and settles upset tummies.

Tahini Ginger Dressing

Enjoy the nutty flavors and delicate textures of this wonderful nutrient-rich dressing. It's ideal as an accompaniment to almost any vegetable and delicious as a spread on crackers or bread, too.

Yield:	Serving size:	Prep time:	Cook time:
2 cups	2 tablespoons	10 minutes	None

1 cup sunflower seeds, soaked in filtered water

1 cup fresh apple juice or filtered water

2 TB. raw tahini

2 TB. raw apple cider vinegar

1 tsp. fresh ginger, chopped finely

1 tsp. curry powder

$\frac{1}{2}$ tsp. Bragg Liquid Aminos

$\frac{1}{4}$ tsp. cayenne pepper

1. In a food processor or blender, add sunflower seeds, apple juice, tahini, vinegar, ginger, curry powder, amino acids, and cayenne pepper.

2. Blend until smooth.

3. Serve immediately or refrigerate until ready to use.

HEART-HEALTHY TIP

Sesame seeds are an excellent source of DASH minerals such as magnesium, calcium, and zinc, as well as vitamin B$_1$. They are a good source of copper, iron, and tryptophan. Copper is known for its use in reducing pain and swelling associated with rheumatoid arthritis.

Creamy Miso Dressing

Enjoy the rich flavors of this creamy dressing that goes well with any salad or cold grain dishes. The addition of flax seed oil rounds out the flavors, as well as adding heart-healthy omega-3s.

Yield:	Serving size:	Prep time:	Cook time:
¾ cup	2 tablespoons	10 minutes	None

3 TB. lemon or lime juice

1 TB. mellow miso, low sodium

1 TB. flax seed oil

1 tsp. ginger, chopped

1 clove garlic, chopped

½ cup filtered water

Dash cayenne pepper (optional)

1. Combine lemon or lime juice, miso, flax seed oil, ginger, garlic, water, and cayenne pepper in a small bowl, or a jar with a lid.

2. Stir or shake for 30 seconds.

3. Serve immediately or refrigerate until ready to use.

HEART-HEALTHY TIP

Miso is made from fermented soybeans and is rich in minerals such as manganese, zinc, and copper. It has a salty taste to it and is loaded with enzymes, which supports a healthy digestive tract.

Guacamole Dressing

You can't go wrong with this delicious guacamole that's got zingy flavors to match its nutrient density and antioxidants. Spread it over toast or crackers and enjoy it as an anytime snack or appetizer.

Yield:	Serving size:	Prep time:	Cook time:
1 cup	½ cup	10 minutes	None

1 avocado

1 tomato, diced

¼ cup lemon or lime juice

2 TB. raw apple cider vinegar

1 TB. Bragg Liquid Aminos

1 TB. fresh cilantro, chopped

2 shallots, chopped

1 clove garlic, chopped

¼ tsp. cayenne pepper

1. Place avocado, tomato, lemon or lime juice, vinegar, amino acids, cilantro, onion, garlic, and cayenne pepper in a blender or food processor.

2. Blend until coarse in texture.

3. Serve immediately or refrigerate until ready to use.

HEART-HEALTHY TIP

Avocados are known to have anti-inflammatory nutrients and are an excellent source of essential fatty acids. This delicious food is high in vitamins C and E, as well as the DASH-healthy minerals magnesium, selenium, and zinc.

Sweet-'n'-Sour Dressing

Sunflower seeds are creamy and delicious, especially when you increase their amazing healing potency by adding some sweet and spicy citrus flavors. Laced with antioxidants, this delightful dressing is worth the dip.

Yield:	Serving size:	Prep time:	Cook time:
1 cup	$\frac{1}{2}$ cup	10 minutes	None

1 large tomato

$\frac{1}{2}$ cup sunflower seeds, soaked

3 TB. apple cider vinegar

2 TB. lemon or lime juice

1 TB. raw honey

2 dates, pitted

1 tsp. Bragg Liquid Aminos

1 clove garlic, chopped (optional)

1 small red or green chile, chopped (optional)

1 cup filtered water

1. Place tomato, sunflower seeds, vinegar, lemon or lime juice, honey, dates, amino acids, garlic, chile, and water in a food processor or blender.

2. Blend until smooth.

3. Serve immediately or refrigerate until ready to use.

GOOD TO KNOW

Chile peppers, including cayenne, have powerful cardiovascular benefits that improve circulation. They increase the body's ability to dissolve a substance, called capsaicin, that's responsible for stopping hemorrhaging when bleeding.

Tofu Honey Mayonnaise

Called "the cheese of Asia" in China mainly because of its resemblance to a block of farmer's cheese, tofu is highly nutritious. Lusciously delicious, this tofu mayonnaise combines the delightful flavors of citrus and dried herbs with a little bit of honey.

Yield:	Serving size:	Prep time:	Cook time:
2 cups	$\frac{1}{2}$ cup	15 minutes	None

1 cake tofu, soft	1 tsp. raw honey
1 cup filtered water	2 TB. lemon or lime juice
2 TB. Bragg Liquid Aminos	$\frac{1}{4}$ tsp. ground coriander
1 tsp. sesame oil	Dash cayenne pepper (optional)

1. Place tofu, water, amino acids, sesame oil, honey, lemon or lime juice, coriander, and cayenne pepper in a food processor or blender.

2. Blend until smooth. Add more water or cayenne pepper as needed.

3. Serve immediately or refrigerate until ready to use.

GOOD TO KNOW

Coriander has been given top ranking as a powerful blood sugar and insulin level moderator. It has undergone numerous studies supporting its anti-diabetic as well as cholesterol-lowering abilities.

Lemon Sesame and Spice Dressing

The nutrients alone in sesame seeds cannot be understated or underestimated. High in copper, which aids inflammation and arthritis, sesame seeds are a potent ally in lowering your cholesterol. The addition of antioxidant-rich herbs, and the spices means you can easily enjoy this dish and not worry about calories either. High in DASH-friendly minerals magnesium and calcium is an added plus.

Yield:	Serving size:	Prep time:	Cook time:
1 cup	2 tablespoons	15 minutes	3 minutes

3 TB. sesame seeds

¼ cup extra virgin olive oil

3 TB. fresh lemon juice

1 clove garlic, chopped

2 TB. onions, finely chopped

1½ TB. tamari

1 tsp. paprika, ground

3 TB. tahini

½ tsp. celery seeds

½ cup filtered water

⅛ tsp. ground black pepper

Dash cayenne pepper (optional)

1. In a small skillet, dry roast sesame seeds on medium heat for approximately 3 minutes, stirring constantly, until seeds begin to brown. Remove and let cool for 5 minutes.

2. In a blender or food processor, combine cooled seeds, olive oil, lemon juice, garlic, onions, tamari, paprika, tahini, celery seeds, water, black pepper, and cayenne pepper.

3. Blend until smooth.

4. Serve immediately or refrigerate until ready to use.

HEART-HEALTHY TIP

Tamari is made from fermented soybeans and is thicker and richer than its counterpart, soy sauce. It is less salty and I think of it as kinder and gentler on your system. It is high in tryptophan, vitamin B₃, and manganese, all of which are soothing to the central nervous system.

DASH-ing and Lively Salsa

The combination of the tomatoes with oils ignites triple potency and releases more lycopene in this process. The powerful antioxidants reign supreme, and with too-numerous-to-mention health benefits, you can imagine the goodness. It's easy to have seconds with this delicious salsa.

Yield:	Serving size:	Prep time:	Cook time:
5–6 cups	1 cup	15 minutes	None

1 cup canned crushed tomatoes, organic

2½ cups fresh tomatoes, organic, diced

¾ cup red onions, diced

¾ cup green bell pepper, diced

2 TB. fresh cilantro, chopped

¾ TB. extra virgin olive oil

2 TB. flax seed oil

½ TB. balsamic vinegar

1 tsp. jalapeño peppers, diced, to taste

2 tsp. garlic, diced

2 TB. lemon or lime juice

½ tsp. Celtic or Himalayan salt (optional)

⅛ tsp. ground black pepper

Dash cayenne pepper or hot pepper sauce (optional)

1. In a large bowl, combine tomatoes, onions, bell pepper, cilantro, olive oil, flax seed oil, vinegar, jalapeño, garlic, lemon or lime juice, salt, black pepper, and cayenne pepper.

2. Mix together well.

3. Serve immediately or refrigerate until ready to serve.

HEART-HEALTHY TIP

When purchasing ketchup, look for organic, which has the most potent lycopene content. Lycopene, a powerful antioxidant, has the ability to lower the risk of damage to lipids, or fat, in the bloodstream and thereby reduce inflammation that could lead to heart disease.

Balsamic Vinaigrette Straight Up with a Twist

This creamy dressing is not only heart healthy and brain friendly, it's delicious beyond belief. It's high in omega-9 essential fatty acids from the olive oil and omega-3s from the flax oil. I keep a jar on hand at all times as a base jump for any salad you've got going on any given day. It's soul food for you.

Yield:	Serving size:	Prep time:	Cook time:
2 cups	2 tablespoons	5 minutes	None

⅓ cup fresh orange juice

1 TB. fresh lemon or lime juice

2 TB. balsamic vinegar

¼ cup extra virgin olive oil

2 TB. flax seed oil

1 tsp. Dijon-style mustard,

1 tsp. garlic, chopped

½ tsp. Celtic or Himalayan salt (optional)

½ tsp. black ground pepper

Dash cayenne pepper (optional)

1. In a medium-size bowl, combine orange juice, lemon or lime juice, vinegar, olive oil, flax seed oil, mustard, garlic, salt, black pepper, and cayenne pepper.

2. Stir together with a fork until well blended.

3. Serve immediately or refrigerate until ready to use.

GOOD TO KNOW

Flax seeds and their oil both have high anti-inflammatory benefits. The seeds are best fresh ground into a coarse powder in your coffee mill and stored in the freezer in small batches only. Use them in smoothies and breakfast cereals when you want to increase fiber and detoxify your system. They will help you shed pounds and make your metabolism more efficient. The oils work wonders for balancing your hormones.

Lunch Box-Worthy Sandwiches

In This Chapter

- Balancing sandwiches that go anywhere with you
- Fresh, tasty ingredients that nourish your heart

There's nothing more delicious than a comforting sandwich or burger to make you feel well satisfied, as well as nourished. It's always a treat when you have a great lunch to look forward to, and that's what you have with these great selections.

I've included all of my family's favorite lunch box–worthy sandwiches that are made from fresh whole foods and with your healthy heart in mind. You'll find tons of fiber, minerals, phytonutrients, and antioxidants galore.

These recipes have the right amount of macronutrients to balance your metabolism, as well as round out your appetite. Go ahead and add an apple a day to your lunch box and you're good to go. There are also some good gluten-free and vegetarian selections to choose from.

Spicy Cheddar-Stuffed Turkey Burgers

Not only will you be boosting your immune system and enhancing your mood with the tryptophan that's abundant in turkey, your cholesterol will improve, too. The additional flavors of curry and cayenne pepper are friendly allies to your heart's desire. These burgers are simply delicious.

Yield:	Serving size:	Prep time:	Cook time:
12 burgers	1 burger	10 minutes	20 minutes

1 small Spanish onion, chopped

$\frac{1}{2}$ cup fresh cilantro, chopped

2 TB. extra virgin olive oil

$1\frac{1}{2}$ lb. ground white turkey meat

1 egg

1 medium carrot, grated

3 TB. raisins

1 tsp. curry powder

$\frac{1}{2}$ tsp. Celtic or Himalayan salt

$\frac{1}{2}$ tsp. ground black pepper

2 tsp. tamari sauce or Bragg Liquid Aminos

$\frac{3}{4}$ cup cheddar cheese, low sodium, grated

1 tsp. cayenne pepper

12 whole-wheat buns, split

1. Preheat oven to 350°F.

2. In a small sauté pan, heat 1 tablespoon extra virgin olive oil over medium heat.

3. Add onions and sauté until caramelized. Set aside to cool.

4. In a large bowl, blend cilantro with 2 tablespoons oil.

5. Add turkey, egg, carrot, raisins, curry powder, $\frac{1}{2}$ teaspoon salt, black pepper, and tamari sauce or amino acids. Mix well. Set aside.

6. Add the caramelized onions, cheese, cayenne pepper, and salt. Blend well.

7. Divide turkey into 12 equal balls (approximately 3-4 inches). Stuff each ball with a twelfth of the cheese mixture and form balls into patties and place on baking sheet.

8. Bake burgers for about 20 minutes; you may also grill them.

9. Serve burgers on whole-wheat buns with Tomato and Hearts of Palm Salad (Chapter 7).

GOOD TO KNOW

The skinless white meat of turkey is an excellent source of the amino acid tryptophan, vitamins B$_6$ and B$_3$, plus the antioxidant selenium. A great low-fat, protein-laden choice for people following the DASH diet.

Falafel Burgers with Hummus

Delicious with herbs and spices, these chickpea burgers are a good source of protein and heart-healthy minerals. Falafel originated in Persia and were also a staple of the ancient Romans and Greeks. They're strengthening and nourishing.

Yield:	Serving size:	Prep time:	Cook time:
4–6 burgers	1 burger	20 minutes	10–12 minutes

$1\frac{1}{2}$ cups onions, minced

3 cloves garlic, minced

1 tsp. cumin seeds, ground

1 cup carrot, finely chopped

1 (15-oz.) can cooked chickpeas, drained

$1\frac{1}{2}$ TB. tahini (sesame paste)

$\frac{1}{4}$ cup fresh parsley, minced

$\frac{1}{3}$ cup plus 1 TB. chickpea flour (or whole-wheat flour)

$\frac{1}{2}$ tsp. baking soda

Dash cayenne pepper

1 tsp. Celtic or Himalayan salt

Juice of $\frac{1}{2}$ medium lemon

1. In a large skillet over medium heat, sauté onions in 1 tablespoon extra virgin olive oil until soft.

2. Add garlic, cumin seeds, and carrot. Sauté for 2 more minutes. Transfer to a large bowl.

3. Mash chickpeas by hand or in a food processor. Add to onions.

4. Add tahini and parsley.

5. In a smaller bowl, combine $\frac{1}{3}$ cup chickpea flour, baking soda, cayenne pepper, and salt.

6. Add dry mixture to mashed chickpea mixture in the large bowl. Mix well.

7. With floured hand, form four to six patties (approximately 4 inches round) and lightly dust with remaining 1 tablespoon chickpea flour.

8. In a large skillet over medium heat, heat 1 tablespoon grape seed oil.

9. Add patties to skillet. Flip after 1 minute or when browning begins. Cook approximately 2 more minutes before flipping again.

10. Keep cooking, turning every 1 to 2 minutes, until patties are deep golden brown on both sides.

11. Squeeze fresh lemon juice on top.

12. Serve immediately with hummus.

GOOD TO KNOW

Chickpeas have a low glycemic index of between 28 and 30, making them an ideal food for diabetics and people with high triglycerides, which are a type of fat found in your blood. While you need some triglycerides for good health, they can raise your risk of heart disease if too high.

Luscious Lentil Burgers

Keeping it simple while nourishing your heart's health doesn't get any more delicious than this. You'll enjoy the fine flavors and aromas and especially love the calming, grounding effects the lentils offer in this luscious meal.

Yield:	Serving size:	Prep time:	Cook time:
6–8 burgers	1–2 burgers	15 minutes	40 minutes

1 carrot, finely grated	3 TB. sesame seeds, roasted
2 garlic cloves, chopped finely	1 TB. Bragg Liquid Aminos
1 onion, minced	1 tsp. fresh or dried sage
2 cups cooked lentils	1 tsp. fresh or dried thyme
1/4 cup whole-grain breadcrumbs, plain, unseasoned	1/2 cup fresh parsley, chopped
	1 egg, beaten (optional)

1. Preheat oven to 375°F.

2. In a large saucepan, heat 1 teaspoon sesame oil over a moderate heat and add chopped carrot, garlic, and onion. Lightly sauté, then cover and cook on low heat for 5 minutes.

3. In a large bowl, mix lentils, breadcrumbs, sesame seeds, amino acids, sage, thyme, and parsley.

4. Add the cooked ingredients and shape into six to eight burgers. If needed, add a small amount of water until they hold, or you can add an egg.

5. Bake in a dish or oiled tray for 40 minutes or until crisp on the surface. If preferable, put entire contents into baking dish and make into a loaf.

6. Serve burgers with all the trimmings, such as mustard, pickles, hummus, or tofu mayo.

GOOD TO KNOW

High in folate for heart health, lentils are loaded with magnesium and fiber, too.

Gluten-Free Veggie Pizza

This gluten-free vegetarian pizza may be meat-free, but it's certainly not flavor-free. It's simple and easy to cook up, even if you don't normally cook. Feel free to add shrimp or chicken on top if you want extra protein.

Yield:	Serving size:	Prep time:	Cook time:
1 pizza	2 slices	10 minutes	15 minutes

1 cup of gluten-free pizza dough mix, prepared (or use chickpea flour)

½ red onion, chopped or thinly sliced

½ red bell pepper, thinly sliced

1 TB. oregano, fresh or dried, chopped finely

1 small zucchini, thinly sliced

3 garlic cloves, chopped finely

1 cup mushrooms, thinly sliced

Dash of ground black pepper

Dash cayenne pepper

2 TB. extra virgin olive oil

1 cup part skim milk mozzarella, shredded

4 ripe tomatoes, thinly sliced (or sun-dried tomatoes if preferred)

1 cup Parmesan cheese, grated

½ cup provolone cheese, shredded

1. Preheat oven to 400°F.

2. In a large saucepan, heat 1 tablespoon extra virgin olive oil over medium heat. Add onion, red bell pepper, and oregano and sauté for 5 minutes.

3. Stir in zucchini, garlic, and mushrooms. Sauté 5 more minutes.

4. Remove from heat and add black pepper and cayenne pepper.

5. Brush prepared crust with remaining olive oil. Sprinkle mozzarella cheese over crust. Top with tomatoes.

6. Mound the cooked vegetables on top. Sprinkle with Parmesan and provolone cheeses.

7. Bake 10 to 20 minutes or until cheeses melt and brown slightly.

8. Serve hot with a tossed salad.

HEART-HEALTHY TIP

A strict gluten-free diet means uncontaminated oats, wheat, rye, barley, or malt flavorings are off limits. You don't have to be diagnosed with celiac disease to enjoy the relief of digestive symptoms from following a gluten-free diet. Try it and see for yourself!

Millet Buckwheat Tortillas with Avocado and Onions

Enjoy the strengthening of heart and spirit you will obtain with these delicious buckwheat treats that are packed full of many B vitamins as well as DASH-healthy minerals. The herb-mixed avocado spread will delight your taste buds. It's loaded with fiber and goodness.

Yield:	Serving size:	Prep time:	Cook time:
6–10 wraps	1–2 wraps	20 minutes	10–15 minutes

1 cup millet flour	1 TB. fresh lemon or lime juice
½ cup buckwheat flour	2 dashes Celtic or Himalayan salt
½ cup sorghum flour	1 garlic clove, chopped finely
½ cup arrowroot or tapioca starch	1 tsp. baking powder
2 tsp. xanthan gum	1 TB. onion, minced
1 cup warm filtered water	1 tsp. thyme
½ cup almond or rice milk	1 avocado, mashed
1–2 fresh dates, chopped finely	1 TB. fresh lemon or lime juice
2 eggs, beaten with 2–4 TB. water	Dash cayenne pepper

1. To a large bowl add the buckwheat flour, sorghum flour, arrowroot or tapioca starch, xanthan gum, water, and milk and blend together.

2. Add eggs, fresh dates, garlic, baking powder, onion, and thyme and beat into a smooth thick pancake batter.

3. In a large skillet, heat the oil over medium-high heat. Drop a spoonful of batter onto the hot pan and spread batter thin. Lift edges and flip when cooked.

4. After cooking both sides place the cooked wrap on a flat surface to cool. Repeat process to make a total of 6 to 10 wraps.

5. Mash avocado with lemon juice, cayenne pepper, and dash of salt.

6. Spread a tortilla with the avocado and enjoy with a raw salad or on its own.

GOOD TO KNOW

Buckwheat is actually a fruit seed and is a wonderful gluten-free alternative to grains. It contains the eight essential amino acids that make up a complete protein that your body needs to function efficiently.

Turkey with Salad Sandwiches

You can't beat the simplicity and ease of a wholesome and heart-healthy turkey salad sandwich. Turkey contains selenium, which is essential for the healthy function of the thyroid, heart, and immune system. You'll get tons of fiber, B vitamins, and DASH minerals with this delicious combo. You'll enjoy every bite.

Yield:	Serving size:	Prep time:	Cook time:
1 sandwich	1 sandwich	10 minutes	None

¼ avocado, mashed

Dash of Celtic or Himalayan salt

Dash of cayenne pepper

2 slices of whole-grain or sour-dough bread

½–1 cup thinly sliced turkey

1 small tomato, sliced thinly

¼–½ cup red onion, sliced thinly

1–2 medium-size Romaine lettuce leaves

½ cup sprouts

1. Mash the avocado, and add salt and cayenne pepper.

2. Spread the avocado on the bread.

3. Fill the bread with turkey, tomato, onion, lettuce, and sprouts.

4. Slice and serve.

HEART-HEALTHY TIP

Organic, pasture-based turkey that's been grass-fed has the most health benefits, as they offer higher nutritional value compared to birds given antibiotics or raised indoors. Turkey is a good source of amino acids and is low in saturated fat, too.

Nut Butter and Raisin Sandwich

This is one of my all-time favorites, and probably will be one of yours, too. You'll receive more than your daily nourishment of healthy fats and proteins with the mineral-filled nut butter. Toss in some juicy raisins with more daily fiber from fresh Romaine lettuce, and you'll enjoy every bite.

Yield:	Serving size:	Prep time:	Cook time:
1 sandwich	1 sandwich	10 minutes	None

2 slices of whole multigrain or
  sourdough bread
2 TB. nut butter, your choice
  (cashew, almond, hazelnut,
  peanut)

2 TB. raisins, or 1 TB. raw honey
1–2 Romaine lettuce leaves

1. Spread the nut butter on bread.

2. Add raisins or honey.

3. Add lettuce and serve.

HEART-HEALTHY TIP

Almonds and almond butter are nutrition powerhouses that contain significant amounts of protein, calcium, fiber, magnesium, potassium, folic acid, and vitamin E.

Fresh Vegetables and Cream Cheese with Chutney Sandwich

This seemingly indulgent delight is delicious, highly nutritious, and as DASH friendly as you can get. Who can get past the creamy yet spicy combination of flavors with the chutney and cream cheese? Simply sumptuous!

Yield:	Serving size:	Prep time:	Cook time:
1 sandwich	1 sandwich	10 minutes	None

2 slices of whole multigrain or
  sourdough bread

1 TB. organic cream cheese,

1 TB. raisin chutney, low sodium

⅓ cup cucumber, sliced thin, with
  or without skin

1 radish, sliced thin

¼ red onion, sliced thin

1–2 Romaine lettuce leaves,
  chopped or torn

1. Spread the cream cheese and chutney on the bread.

2. Add cucumber, radish, onion, and lettuce.

3. Serve immediately.

GOOD TO KNOW

A 1-oz. serving of cream cheese provides about 4 percent of your daily intake of sodium and can be considered a low-sodium food.

Sumptuous Soups

In This Chapter

- Slimming and low-calorie soups
- Recipes to get your heart pumping

Soups play an important role in our DASH-healthy diets. Soups are usually the entrée for the evening meal, and this is because the digestive power decreases in the evening—soups make an easy choice for our system.

In this chapter you'll find numerous versatile and tempting recipes to complement any meal. Soups are a great way to provide you with nutrient density, and are easy on your waistline, too.

As you prepare your recipes, remember to add a big dose of love into everything you cook. It truly is remarkable how some conscious attention of nourishing your body makes its way into your heart through your stomach.

Soup Stock—Veggie or Chicken

Homemade soup stock, be it vegetable or chicken flavor, gives any soup a special, rich flavor. It's loaded with potassium and numerous other DASH-healthy minerals. Feel free to use this stock in all of the following recipes as needed.

Yield:	Serving size:	Prep time:	Cook time:
6 quarts	2 cups	20 minutes	2–3 hours

1 whole chicken

4–5 quarts of filtered water

1 large onion, cut into chunks (about 1 cup)

2 carrots, cut into chunks (about 1 cup)

1 turnip, cut into chunks (about $\frac{1}{2}$ cup)

2 celery stalks, cut into 1-inch pieces (about 1 cup)

$\frac{1}{4}$ bunch fresh parsley stems (no leaves)

1 medium leek, sliced (about $\frac{1}{2}$ cup)

3–4 sprigs fresh thyme

1 TB. peppercorns

2 bay leaves

1 5-inch piece kombu (dried sea vegetable)

1 TB. extra virgin olive oil

1 tsp. sage

1 TB. brown rice

1 TB. apple cider vinegar (if adding chicken bones)

5 mushrooms with stems (optional)

1. Bring chicken bones, skin, meat, and water to a boil in an 8-quart pot. Skim off foam and discard.

2. Add onions, carrots, turnips, celery, parsley, leeks, thyme, peppercorns, bay leaves, kombu, olive oil, sage, brown rice, vinegar, and mushrooms.

3. Bring up to a boil, and then cover and simmer for approximately 2 hours.

4. Strain liquid and discard bones, skin, and meat of chicken. Also discard cooked vegetables.

5. Place liquid in fridge and let fat congeal overnight. Skim off fat. You can freeze the broth for up to 2 months.

GOOD TO KNOW

Save the ends and bits whenever you cut vegetables (outer leaves of cabbage, tops of celery, parsley, stems, stalks, etc.). Keep them in a container in the fridge for up to one week. When you have plenty, simmer them in a quart of water for 20 to 30 minutes. Strain and refrigerate. This gives you a good supply of vegetable broth stock.

Cauliflower Cheddar Cheese Soup

Enjoy the creamy textures of dairy combined with this antioxidant- and mineral-rich soup. It's more like a savory dessert that's loaded with fiber and DASH-healthy ingredients.

Yield:	Serving size:	Prep time:	Cook time:
1 quart	1 cup	15 minutes	15 minutes

1 cup onion, chopped

3 cups cauliflower, coarsely chopped, plus 1 cup florets

1½ cups red potatoes, cubed

2 cups filtered water

Pinch salt

1 TB. fresh parsley, chopped

¾ cup skim milk

1 cup shredded cheddar cheese, low sodium, organic

¼ tsp. dried dill, or 1 tsp. fresh dill, chopped

½ tsp. ground mustard

⅛ tsp. ground white pepper

Pinch ground black pepper

Pinch nutmeg

Dash cayenne pepper (optional)

1. In a large pot, over medium heat, melt 1 tablespoon butter and sauté onions for 3 to 5 minutes, or until translucent.

2. Add 3 cups chopped cauliflower, potatoes, water, and salt and bring to a boil.

3. Boil for 10 minutes, or until potatoes are tender. Remove from heat.

4. In a blender or food processor, purée cauliflower mixture with the parsley and milk until smooth and creamy.

5. Return the mixture to the pot and reheat over medium heat.

6. Add cheddar cheese.

7. Stir in dill, mustard, white and black pepper, nutmeg, and cayenne pepper.

8. Add cauliflower florets and simmer for 5 to 10 minutes, or until the florets are tender.

9. Serve immediately.

GOOD TO KNOW

Cauliflower is one of the healthiest vegetables around due to its high vitamin C and antioxidant benefits. Antioxidants are powerful weapons for reducing chronic inflammation and oxidation, which causes aging. They have known cardio-protective qualities and are great eaten any time of the year.

Curry Cream of Tomato Soup

You won't go wrong with the deliciously creamy mixture of flavorful tomatoes blended with curry and herbs in this soup. The health benefits in tomatoes are great, with their high levels of antioxidants, lycopene, and vitamin C. This recipe is excellent for cardio health as well as hormones and men's prostates.

Yield:	Serving size:	Prep time:	Cook time:
2 quarts	2 cups	15 minutes	1 hour

2 cups onion, sliced

2 TB. garlic, chopped

1 tsp. Celtic or Himalayan salt (optional)

2 cups carrots, diced, with skin

3 (16-oz.) cans whole plum tomatoes, organic

¾ cup canned tomato sauce, organic

¼ cup canned tomato paste, organic

1 TB. extra virgin olive oil

½ TB. dried basil, or 1½ TB. fresh basil, chopped

2 TB. fresh parsley, chopped

¼ tsp. ground black pepper

¼ tsp. curry powder

Pinch ground nutmeg

Dash cayenne pepper

½ cup skim milk

½ cup light cream

1. In a large pot, over medium heat, melt 1 tablespoon butter and sauté onions and garlic for 3 to 5 minutes, or until onions are translucent.

2. Mix in salt, carrots, plum tomatoes, tomato sauce, tomato paste, olive oil, basil, parsley, black pepper, curry powder, nutmeg, and cayenne pepper.

3. Cook for approximately 1 hour over medium heat, stirring occasionally.

4. In a blender or food processor, purée the tomato mixture with the milk and cream until smooth and creamy.

5. Return mixture to the pot, and reheat over medium heat.

6. Serve immediately.

 GOOD TO KNOW

This recipe can be stored overnight in the refrigerator. For a nondairy version, use 1 cup soy milk instead of the milk and cream.

Carrot Ginger Soup with Chives

Tangy and tasty, the combination of carrots with ginger will delight not only your taste buds but your entire digestive system. This soup is packed with antioxidants vitamin A and beta-carotene, together with tons of fiber and B-complex vitamins. It doesn't get better than this for high-energy, nutrient-dense soups.

Yield:	Serving size:	Prep time:	Cook time:
2 quarts	1–2 cups	15 minutes	45 minutes

1½ cups onions, chopped

1½ TB. fresh ginger, peeled and chopped

4 cups carrots, chopped (5–6 large carrots)

2 cups vegetable stock, homemade or low-sodium canned

2 cups filtered water

½ tsp. Celtic or Himalayan salt

½ cup soy milk or light cream (optional)

½ tsp. ground black pepper

¼ cup fresh chives, chopped

1. In a large pot, heat 1 tablespoon extra virgin olive oil over medium heat and sauté onions for 3 to 5 minutes or until translucent.

2. Add ginger and sauté for 1 minute.

3. Stir in carrots, stock, and water. Bring to a boil. Add salt.

4. Reduce heat over simmer and cook, stirring occasionally, for 40 minutes. Remove from heat.

5. In a blender or food processor, purée the mixture until creamy, adding soy milk or cream, if desired.

6. Return mixture to pot, reheat over medium heat, and stir in black pepper and chives.

7. Serve immediately.

HEART-HEALTHY TIP

When selecting carrots, you should look for vegetables which are firm, smooth, and bright in color. The deeper the color, the higher nutritional and beta-carotene properties present in the carrots. If tops are attached, make sure they are not wilted and remove the tops before storing them in the fridge. Use the tops in your vegetable stock, too.

A-maizing Corn Chowder

Enjoy the digestive qualities along with the delicious flavors of this wonderful soup. Known for its high fiber, antioxidants, minerals, and vitamins, corn (a.k.a., maize) provides tons of chewing satisfaction in every mouthful. You'll love the combination of herbs and vegetables added to this dish.

Yield:	Serving size:	Prep time:	Cook time:
2 quarts	1–2 cups	15 minutes	20 minutes

1½ cups onions, chopped

4 cups fresh or frozen corn

2 tsp. apple cider vinegar

½ tsp. ground white pepper

2 cups red potatoes, diced

2 cups filtered water

2 cups vegetable stock

1 cup celery, chopped

1 cup red bell pepper, chopped

1 tsp. Celtic or Himalayan salt

2¼ tsp. onion powder

1 tsp. ground cumin

1 tsp. ground paprika

⅛ tsp. black pepper

Dash cayenne pepper (optional)

½ TB. tamari

¼ cup fresh cilantro, chopped

1. In a large pot, heat 2 tablespoons olive oil over medium heat and sauté onions 3 to 5 minutes or until translucent.

2. Add corn, vinegar, and white pepper. Sauté for 5 more minutes.

3. Stir in potatoes, water, and stock. Bring to a boil.

4. Reduce heat over simmer and cook for 10 minutes.

5. Separate ⅓ of mixture into a blender or food processor. Blend mixture. Return to pot.

6. Add celery, red bell pepper, salt, onion powder, cumin, paprika, black pepper, cayenne pepper, and tamari. Simmer for 5 minutes.

7. Add fresh cilantro just before serving. Serve immediately.

GOOD TO KNOW

Adding corn to chowder or chili enhances the meal's fiber and nutritional profile. It adds flavor as well as hardiness and is quick and easy to prepare.

White Bean Kale Soup

This kale soup with white beans is a heart-healthy meal with some special cholesterol-lowering benefits. It's loaded with antioxidants to support your DASH eating plan and has numerous minerals and vitamins, enough to provide plenty of health advantages. It's very tasty and delicious.

Yield:	Serving size:	Prep time:	Cook time:
2 quarts	1–2 cups	20 minutes	40 minutes

2 cups dried navy beans

1 2-inch strip kombu (dried sea vegetable)

3 cups vegetable stock

3 cups filtered water

$1\frac{1}{2}$ cups onion, chopped

$\frac{1}{2}$ tsp. Celtic or Himalayan salt

3 TB. white miso diluted in $\frac{1}{2}$ cup warm water

$\frac{1}{3}$ cup prepared brown mustard

2 cups fresh kale, de-veined, washed, and chopped

Dash cayenne pepper (optional)

1. Rinse navy beans. Soak overnight in filtered water.

2. In a large pot, combine beans, kombu, stock, and water. Bring to a boil over high heat.

3. Reduce heat to medium-low and cook, stirring occasionally, for 1 hour or until beans are soft.

4. Meanwhile, in a medium-size skillet, heat 1 tablespoon extra virgin olive oil over medium heat and sauté onion for 3 to 5 minutes or until translucent.

5. Add onions to beans.

6. When beans are soft, add salt.

7. Separate $\frac{2}{3}$ of the bean mixture into blender or food processor. Blend until smooth.

8. Return mixture to pot.

9. Stir in diluted miso and mustard. Simmer over low heat for 10 minutes. Add kale and cayenne pepper. Let stand for 5 minutes and serve.

GOOD TO KNOW

Navy beans are a great source of plant protein, folate, vitamin B_1, and heart-healthy minerals like magnesium, copper, and manganese. They are low on the glycemic index and keep your blood sugar levels stable for hours—high in fiber, too!

Red and Black Bean Chili

Delicious and nutritious, your DASH diet would not be complete without a dish of red and black bean chili. This heart-healthy combination of flavors is not only easy on your waistline but will improve your energy and vitality.

Yield:	Serving size:	Prep time:	Cook time:
1 gallon	1–2 cups	50 minutes	2 hours

2 cups dried kidney beans

1½ cups dried black beans

12 cups water

2 cups vegetable stock

2 bay leaves

2 cups onions, chopped

2 TB. garlic, chopped

2 TB. extra virgin olive oil

1½ cups green bell pepper, chopped

4 medium tomatoes, chopped

1 TB. dried oregano

1½ TB. ground cumin

1½ TB. ground paprika

1 tsp. cayenne pepper

1½ TB. chile powder

1 tsp. dried crushed mild chile peppers

2 TB. dried basil

2 tsp. Celtic or Himalayan salt

1½ cups canned tomato paste, organic

¼ cup fresh cilantro, chopped

2 TB. fresh lemon or lime juice

1. Wash beans. Soak beans overnight in filtered water.

2. In a large pot on high heat, add beans, water, and stock and bring to a boil.

3. Reduce heat to medium-high.

4. Add bay leaf and cook, stirring occasionally, for 1½ hours.

5. Meanwhile, in a large, deep skillet, heat 2 TB. extra virgin olive oil over medium heat and sauté onion and garlic for 3 to 5 minutes, or until onion is translucent.

6. Mix in green bell pepper, tomatoes, oregano, cumin, paprika, cayenne pepper, chile powder, chile peppers, and basil and sauté for 5 more minutes. Set aside.

7. Check beans after 1¼ hours. Add reserved vegetable mixture, salt, and tomato paste to beans.

8. Cook for 30 minutes, or until beans are soft.

9. Add cilantro and mix in lemon juice. Serve immediately.

GOOD TO KNOW

Adding beans to your diet helps cut calories without feeling deprived. Beans are an excellent source of plant protein, are high in fiber, and in some nutritional circles are considered a superfood.

Butternut Bisque with Carrot and Parsley

Butternut squash and carrots make a great team—they're sweet, but not so sweet that they spike your blood sugar or insulin levels. The combination and addition of ginger and parsley completes the flavors in this wholesome soup that's high in antioxidants and DASH-healthy minerals—fiber, too.

Yield:	Serving size:	Prep time:	Cook time:
1½ quarts	1–2 cups	15 minutes	30 minutes

1 medium onion, chopped

½ tsp. fresh garlic, chopped

1 medium butternut squash, skin on

2 cups vegetable stock

3 cups filtered water

½ tsp. Celtic or Himalayan salt

¼ tsp. ground cumin

¼ tsp. coriander powder

1 tsp. fresh ginger, chopped

2 large carrots, chopped, skin on

1 cup fresh parsley, regular, chopped

6 TB. low-fat yogurt

1 TB. fresh chives, chopped (for garnish)

1. Place 2 tablespoons extra virgin olive oil in a pan. Add chopped onion and garlic, and cook for 2 to 3 minutes on high heat.

2. Wash butternut squash, cut in half, scoop out seeds, and cut into 1-inch cubes.

3. Place squash in a large soup pot with stock and water, salt, cumin, coriander, and ginger.

4. Add carrots. Bring to a boil and simmer, covered, until you can pierce the pieces easily with a fork, about 15 to 20 minutes.

5. Purée the soup in a blender with fresh parsley.

6. Add 1 tablespoon yogurt to each serving and chopped chives on top.

HEART-HEALTHY TIP

Leave the skin on the butternut squash and carrots, as many vitamins and minerals are found just beneath the surface of the skin. Be sure to scrub them thoroughly using a vegetable brush.

Satisfying Snacks and Sauces

In This Chapter

- Eight amazing anytime snacks
- Eight sumptuous sauces loaded with goodness

All of the recipes in this chapter contain heart-healthy nutrients to sustain and uplift you. You can feel good about snacking in between meals when you are eating such healthy ingredients as these.

With a little bit of planning, it is easier than you may think to eat healthy and satisfying snacks. You need to have a game plan to keep yourself on track when hunger strikes. Stocking the fridge with healthy ingredients for on-the-go people and choices can help you resist the vending machine or that fat-filled cookie on the grocery store shelf.

Keep some of these delicious recipes on hand and be prepared to whip up a quick and easy snack for you or the family. Most are loaded with antioxidants, fiber, and heart-healthy nutrients.

Tuna Radicchio Mozzarella Pizza

Enjoy the delicious flavors of this heart-healthy snack that includes a serving of omega-3 essential fatty acids. The addition of tomatoes adds another DASH-friendly nutrient, lycopene. This pizza is a great all-round snack that's everybody's favorite.

Yield:	Serving size:	Prep time:	Cook time:
1 pizza	1–2 slices	15 minutes	30 minutes

2 cups self-rising flour

¼ tsp. Celtic or Himalayan salt plus a pinch of salt

4 TB. unsalted butter

½ cup milk

1 (14.5-oz.) can tomatoes, organic, chopped

2 garlic cloves

Pinch dried basil

Dash cayenne pepper (optional)

2 leeks, sliced

1 small can tuna, low sodium, packed in spring water

1 cup radicchio, roughly chopped

⅓ cup Parmesan cheese, grated

Freshly ground black pepper

¾ to 1 cup mozzarella cheese, sliced, part skim milk

12 black olives, pitted, sliced

Fresh basil leaves, to garnish

1. Preheat the oven to 425°F and grease a baking sheet.

2. To make dough, mix flour and ¼ teaspoon salt in a medium bowl and rub in butter.

3. Gradually stir in milk to form a soft dough.

4. Roll out dough on a lightly floured surface to make a 10- to 11-inch round. Place on the baking sheet.

5. Pour tomatoes into a small saucepan. Stir in one crushed garlic clove, dried basil, and cayenne pepper.

6. Simmer over medium heat until the mixture is thick and reduced by approximately half.

7. Heat 1½ tablespoons extra virgin olive oil in a large frying pan and fry leeks and remaining crushed garlic clove for 4 to 5 minutes until slightly softened.

8. Add tuna and radicchio and cook, stirring continuously, for approximately 3 minutes, then cover and simmer gently for 5 to 10 more minutes.

9. Stir in Parmesan cheese and season with dash of salt and pepper.

10. Cover dough base with tomato sauce.

11. Spoon over leek, tuna, and radicchio mixture.

12. Arrange mozzarella slices on top and scatter black olives over.

13. Dip a few basil leaves in olive oil and arrange on pizza.

14. Bake for 15 to 20 minutes until the base and top are golden brown.

HEART-HEALTHY TIP

Tuna is a rich source of heart-healthy nutrients such as vitamins B_1, B_3, potassium, magnesium, selenium, and mood-elevating tryptophan. Tuna is also a rich source of vitamin B_6, which, along with folic acid found in radicchio, lowers levels of homocysteine, an amino acid that can damage the lining of blood vessels when too high.

Sesame Squash Spread

The sesame combinations are a match made in heaven, and you won't go astray with the high fiber and other minerals in this heart-healthy spread.

Yield:	Serving size:	Prep time:	Cook time:
1 cup	$\frac{1}{3}$ cup	10 minutes	15 minutes

1 cup buttercup or butternut squash

3 TB. sesame seeds

1 TB. mellow white or chickpea miso

Dash cayenne pepper

Dash cinnamon

$\frac{1}{2}$ cup filtered water

1 clove garlic, chopped

1. Steam the squash, then mash.

2. In a skillet over medium heat, roast sesame seeds by stirring until they smell toasty and crumble easily between thumb and forefinger.

3. In a blender or food processor, blend seeds into a butter.

4. Mix in squash, miso, cayenne pepper, cinnamon, and garlic, and add just enough water to make a creamy spread, 1 tablespoon at a time.

5. Serve with Kale Curry Crackers (see recipe later in chapter).

GOOD TO KNOW

Butternut squash is loaded with vitamin A, which is one of the most powerful natural antioxidants. It's great for vision and cell wall integrity, not to mention boosting your immune system. Butternut squash contains five B-complex vitamins. What's important about this is that blood sugar regulation is closely tied to having a good daily supply of B complex vitamins. These are required for many functions in the body.

Nutrient-Dense Hummus

The spread contains chickpeas—high in folate, tryptophan, and iron—plus it has fiber, antioxidants, and plant protein. It gets a hit of the DASH-healthy minerals calcium and magnesium from the sesame or sunflower seeds. Garlic and cayenne pepper give a boost to your cardiovascular system. It's a delicious tasty spread that is great over flax crackers or freshly sliced vegetables.

Yield:	Serving size:	Prep time:	Cook time:
3 cups	½ cup	2 hours, 15 minutes	5 minutes

2 TB. sesame seeds

2 cups lentils or chickpeas (soak beans for 2 hours)

3 cloves garlic, chopped

1 stalk celery, chopped

1 green onion, chopped

2 TB. parsley, chopped

2 TB. fresh lemon or lime juice

Dash cayenne pepper (optional)

1 tsp. cumin (or turmeric)

Dash paprika

2 tsp. miso or tamari soy sauce

1. In a skillet over medium heat, toast seeds by stirring until they smell and taste nutty.

2. In a blender, grind seeds finely.

3. Mash lentils or chickpeas in a small bowl.

4. In a medium bowl or a blender, add mashed lentils or chickpeas, seeds, garlic, celery, onion, parsley, lemon or lime juice, cayenne pepper, cumin, paprika, and miso. Mix well and adjust seasonings as desired.

5. Serve on rice cakes, whole-wheat pita bread, or flax crackers.

HEART-HEALTHY TIP

The turmeric herb is a plant native to south India that's used medicinally as an aromatic stimulant. It's known for its anti-inflammatory properties and being even more potent than certain steroidal drugs, but without the side effects.

Kale Curry Crackers

Rich in calcium and iron, and loaded with antioxidants, kale reigns supreme when it comes to high fiber and your health. Flax seeds are rich with omega-3 essential fatty acids and numerous heart-healthy minerals and vitamins. These crackers are high fiber and nutrient dense in every possible way. And they taste great with any spread you put over them. A dehydrator is a wonderful equipment addition to your kitchen and will open up a new world of food preparation and flavors.

Yield:	Serving size:	Prep time:	Cook time:
40 crackers	6 crackers	8 hours, 15 minutes	4 hours

1 cup almonds, soaked overnight, then drained

1 cup kale, organic, washed

2 cups flax seeds, ground

1 tsp. cumin or turmeric, ground

1 TB. curry powder

Dash Celtic or Himalayan salt

Dash cayenne pepper

$\frac{1}{2}$ cup filtered water

1. Place almonds and kale in a blender or food processor and blend for several minutes. (Or use almond butter if you prefer.)

2. Add ground flax seeds, cumin, curry powder, salt, and cayenne pepper to a large bowl and mix well. Add water as needed so that the mixture is moist and easily spreadable.

3. Using a spatula or trowel, spread mixture approximately $\frac{1}{8}$ inch thick on dehydrator trays with a Teflex sheet. Using a knife, make a 3 inch by 3 inch division line in the mixture.

4. Dehydrate at 120°F for 2 to 3 hours, then turn over, remove Teflex sheet, and continue dehydrating for a further 3 to 4 hours or until desired crispness is reached.

5. Break up the crackers where you made the division line.

6. Store in glass containers or plastic bags. Lasts up to 30 days.

HEART-HEALTHY TIP

Kale has seven times the beta-carotene of broccoli and ten times more lutein. Both are powerful antioxidants that support cardiovascular and eye health.

Turkey Avocado Roll-Ups

Relax and feel nourished with this delicious treat that's easy to make and slimming on the waistline, too. Turkey is high in tryptophan, a feel-good neurochemical that calms your mood. The addition of healthy fats from avocado and heart-healthy cayenne makes this an anytime pick-me-up snack—even at bedtime.

Yield:	Serving size:	Prep time:	Cook time:
6 roll-ups	3 roll-ups	5 minutes	None

½ avocado, mashed or sliced

6 slices of low-sodium, oven-baked turkey, free of nitrates

Dash cayenne pepper (optional)

1 cup Romaine lettuce, chopped

1. Spread avocado over each slice of turkey, sprinkle with cayenne, and roll up.

2. Serve with a sprinkle of Romaine lettuce.

GOOD TO KNOW

Turkey is low in fat, making it a good choice for a heart-healthy diet. Almost all the fat is found in the skin, although the dark meat is higher in fat than the light meat. Look for nitrite-free turkey meats as it's lower in sodium.

Tofu and Sesame Butter–Stuffed Celery

Lower cholesterol and relax your heart muscle with these two potent DASH powerhouses. Celery contains active compounds which can help relax muscles and allow blood vessels to dilate. Sesame seeds are high in important nutrients as well as cholesterol-lowering lignans, which are estrogen-like chemicals found in plants. Sometimes the simplest things are the best.

Yield:	Serving size:	Prep time:	Cook time:
6 pieces	2 pieces	10 minutes	None

1 cup tofu, firm, drained, and crumbled

3 TB. sesame tahini

2 tsp. Bragg Liquid Aminos or tamari

1 TB. fresh lime juice

Dash cayenne pepper

6 celery stalks, cut into 2-inch pieces

1 TB. raw sesame seeds

1. Place tofu, sesame tahini, amino acids, lime juice, and cayenne pepper in a blender or food processor. Mix for 3 to 5 minutes or until creamy.

2. Spoon mixture into celery stalks and top with sesame seeds.

HEART-HEALTHY TIP

Sesame seeds are high in copper, a mineral known for its use in reducing some of the pain and swelling associated with rheumatoid arthritis. They are also loaded with enzymes to aid in digestion.

Crispy Nuts Trail Mix

Many nuts can be eaten raw but roasting them helps intensify their delicious flavor. In a nutshell, nuts are high in protein and fiber, and very high in heart-healthy fatty acids. They are jam-packed with goodness, including tons of DASH-friendly minerals such as magnesium and potassium.

Yield:	Serving size:	Prep time:	Cook time:
4 cup	1 cup	8 hours, 15 minutes	6 hours

4 cups raw, unsalted nuts (e.g., walnuts, almonds, pecans, Brazil nuts)

1 tsp. Celtic or Himalayan salt

2 cups filtered water

$\frac{1}{2}$ cup raisins

$\frac{1}{2}$ cup sunflower seeds

$\frac{1}{2}$ cup dried coconut, chopped

1. Place nuts in a bowl with salt and cover with filtered water. Cover bowl and allow nuts to soak at room temperature overnight.

2. Drain nuts in a colander and scatter onto a baking tray or cookie sheet.

3. Place in oven set at 150°F for up to 6 hours or until completely dry and crisp.

4. Add raisins, sunflower seeds, and coconut.

5. Store in an air-tight container in a cool place or refrigerate.

GOOD TO KNOW

Walnuts are high in essential omega-3 fatty acids. They are shaped like a minisize brain—an interesting tidbit, since they are also brain food.

Love-Your-Heart Lentil Pâté

Loaded with goodness, lentils are known and well studied for their ability to lower the risk for heart attacks and homocysteine, important for healthy metabolic functions, because of their high folate levels. This delicious snack is more than satisfying with its high-fiber nourishment and delicious fresh herbs and spices. You simply have to try it.

Yield:	Serving size:	Prep time:	Cook time:
2 quarts	1–2 cups	40 minutes	30 minutes

1 cup, plus 2 TB. toasted whole-wheat breadcrumbs

4 cups dried lentils

8 cups filtered water, or 4 cups vegetable stock and 4 cups filtered water

1½ tsp. Celtic or Himalayan salt

⅓ cup extra virgin olive oil

4 cups onions, chopped

1 TB. garlic, chopped

2 tsp. oregano, dried or fresh

2 tsp. thyme, dried or fresh

2 TB. basil, chopped

2 TB. dried parsley

1½ cups celery, chopped

1 TB. Bragg Liquid Aminos or balsamic vinegar

1 cup black olives, pitted and chopped

Pinch black pepper

½ cup red bell peppers, chopped

½ cup fresh parsley, chopped

1. Coat the bottom of a 9x12-inch-deep baking pan with 1 cup of the breadcrumbs. Set aside.

2. Rinse lentils, then place in a large pot with stock or water and bring to a boil.

3. Reduce heat to medium-low and cook, stirring occasionally, for 30 to 40 minutes, or until soft and water is absorbed.

4. Add salt.

5. In a large deep skillet, heat oil and sauté onions and garlic for 10 to 15 minutes. Stir in oregano, thyme, basil, dried parsley, and celery. Turn heat off.

6. Add remaining breadcrumbs, onion mixture, amino acids or vinegar, olives, and pepper to the cooked lentils and mix together.

7. Preheat oven to 350°F. Pour mixture into baking pan and bake until set or around 30 minutes.

8. Serve with fresh parsley and bell peppers.

HEART-HEALTHY TIP

Lentils are high in magnesium, which is nature's own calcium channel blocker. It relaxes veins and arteries, allowing blood to flow more easily around the heart and your entire body.

Sauces

Tofu Sour Cream

Made from heart-healthy bean curd which comes from soy milk, tofu contains lots of protein to nourish and sustain you. It's delicious on top of your favorite pasta or rice dish, or try it with vegetables. If you love rich flavors with beneficial nutrients, then tofu can be an exciting addition as it soaks up all flavors of anything it's cooked with.

Yield:	Serving size:	Prep time:	Cook time:
1½ cups	¼ cup	15 minutes	None

¼ cup onions, chopped

1 TB. garlic, chopped (optional)

1 TB. fresh lemon or lime juice

1 (12-oz.) package firm tofu, rinsed and drained

1 TB. Umeboshi vinegar (or use balsamic)

2 TB. fresh chives, chopped

Pinch ground black pepper

Pinch nutmeg

Dash of cayenne pepper

2 TB. extra virgin olive oil

1. In a blender or food processor, blend together onions, garlic, lemon or lime juice, tofu, vinegar, chives, black pepper, nutmeg, and cayenne.

2. Pour oil in slowly while blending and blend until smooth.

3. Serve at room temperature, or chill and serve later.

HEART-HEALTHY TIP

Soybeans are rich in minerals and plant phytonutrients called isoflavones. These act as a natural form of estrogen hormone in the body. This combination, with its low sodium and fat content, delivers some significant health benefits.

Coconut Cilantro Chutney

Coconuts are highly nutritious and rich in important fiber, vitamins, and minerals. The inclusion of cilantro, fresh ginger, and lime juice give this chutney an antioxidant edge that's highly medicinal, too. This chutney tastes divine—you'll definitely enjoy this one.

Yield:	Serving size:	Prep time:	Cook time:
2 cups	½ cup	15 minutes	None

½ cup raisins

½ cup coconut, shredded

2 TB. cilantro, chopped

3 TB. fresh lemon or lime juice

¼ tsp. fresh ginger, chopped

1 TB. fresh basil, chopped

1 cup apple, organic, chopped

½ tsp. Celtic or Himalayan salt

Dash cayenne pepper (optional)

1. Cover raisins in filtered water and soak for 5 to 10 minutes.

2. Place raisins, coconut, cilantro, lemon or lime juice, ginger, basil, apple, salt, and cayenne in blender and blend until smooth and creamy.

3. Refrigerate immediately and serve with your favorite dishes and snacks.

GOOD TO KNOW

Coconuts improve insulin secretions and utilization of blood glucose, making them particularly favored for people with diabetes.

Tomato Basil Sauce

Rich red tomatoes contain lycopene, which gives them their red pigment. Lycopene is a powerful antioxidant and has so many uses, which include lowering the risk of hypertension. You'll enjoy the spices and taste of this tomato fresh herb sauce.

Yield:	Serving size:	Prep time:	Cook time:
1 quart	1 cup	10 minutes	20 minutes

2 cups onions, chopped

2 TB. garlic, chopped

2 cups canned tomato sauce or 1 cup canned tomato paste, organic

2 cups canned whole plum tomatoes, organic

1 tsp. Celtic or Himalayan salt

Pinch of ground black pepper

Dash cayenne pepper

½ cup fresh basil, chopped

1. In a large pot, heat 2 tablespoons extra virgin olive oil over medium heat and sauté onions and garlic for 3 to 5 minutes, or until onions are translucent.

2. Stir in tomato sauce or paste.

3. Crush whole plum tomatoes by hand and add to pot.

4. Add salt, black pepper, and cayenne pepper and simmer over low heat for 20 minutes.

5. Add basil and simmer over low heat for 5 minutes.

6. Serve over favorite pasta or brown rice.

GOOD TO KNOW

Niacin present in tomatoes help in reducing blood cholesterol levels, making them helpful in preventing heart problems. The vitamin K content in tomatoes also helps prevent bleeding by aiding in clotting.

Plum Delicious Sauce

Known for their vitality building abilities, the prunes give this tangy sauce its plum-like flavor when combined with fresh herbs and spices. It's aptly named because it's simply delicious.

Yield:	Serving size:	Prep time:	Cook time:
1½ quarts	⅓ cup	10 minutes	15 minutes

1¾ cups red onions, chopped

½ cup canned crushed pineapple, low syrup, less sugar

½ tsp. dried mild chile peppers, crushed

¾ cup prunes, pitted and diced

2½ cups apple cider

3 TB. canned tomato paste, organic

1 (8-oz.) can tomato sauce, organic, no salt added

1 TB. apple cider vinegar

2 tsp. Celtic or Himalayan salt

½ TB. fresh lemon or lime juice

¼ tsp. ground black pepper

Dash cayenne pepper (optional)

1 tsp. coconut, shredded

1. In a large saucepan, heat 1 tablespoon sesame oil over medium heat and sauté onions for 3 to 5 minutes, or until translucent.

2. Add pineapple and chile peppers and continue to sauté over low heat.

3. Meanwhile, in a blender or food processor, blend together prunes, cider, and tomato paste.

4. Add prune mixture to onion mixture and mix together well.

5. Stir in tomato sauce, vinegar, salt, lemon or lime juice, black pepper, and cayenne pepper. Simmer over low heat for 10 minutes.

6. Serve with shredded coconut on top. Tastes great served over rice, pasta, or egg noodles.

HEART-HEALTHY TIP

Prunes are high in fiber and are helpful in maintaining normal blood circulation. They help slow brain aging and are high in antioxidants. Prunes are basically dried plums.

Lemon Tahini Sauce

As far as health foods go, there aren't many that are as versatile or that pack the same nutritional punch as tahini. It's loaded with heart-healthy nutrients such as calcium and almost a full range of B-complex vitamins for helping you reduce stress and feel calmer, and is excellent for lowering hypertension—and it tastes delicious.

Yield:	Serving size:	Prep time:	Cook time:
2 cups	⅓ cup	15 minutes	None

1 cup tahini

¾ cup filtered water

2 TB. Bragg Liquid Aminos

3 TB. fresh lemon or lime juice

1 tsp. cilantro, chopped

Dash cayenne pepper (optional)

1. In a blender or with a fork in a small bowl, blend tahini, water, amino acids, lemon or lime juice, cilantro, and cayenne pepper, until smooth.

2. Serve immediately with pita chips or kale crackers.

HEART-HEALTHY TIP

Sesame seeds contain phytosterols, which are compounds found in plants that have a chemical structure similar to cholesterol. They are believed to reduce blood levels of cholesterol and boost immunity.

DASH-Perfect Pesto

Enjoy this delicious all-natural pesto made with heart-healthy walnuts and basil. Walnuts are higher in omega-3 fatty acids than a serving of salmon and known for their inflammation-lowering effects. High in antioxidants, this pesto is also a good source of plant protein.

Yield:	Serving size:	Prep time:	Cook time:
2 cups	⅓ cup	2 hours, 15 minutes	None

1 cup walnuts, soaked in filtered water

1 cup basil

½ cup pine nuts

3 cloves garlic, chopped

Dash cayenne pepper (optional)

2 TB. filtered water

1. Soak walnuts in water for 2 hours and pour off the soaking water.

2. Blend walnuts, basil, pine nuts, garlic, cayenne pepper, and water in a blender or food processor until smooth and creamy.

3. Mix with your favorite pasta or rice dish.

HEART-HEALTHY TIP

Add a few heart-healthy walnuts to your salads, oatmeal, muesli, rice, chicken dishes, yogurt, or trail mix each day.

Spiced Peanut Sauce

Enjoy the tasty flavors of peanuts spiced with herbs and rich in energy. This sauce is packed with numerous heart-healthy antioxidants, fiber, and tons of minerals and vitamins … simply delicious.

Yield:	Serving size:	Prep time:	Cook time:
3 cups	⅓ cup	15 minutes	5–10 minutes

1 TB. cumin, ground

½ TB. dried mild chile peppers, crushed

1 tsp. coriander, ground

Dash cayenne pepper

1½ cups natural smooth peanut butter, no additives

1 TB. fresh parsley, chopped

2½ TB. tamari

1 tsp. Celtic or Himalayan salt

½ tsp. fresh ground black pepper

2 cups filtered water

1. In a small skillet, heat 2½ tablespoons sesame oil over medium heat and sauté cumin, chile peppers, coriander, and cayenne pepper for 1 to 2 minutes.

2. In a blender or food processor, slowly blend together cumin mixture, peanut butter, parsley, tamari, salt, and black pepper. Add the water slowly while blending until desired thickness.

3. In a medium-size saucepan, combine and heat the mixture over low heat until warm.

4. Serve over brown rice.

GOOD TO KNOW

Studies show that peanuts have been associated with lowering LDL or "bad" cholesterol and triglyceride levels, which are associated with lower cardiovascular disease risk.

Thai Coconut Sauce

Increase your metabolism and your energy with the delicious flavors of this coconut Thai spice sauce. People living in tropical areas who eat coconut daily are usually not overweight and have very little heart disease. Sauce it up and enjoy.

Yield:	Serving size:	Prep time:	Cook time:
2½ cups	⅓ cup	15 minutes	None

2 cups, or 1 (14-oz.) can light
  coconut milk

3 TB. cilantro

1 garlic clove, chopped

3 TB. parsley, chopped

1 TB. oregano, chopped

½ Thai chile pepper, chopped

2 fresh basil leaves, chopped

1. Place coconut milk, cilantro, garlic, parsley, oregano, chile, and fresh basil into blender and blend for 3 to 5 minutes until smooth.

2. Serve with fish, chicken, or rice dishes.

HEART-HEALTHY TIP

Coconut oil contains approximately 50 percent lauric acid, which studies have shown helps in preventing heart problems by increasing HDL the "good" cholesterol and reducing LDL the "bad" cholesterol.

On the Dinner Menu

All the recipes in this part go beyond simply qualifying as heart healthy. That's because in addition to traditional heart-healthy dinner menus, I've included plenty of Mediterranean-style dishes, which are considered the most heart healthy in the world.

Remember to include lots of brightly colored fruits and vegetables, whole grains, beans, and fermented soy products in your diet on a daily basis. These are the highest in antioxidants and fiber and are the most beneficial for your heart. By eating this way and adding a good dose of daily exercise, you'll be on your way to lower blood pressure and cholesterol in no time.

Hearty Beef Entrées

In This Chapter

- High-protein nourishment from grass-fed beef
- Red-meat selections you'll simply love

When it comes to dining DASH with panache, you will want to include some succulent red meat in your diet. It's all in the way you prepare your food that determines how healthy it will be for your body.

The main things you will want to remember when including red meat in your diet is to pick lean cuts of meat to reduce the saturated fat content. In addition, keep in mind that it's the processed meats which are most likely to increase your risk for obesity, heart disease, and hypertension.

Something else to keep in mind: you should avoid charring your meats over a flame. This process creates oxidation and can cause free radical damage in your body. When at the market, choose grass-fed beef over grain fed, if you can, as these are the healthiest. And, of course, feel free to substitute the beef with chicken or turkey in any of the following recipes.

Easy Beef Stir-Fry with Fresh Herbs

Eating beef occasionally—especially when it's grass fed, is a healthy way to go because it gives you two to six times more omega-3s—than commercial farmed beef. The goodness is enhanced by the vegetables you add to the dish. This one has got your heart health covered. Enjoy!

Yield:	Serving size:	Prep time:	Cook time:
4 cups	1 cup	20 minutes	10 minutes

2 cloves garlic, minced

1 small chile pepper, minced

1 medium onion, minced

4–6 oz. grass-fed beef, chopped into 1- to 2-inch cubes

1 cup zucchini, sliced

3 large carrots, with skin, sliced

8 crimini mushrooms, sliced

1 large green bell pepper, chopped

2 TB. tamari

Dash Celtic or Himalayan salt

Pinch ground black pepper

2 TB. fresh parsley, chopped

1. In a skillet over medium-high heat, add 2 tablespoons olive oil and sauté garlic, chile pepper, and onion until softened.

2. Add beef cubes and cook until tender.

3. Add zucchini, carrots, mushrooms, green pepper, tamari, salt, and black pepper.

4. Cook, stirring often, until vegetables are crisp-tender. Add the fresh parsley at the end.

5. Serve immediately.

HEART-HEALTHY TIP

Switching to grass-fed beef will provide essential omega-3 fatty acids and save you calories without requiring much effort or change in eating habits. This is healthier for your heart.

Moroccan-Style Beef Stew

Enjoy the rich, hearty flavors and substance of this spicy Moroccan beef stew. The combination of herbs and spices will nourish your soul and replenish your energy.

Yield:	Serving size:	Prep time:	Cook time:
1 quart	2 cups	8 hours, 15 minutes	1–2 hours

⅓ cup extra virgin olive oil

5 garlic cloves, chopped finely

1 TB. fresh ginger, chopped finely

4 tsp. ground cumin

1 tsp. ground turmeric

1 tsp. paprika

1 tsp. ground cinnamon

1 tsp. ground black pepper

½ tsp. Celtic or Himalayan salt

8 oz. lean beef, cut into 2-inch chunks

2–4 cups vegetable or low-salt beef stock

2 TB. arrowroot blended with 2 TB. filtered water

2 TB. grated lemon rind

1 cup prunes, pitted

¼ cup cilantro

1. Preheat oven to 300°F.

2. In a medium bowl, make a mixture of olive oil, garlic, ginger, cumin, turmeric, paprika, cinnamon, black pepper, and salt. Add the beef chunks to the marinade for several hours or overnight.

3. Place the marinated beef and marinade in a heavy, flameproof casserole, along with stock. Bring to a boil and skim off any fat.

4. Reduce heat to a simmer and stir in lemon rind and prunes. Add the arrowroot and water.

5. Cover casserole and bake in oven for about 1 hour or until meat is tender.

6. Add the cilantro just before serving for garnish. Serve with fresh vegetables or a raw salad.

GOOD TO KNOW

Beef is healthiest when grass fed and not grain. It tends to lose its valuable store of omega-3 fatty acids when grain fed.

Veal Scaloppini with Fresh Herbs

Enjoy the succulent flavors of this low-fat veal dish that's high in B vitamins and bio-available iron. This recipe offers plenty of lean protein and is simply delicious.

Yield:	Serving size:	Prep time:	Cook time:
4 fillets	1 fillet	1 hour, 15 minutes	20 minutes

1 lb. pasture-fed veal fillet

2 lemons or limes, juiced

1 tsp. freshly ground black pepper

½ cup unbleached flour

½ cup dry white wine

2 cups vegetable or low-salt beef stock

½ cup cream, organic

2 TB. fresh parsley, chopped

1. In a medium bowl place the meat in lemon or lime juice for 1 hour. Remove and pat dry with paper towels.

2. Mix the black pepper into the flour and dredge it over the meat.

3. In a heavy skillet, brown the scaloppini in batches in 2 tablespoons organic butter and 3 tablespoons extra virgin olive oil. Transfer to a heated dish when cooked.

4. Place veal in oven to warm while preparing sauce.

5. Place wine in pan and bring to a boil. Add the stock and stir consistently. Add cream and let liquid boil down. Reduce down to half a cup.

6. Season sauce with black pepper and add parsley.

7. Pour sauce over veal and serve with vegetables or salad.

GOOD TO KNOW

Veal is meat from young calves and is naturally lower in fat. It's a DASH-friendly animal protein.

Favorite Spicy Meatloaf

This dish is enjoyed the most on heartwarming nights when you eat by the fire.

Yield:	Serving size:	Prep time:	Cook time:
1¼ quarts	2 cups	20 minutes	1 hour, 20 minutes

1 large onion, chopped

3 garlic cloves, chopped

1 medium carrot, chopped finely, skin on

2 stalks celery, chopped finely

1 small chile, chopped finely

4 shiitake mushrooms, chopped

1 tsp. thyme, chopped finely

4 TB. organic tomato paste

1 cup whole-grain breadcrumbs, plain, unseasoned

½ cup low-fat milk or 1 cup yogurt

1 lb. ground beef, or other lean, ground red meat

1–2 small eggs, beaten (organic)

1 TB. Bragg Liquid Aminos

Dash Celtic or Himalayan salt

Dash cayenne pepper

1. Preheat oven to 350°F.

2. In a large sauce pan, sauté onion, garlic, carrots, and celery in 2 tablespoons unsalted, organic butter until soft.

3. Add chile, mushrooms, thyme, and tomato paste, and stir.

4. Presoak breadcrumbs in yogurt or whole milk until moist.

5. With your hands, blend in meat with sautéed vegetables, soaked bread, egg, amino acids, salt, and cayenne.

6. Place mixture into a greased 9x13-inch baking dish.

7. Bake for 1 hour.

8. Serve with tomato sauce and steamed carrots or brussels sprouts.

GOOD TO KNOW

Organic farmers are required by law to raise animals without the use of antibiotics or synthetic growth hormones. This is a bonus to your health!

Perfect Poultry Dishes

In This Chapter

- Healthy recipes for the most versatile protein
- Nourishment that ranges from roasting to sautéing

Your DASH diet cooking would not be complete without a good selection of delicious chicken recipes. It's easy to prepare a low-fat chicken recipe; chicken has low-fat content to begin with, and when you add the heart-healthy ingredients that you'll find here—violá!

Apart from the fact that you will lose weight as a result of eating low-fat chicken recipes, it makes cooking and eating a pleasure. Chicken is just about one of the most nourishing meats available and is associated with numerous positive benefits on your health.

Chicken is high in essential nutrients and vitamins, including selenium, an antioxidant that's good for your metabolism, as well as being healthy for your heart. Chicken is high in pyridoxine, as well as vitamin B_6, both nutrients that play an important role in energy production and supports blood flow.

Grilled Chicken Burritos

Who doesn't love the flavor of delicious burritos? These are filled with nourishment and plenty of lean protein, healthy fats, and the right amount of antioxidants to keep you fully satisfied. Serve with your favorite mixed green salad, and don't spare the vegetables, either. It's a tasty choice as a snack—or even for breakfast!

Yield:	Serving size:	Prep time:	Cook time:
8 burritos	2 burritos	15 minutes	5–10 minutes

8 flour tortillas, small

1 TB. grape seed or extra virgin olive oil

1 TB. plus dash fresh lemon or lime juice

1 tsp. fresh ginger, chopped finely

2 TB. garlic, chopped finely

½ cup cilantro, chopped

2 TB. shallots, chopped finely

1 tsp. fresh ground black pepper

Dash cayenne pepper (optional)

1 lb. organic chicken breast, chopped into 2-inch pieces

1 avocado, peeled and mashed

1 medium tomato, chopped

1. Preheat oven to 250°F.

2. Place tortillas in oven and warm for 10 minutes.

3. In a medium bowl mix 1 tablespoon lemon or lime juice, ginger, garlic, cilantro, shallots, black pepper, and cayenne pepper. Add the chicken to marinate for 30 minutes in refrigerator.

4. In a small bowl, combine the avocado and tomato with a dash of lemon juice.

5. In a medium skillet, heat the oil over a medium flame and add the chicken pieces.

6. Spread the warmed tortilla with avocado and fill with the chicken. Roll up the tortilla and serve with chopped tomato.

GOOD TO KNOW

Burritos are enjoyed around the world in many countries often as a breakfast. In Mexico they add beans or meat; in India, a variety of delicious vegetables and gravy; and in the United States, we enjoy a combination of ingredients such as beans, avocado, salsa, lettuce, and cheese.

Vegetable Biryani with Chicken and Herbs

Enjoy the delicious spices from this popular Indian rice dish that's served all around the world. I've added a couple of extra herbs and spices to make your own heart-healthy version. See if you can guess what they are.

Yield:	Serving size:	Prep time:	Cook time:
1 quart	2 cups	20 minutes	20–30 minutes

1 cup basmati rice

1½ cups filtered water, hot, plus 1 cup

Pinch saffron

2 tsp. fresh ginger, minced

2 TB. garlic, minced

1 lb. chicken breast, chopped into 2-inch cubes

½ tsp. turmeric

½ small carrot, skin on, chopped

½ small onion, chopped

1 small chile, chopped finely, (optional)

1¼ tsp. Celtic or Himalayan salt

½ cup frozen green peas

¼ cup raisins

¼ cup cashews, unsalted and raw

1. Rinse rice and cover with hot water in a large bowl for 15 minutes.

2. Drain rice and combine with water and saffron in a small pot.

3. In a separate sauté pan, heat 1 tablespoon sesame oil or ghee (a.k.a., clarified butter) over medium heat. Add ginger and garlic and sauté for 3 minutes.

4. Add the chicken and sauté for several minutes until cooked on both sides.

5. Add turmeric and stir.

6. Add carrots, onions, and chile, and sauté until onions start to brown.

7. Add salt and transfer mixture to the rice pot and stir to combine with rice.

8. Bring to a boil over medium-high heat and then reduce heat to a low simmer. Cover and cook for 12 minutes until rice is cooked through.

9. Add frozen green peas and raisins and allow to cook in covered pot for 3 to 5 minutes to warm peas and soften raisins.

10. Serve immediately with cashews sprinkled over top.

GOOD TO KNOW

Use tofu in place of chicken if you prefer something lighter or are a vegan or vegetarian.

Spinach, Cheese, and Chicken Lasagna

Enjoy this delicious chicken and spinach lasagna as is, or you can substitute the meat using tofu and use whole-wheat pasta. This is a perfect dish to see how much better your body can feel by way of healthier blood pressure and cholesterol levels.

Yield:	Serving size:	Prep time:	Cook time:
6–8 cups	2 cups	20 minutes	1 hour, 20 minutes

1 large onion, chopped

6 cloves garlic, chopped finely

1 TB. filtered water

2 large chicken breasts (6-8 oz. each), chopped into 1 inch cubes

4 cups tomato purée, organic

2 cups zucchini, chopped

3 tsp. onion powder

1 TB. dried Italian seasonings (oregano, basil, and thyme)

Dash nutmeg

$\frac{1}{4}$ tsp. freshly ground black pepper

1 large bay leaf

1 lb. whole-wheat or gluten-free lasagna noodles

4 cups low-fat, low-sodium cottage cheese, whipped

Dash cayenne pepper

$\frac{1}{2}$ tsp. garlic powder

6 cups chopped spinach, washed, dried

1. Preheat the oven to 350°F.

2. In a nonstick frying pan over medium heat, sauté onion and garlic, adding water as needed to keep onion from sticking and burning.

3. Add the chicken pieces and brown them on both sides until just cooked (approximately 5 minutes).

4. When onions are soft, add tomato purée, zucchini, 1 teaspoon onion powder, Italian seasonings, nutmeg, black pepper, and bay leaf.

5. Simmer sauce slowly for 25 minutes and remove from heat. Remove bay leaf.

6. Meanwhile, in a large pot, heat water for lasagna noodles over high heat until water is boiling rapidly.

7. Add noodles and cook according to instructions on package.

8. Rinse and leave noodles in cool water until ready to use.

9. Drain noodles well just before assembling lasagna.

10. In a medium bowl, mix together whipped cottage cheese, 2 teaspoons onion powder, cayenne pepper, and garlic powder and set aside.

11. In a 9x13-inch nonstick or glass oven-proof baking pan, layer lasagna in the following order: (1) 1 cup tomato sauce for bottom of pan, (2) one layer noodles, (3) ¾ cup sauce spread over noodles, (4) ½ cup cottage cheese, (5) ½ spinach, (6) another layer of noodles. Repeat process and finish with a layer of sauce on top.

12. Cover with foil and bake lasagna for 1 hour, or until hot and bubbly, and light brown on top.

13. Let stand for 5 minutes before serving. Serve with a tossed green salad or steamed vegetables.

HEART-HEALTHY TIP

Spinach is one of the healthiest vegetables because it's loaded with significant amounts of vitamins and minerals. Spinach is also a significant source of vitamin K which can have a clotting effect on the blood. This may affect any blood thinning medications you are on so speak to your nutritionist about consuming a balanced diet containing adequate amounts of vitamin K.

Thanksgiving Turkey Loaf

Get your daily fiber in a tasty way with Thanksgiving turkey meat loaf to live for. Not only packed with goodness and the love of its maker, you will enjoy the calm feeling you experience after eating the turkey.

Yield:	Serving size:	Prep time:	Cook time:
2 quarts	2 cups	20 minutes	1 hour

2 TB. extra virgin olive oil

2 onions, chopped

6 cloves garlic, chopped

2 celery stalks, chopped

3 large carrots, shredded, skin on

3 tomatoes, chopped

6 cups filtered water

2 tsp. oregano

1 tsp. sage

1 tsp. rosemary

$1\frac{1}{2}$ tsp. fresh ground black pepper

Dash cayenne pepper

1 lb. ground turkey

$2\frac{1}{2}$ cups brown rice, raw

$\frac{1}{2}$ cup white wine

2 TB. onion powder

2 tsp. celery seed

8 cups toasted whole-wheat breadcrumbs or bran flakes

$\frac{1}{3}$ cup walnuts, chopped

$\frac{1}{3}$ cup almonds, chopped

4 cups low-fat cottage cheese, low-sodium, whipped

1 TB. garlic powder

$1\frac{1}{2}$ cups pecans, ground

1. Preheat the oven to 375°F.

2. In a large saucepan add the olive oil, onions, and garlic and sauté for 3-5 minutes over medium heat.

3. Add celery, carrots, tomatoes, 1 cup water, oregano, sage, rosemary, 1 teaspoon black pepper, and cayenne pepper for approximately 30 minutes or until celery is soft.

4. Add the ground turkey and cook a further 10 minutes.

5. Reserve $1\frac{1}{2}$ cups of liquid from vegetables for topping and use remaining juice and vegetables in the loaf.

6. Meanwhile, in a medium pot, cook rice in 5 cups water, wine, 1 tablespoon onion powder, celery seed, and $\frac{1}{2}$ teaspoon black pepper, bringing to a boil; then reduce to a simmer partially covered over low heat for approximately 45 minutes.

7. In a large bowl, mix together vegetable mixture, rice, 4 cups breadcrumbs, walnuts, $\frac{1}{3}$ cup almonds, 3 cups cottage cheese, 1 tablespoon onion powder, and garlic powder.

8. Form into one loaf.

9. Place loaf in a 10x15-inch nonstick pan or large roasting pan. Set aside.

10. In a large bowl, mix together ground pecans, 1 cup ground almonds, 4 cups breadcrumbs, and 1 cup cottage cheese.

11. Add $1\frac{1}{2}$ cups reserved vegetable liquid slowly until mixture becomes a dough.

12. Pat mixture all over loaf to cover well with fingers, a little at a time.

13. Bake, covered, for 30 minutes, then uncovered for 30 minutes or until nut topping is golden brown.

14. Serve immediately with Mushroom Chicken Gravy (see following recipe).

HEART-HEALTHY TIP

Turkey contains an essential amino acid called tryptophan. It's called essential because your body needs it and turkey is a low-fat protein that's very DASH healthy for you.

Mushroom Chicken Gravy

Serve this delicious mushroom chicken gravy over your favorite meat loaf. It's loaded with goodness.

Yield:	Serving size:	Prep time:	Cook time:
1 quart	1 cup	20 minutes	30 minutes

1 TB. extra virgin olive oil

2½ cups onions, chopped

7 cloves garlic, chopped finely

¼ tsp. fresh ground black pepper

½ tsp. oregano

1 tsp. thyme

Dash cayenne pepper

2 TB. plus ¼ cup filtered water

4 cups portobello or shiitake mushrooms, sliced

1 cup chicken stock or 1 cup evaporated skim milk

1. In a large nonstick frying pan over medium heat, add olive oil and sauté onions, garlic, black pepper, oregano, thyme, and cayenne pepper until onions are softened and lightly browned.

2. Add 1 or 2 tablespoons of water as needed to keep mixture from sticking or burning.

3. Stir in mushrooms and cook for 25 to 30 minutes over low heat, stirring occasionally.

4. Cool slightly and purée half of mushroom mixture in a food processor or blender.

5. Stir in puréed mixture to the remaining portion in frying pan.

6. Add stock or milk and water. Heat over medium heat. Do not boil.

7. Serve over your favorite meat loaf.

HEART-HEALTHY TIP

Shiitake mushrooms have been popular in China and Japan for centuries because of their medicinal properties. Shiitakes are long known as a remedy for upper respiratory diseases, and keeping the blood flowing to boost immunity and promote strength.

Chicken and Mushroom Curry

This traditional chicken curry dish originated in India and became famous for its medicinal benefits. Curry has numerous positive health benefits that reduce inflammation and improve your metabolism. Each bite is full of flavor, and you can be sure it's DASH friendly, too.

Yield:	Serving size:	Prep time:	Cook time:
1 quart	1 cup	20 minutes	20 minutes

½ cup filtered water

1 TB. plus 1 TB. extra virgin olive oil

1 small onion, chopped

1 TB. garlic, chopped

1 lb. chicken breast, chopped into 2-inch cubes

1 cup portobello mushrooms, chopped

¼ cup fresh lemon or lime juice

3 tsp. curry powder

Dash cayenne pepper (optional)

1 tsp. allspice

½ tsp. Celtic or Himalayan salt

½ tsp. ground black pepper

2 cups cooked quinoa

1 bunch green onions, diced

1 medium red bell pepper, chopped

1 cup raisins

½ cup cooked or canned chickpeas

1. In a medium saucepan, heat the water and 1 tablespoon oil over a medium-high heat and add the onions and garlic. Cook 5 minutes and add chicken. Add mushrooms and cook a further 5 minutes. When cooked, remove from pan and set aside.

2. To make dressing: In a small bowl, whisk together lemon juice, curry powder, cayenne pepper, allspice, salt, and black pepper. Gradually add remaining oil in a thin stream, whisking until all is blended. Set dressing aside.

3. Fluff quinoa with a fork. Add green onions, bell pepper, raisins, and chickpeas. Mix well.

4. Add dressing and toss. Add chicken and serve hot or cold.

HEART-HEALTHY TIP

Curry contains curcumin, a powerful antioxidant and anti-inflammatory agent that also gives curry its yellow ocher color.

Poached Chicken Breast in Spicy Broth

Enjoy the delicious spicy blend of flavors with the packed-in goodness inside this dish. Chicken is known as one of the healthiest foods because of all the vitamins and minerals it contains, and when you add the delicious flavors of fresh okra, fennel, and other delights, your heart will sing.

Yield:	Serving size:	Prep time:	Cook time:
2 quarts	2 cups	20 minutes	15–20 minutes

2 cloves garlic, chopped

1 small chile, chopped finely

2 TB. tomato paste, organic

2 TB. dry white wine

4 cups chicken or vegetable stock

2 tsp. tarragon, chopped

1 TB. orange peel, grated (zest)

1 tsp. saffron

1 bay leaf

2 TB. fennel, chopped finely

1 cup okra, chopped

1 cup leeks, chopped

1 lb. chicken breast, cut in 2-inch pieces, organic

2 cups tomatoes, chopped

Dash cayenne pepper

Dash Celtic or Himalayan salt

Dash fresh ground black pepper

1 TB. fresh lemon or lime juice

1. In a large skillet, heat 1 tablespoon extra virgin olive oil or grape seed oil, and add the garlic and chile. Sauté lightly, then add tomato paste and cook until brown.

2. Add the wine and deglaze the pan by loosening any stuck pieces in the pan. Add the 1 cup stock, tarragon, orange peel, saffron, and bay leaf. Simmer 10 to 15 minutes. Turn heat down, remove bay leaf and orange peel, and keep warm.

3. In a large sauce pan, heat the 3 cups chicken or vegetable stock.

4. Add the fennel, okra, and leeks. Simmer until vegetables soften.

5. Add chicken and poach gently until thoroughly cooked, about 8 to 10 minutes.

6. Add the tomatoes and cayenne pepper and cook for several minutes.

7. Season with salt, pepper, and lemon juice.

GOOD TO KNOW

Chicken soup has long been called a panacea for many different ailments. This is for good reason. Studies have shown that chicken soup can help reduce inflammation and is a rich source of protein, which provides amino acids that your body needs to build muscles, including your heart.

DASH Roast Chicken

Your DASH diet cooking would not be complete without a nourishing roast chicken recipe. This one's complete with every flavor to satisfy your most wholesome urge.

Yield:	Serving size:	Prep time:	Cook time:
4 pounds	6–8 ounces	20 minutes	2 hours

1 (4–5 lb.) roasting chicken, giblets removed

1 large onion, sliced thinly

2 garlic cloves, chopped

Several sprigs fresh herbs; parsley, thyme, oregano, or tarragon

2–3 TB. unsalted butter, melted

½ tsp. Celtic or Himalayan salt

4 cups chicken or vegetable stock

½ tsp. fresh ground black pepper

1. Preheat oven to 375°F.

2. In a large stainless steel roasting pan, place the onions and garlic.

3. Stuff chicken with fresh herbs of parsley, thyme, oregano, or tarragon and baste the outside of the chicken with melted butter and salt.

4. Place chicken in the roasting pan to which 4 cups chicken or vegetable stock has been added and bake for 1 hour.

5. Baste chicken again with the stock, and ground black pepper, in 1 hour.

6. Remove chicken and place on a carving board and cut into pieces.

7. Reserve the juices and chicken pieces to make into a sauce, if desired.

8. To make gravy, stir in wine and heat on high heat and reduce it to about half.

HEART-HEALTHY TIP

Chicken is an excellent source of the trace mineral selenium. Studies show that this antioxidant is an essential component of several major metabolic pathways and systems in the body.

Spicy Sesame Chicken Wings

Who wouldn't enjoy a special treat when you are breaking out of your daily fare by indulging in these delicious and nutritious chicken wings? They are flavorful to the maximum, and your taste buds and waistline will be glad you chose them over any other treat. You can even enjoy them for breakfast the next morning!

Yield:	Serving size:	Prep time:	Cook time:
24 wings	4 wings	20 minutes	1¼ hours

½ cup Bragg Liquid Aminos

½ cup rice vinegar

2 TB. raw honey

1–2 garlic cloves, chopped

Grated rind of 2 lemon or limes

Juice of 2 lemon or limes

1 tsp. curry powder

1 tsp. fresh ginger, chopped finely

½ tsp. dried oregano

¼ tsp. nutmeg

½ tsp. dried thyme

¼ cup and 1 TB. sesame seeds

½ tsp. fresh ground black pepper

24 chicken wings, separated at joints

3 TB. unsalted butter, melted (organic)

1. Preheat oven to 350°F.

2. In a large bowl, mix the amino acids, vinegar, honey, garlic, lemon or lime rind, curry, ginger, oregano, nutmeg, thyme, ¼ cup sesame seeds, and black pepper.

3. Add the wings to the marinade and let sit for several hours or overnight in refrigerator.

4. Remove wings from mixture and pat dry with paper towel.

5. Place wings in a stainless steel baking pan, brush with butter, sprinkle with 1 tablespoon sesame seeds, and bake for about 1¼ hours.

6. Serve with Plum Delicious Sauce (Chapter 11).

HEART-HEALTHY TIP

Chicken wings are loaded with collagen, which supports healthy blood vessels and connective tissues. Studies have shown that collagen has the ability to reduce blood pressure.

Seafood Suppers

In This Chapter

- Highly nourishing and cholesterol-lowering fish dishes
- Heart-healthy recipes that help you lose weight

It simply doesn't get any heart healthier as far as your DASH diet goes than by eating fish several times a week. Rich in essential omega-3 fatty acids that help lower triglycerides, fish is a superfood in the DASH menu plan. Since these fats can be a risk factor for cardiovascular problems, fish is a great choice for many reasons.

When selecting and purchasing fish, always go first for what's freshest. You will want the fish eyes to be clear and not cloudy and for there to be no odor. Wild caught, deep sea cold water fish is preferable to farm raised, as the omega-3 content and protein quality is higher.

I've made these recipes as simple as possible yet suitable for any table or meal. Let's face it, fish is delicious and nutritious and you don't need a lot of fancy ingredients to make it taste good. Add a tossed green salad on the side or steam, bake, or sauté your favorite vegetables. Your heart will sing with joy.

Garlic Ginger Fish

The garlic and ginger in this recipe add flavor as well as medicinal compounds to support your DASH diet.

Yield:	Serving size:	Prep time:	Cook time:
1 fillet	1 fillet	15 minutes	15 minutes

1 piece fish fillet (tilapia, flounder, sea bass)

Freshly ground black pepper

1 clove garlic

1–2 slices fresh ginger, approximately 2 inches

Pinch salt

Dash cayenne pepper

2 TB. dry white wine

1. Wash and dry fish fillet. Sprinkle with black pepper.

2. Finely dice garlic and ginger.

3. In a large fry pan, heat $\frac{1}{2}$ tablespoon olive oil over medium heat and sauté approximately one-third garlic and ginger until crisp, then remove from pan.

4. Add another $\frac{1}{2}$ tablespoon olive oil, add wine, and pan-fry fillets over medium-low heat. Cover and cook for 10 minutes.

5. Add remaining garlic and ginger. Cook for 5 more minutes.

6. Remove from heat and add cayenne and salt.

7. Serve immediately.

GOOD TO KNOW

Studies have shown that fish oil reduces inflammation associated with peptic ulcers, and boosts immunity to prevent recurrence of the ulcers.

DASH Seafood Paella

The delicious mixture of flavors in this dish will have you coming back for seconds.

Yield:	Serving size:	Prep time:	Cook time:
2 quarts	2 cups	20 minutes	20 minutes

1 medium onion, chopped

3 garlic cloves, chopped

$\frac{1}{2}$ tsp. saffron (optional)

8 shrimp, peeled

$\frac{1}{2}$ each green and red bell peppers, medium, chopped

1 cup grape or cherry tomatoes, halved

Dash Celtic or Himalayan salt

Dash fresh ground black pepper

$\frac{1}{4}$ cup dry white wine

$1\frac{1}{2}$ cups paella rice

1–2 cups vegetable stock

12 mussels, well rinsed

$\frac{1}{2}$ cup peas, frozen or fresh

$\frac{1}{2}$ lb. of either halibut, sea bass, or black cod, cut into small pieces

1 cup spicy turkey or chicken sausage, cut into small pieces (optional)

$\frac{1}{4}$ cup parsley, chopped

1 fresh lemon, cut in wedges

1. Preheat oven to 350°F.

2. In a large paella pan or skillet, heat 2 tablespoons extra virgin olive oil over medium to high flame.

3. Add onions and sauté until they become translucent.

4. Add chopped garlic and saffron and stir.

5. Push onions to the side of the pan and add fish and shrimp, searing on each side for a minute until partially cooked. Then remove and set aside.

6. Add bell peppers and tomatoes, plus sausage if using.

7. Add salt and black pepper to sauté.

8. Deglaze pan with wine. Add the rice and stir quickly to coat the rice well.

9. Add the stock a little at a time while simmering (do not stir). Cook until rice begins to soften. When rice is almost fully cooked, finish as follows.

10. Place fish and shrimp in rice and lay mussels and peas on top of paella. Remove from heat and cover in oven about 10 minutes, until mussels open.

11. Serve with chopped parsley and lemon wedges.

HEART-HEALTHY TIP

Fish oil has been well researched for its many benefits, which includes reducing the activity of enzymes that destroy joint and bone tissue cartilage.

Baked Halibut or Salmon

Fish cooks fast, which makes it a quick, easy dish to prepare. It absorbs the flavors around it while still holding its own. You'll enjoy the flavors in this recipe and your heart health will strengthen, too.

Yield:	Serving size:	Prep time:	Cook time:
1 fillet	1 fillet	15 minutes	15–20 minutes

1 salmon or halibut fillet,
   approximately 4 oz. each.

2 TB. fresh lemon or lime juice

1 TB. unsalted butter, melted

1 TB. unbleached flour

$\frac{1}{4}$ tsp. paprika

Dash Celtic or Himalayan salt

Dash of black pepper

Dash cayenne pepper (optional)

2 TB. fresh parsley, chopped

1. Preheat oven to 350°F.

2. Place fillet in a buttered baking dish. Pour lemon juice on top and brush with butter.

3. Sprinkle on flour and coat evenly.

4. Sprinkle on paprika, salt, black pepper, and cayenne pepper.

5. Bake for 15 minutes or until fish is almost cooked. Place under broiler for about 1 minute until flour browns.

6. Sprinkle with parsley and serve.

HEART-HEALTHY TIP

Dry-heat methods such as baking, broiling, and grilling work well for fish naturally higher in fat, such as halibut and salmon.

Dashing Fish Cakes

These nourishing fish cakes are simply easy to make and great for breakfast, lunch, dinner, or an anytime snack. I like mine accompanied by a fresh mixed green salad, but feel free to serve them with a plate of steamed broccoli or asparagus also. Either way, you'll love them.

Yield:	Serving size:	Prep time:	Cook time:
8 cakes	2 cakes	20 minutes	10 minutes

½ cup filtered water

1 lb. white fish (halibut, sea bass, orange roughy)

2 eggs, beaten lightly

1 large onion, chopped finely

2 TB. Dijon-style mustard

1 cup whole-grain breadcrumbs

Dash cayenne pepper

1 cup cilantro, chopped (optional)

1 tsp. lemon rind, grated

1–2 TB. Bragg Liquid Aminos

¼ cup grape seed oil, or
    ¼ cup ghee (clarified butter)

2 TB. fresh parsley, chopped

1. In a large pan add water and place the fish, simmer gently until fish is tender. Remove with slotted spoon, place in a bowl, and break up using fork.

2. In a separate bowl, combine eggs, onions, mustard, breadcrumbs, cayenne pepper, cilantro, lemon rind, and amino acids.

3. Add to fish and mix well. Form into cakes.

4. Sauté cakes in ¼ cup grape seed oil or clarified butter (ghee) until golden brown, a few minutes for each side.

5. Sprinkle with parsley and serve.

GOOD TO KNOW

Studies have shown that infants whose mothers consumed fish or omega-3 essential fatty acids during pregnancy or while nursing tend to have healthy vision and brain development. Always look for the highest quality or substitute with flax seed oil instead of fish oil if in doubt.

Poached Salmon and Shiitake

You simply can't beat the health benefits of certain fish when it comes to your heart's health. Always select only the freshest wild-caught fish that's available to you, and your heart will thrive.

Yield:	Serving size:	Prep time:	Cook time:
4 fish	1 fish	20 minutes	15 minutes

4 cups filtered water

1 large onion, chopped

1 carrot, chopped, skin on

2 celery stalks, chopped

2 TB. fresh ginger, chopped

2 TB. dry white wine

1 TB. Bragg Liquid Aminos

$\frac{1}{2}$ cup plus $\frac{1}{2}$ cup red bell pepper, sliced in 2-inch strips

4 salmon fillets, approximately 4 oz. each

1 cup shiitake mushrooms, sliced

2 cups bok choy, sliced

$\frac{1}{2}$ cup scallions, sliced

2 TB. water chestnuts (optional)

Sprig of fresh parsley or chervil

1. In a large sauce pan, combine the water, onion, carrot, celery, ginger, wine, and amino acids. Simmer for 20 minutes, add $\frac{1}{2}$ cup bell pepper, strain, and discard the vegetables, retaining the liquid bouillon.

2. In a medium sauté pan, heat 2 tablespoons extra virgin olive oil, place one or two fish fillets in the pan, and add enough of the liquid bouillon to cover fish by half.

3. Add the mushrooms, remaining $\frac{1}{2}$ cup bell pepper, bok choy, and scallions to the pan and cook covered for 5 minutes.

4. Add water chestnuts to pan and cook a further 3 minutes until fish is opaque.

5. Serve with vegetables in the bouillon and garnish with fresh parsley or chervil.

GOOD TO KNOW

The body can't make significant amounts of omega-3 essential fatty acids. Fish from deep-sea cold water is a high-protein, healthy fat–food choice that benefits your heart.

Grilled Shrimp Southern Style

Grilling your shrimp this way is not only heart healthier, it's deliciously satisfying with this spicy sauce that I think you'll love. Shrimp is low in calories and saturated fat, and even the cholesterol is HDL, the good kind. This tastes great with bok choy.

Yield:	Serving size:	Prep time:	Cook time:
16 shrimp	8 shrimp	1 hour, 15 minutes	5 minutes

2 garlic cloves, chopped

1 TB. fresh ginger, chopped

2 TB. Bragg Liquid Aminos or dry white wine

1 tsp. fresh chopped chile

Tabasco sauce

1 TB. fresh lemon or lime juice

1 tsp. sesame oil

16 medium-size shrimp, peeled

2 TB. sesame seeds

1. In a large bowl, combine the garlic, ginger, amino acids or wine, chile, tabasco sauce, lemon or lime juice, sesame oil, and shrimp. Let marinate in refrigerator for at least 1 hour.

2. Remove shrimp from marinade and grill until cooked, about 2 minutes each side (do not char).

3. Sprinkle with sesame seeds. Serve immediately.

HEART-HEALTHY TIP

Shrimp is high in magnesium, which helps stabilize blood sugar levels.

Poached Halibut with Tomato Sauce

Besides being a great source of essential nutrients for your heart and body, halibut has a delicately sweet flavor, making it everyone's favorite. Enjoy the delicious flavors of this tasty fish infused with tomato flavors. It contains very few bones and is a great source of high-quality lean protein.

Yield:	Serving size:	Prep time:	Cook time:
4 fillets	1 fillet	15 minutes	15–20 minutes

1 cup vegetable stock

3 TB. tomato paste, organic, no salt added

3 TB. shallots, chopped finely

4 fish fillets, approximately 4 oz. each

2 TB. Bragg Liquid Aminos

½ cup celery, chopped

1 small tomato, chopped

Fresh chives, chopped

1. In a large pan, heat ⅓ cup of stock and add the tomato paste. Cook for about 5 minutes. Remove and keep it warm.

2. Add remaining stock and shallots to the sauce pan and heat gently. Add the fish over top and slowly bring the liquid to a simmer.

3. Cover the pan with lid and let cook gently for about 5 minutes.

4. Remove the fish from the pan and keep warm. Turn up heat and reduce the cooking liquid by two thirds. Add the celery, and tomato with chopped chives.

5. Simmer gently and serve topped over the fish.

GOOD TO KNOW

The omega-3 essential fatty acids present in halibut provide a wide range of cardiovascular benefits. It especially helps in preventing erratic heart rhythms, making blood less likely to clot inside arteries that can cause heart attacks.

Almond Trout

Enjoy the light taste of this trout that doesn't require a long time to cook. It has a mild flavor and is packed with heart-healthy omega-3 essential fatty acids. Try it with steamed vegetables such as kale or bok choy. Delicious.

Yield:	Serving size:	Prep time:	Cook time:
4 fillets	1 trout	10 minutes	20 minutes

4 trout fillets, 4 oz. each approximately

1 cup corn meal

1 tsp. Celtic or Himalayan salt

Dash ground black pepper

1 cup slivered almonds

1. Mix fish in corn meal, salt, and black pepper.

2. In a large heavy skillet, heat 2 tablespoons unsalted, organic butter and 2 tablespoons extra virgin olive oil over a medium-high heat. Sauté fish fillets for 5 to 10 minutes on each side.

3. Remove fish to a serving platter.

4. Add almonds to skillet and heat on medium-high with butter and oil for 2 minutes until golden brown. Serve over top of fish.

HEART-HEALTHY TIP

Trout is low in sodium, and high in lean protein. Trout helps to raise HDL cholesterol levels, which is the "good" kind.

Fillet of Sole Florentine

Enjoy the taste as well as the health benefits of this delicious fish dish. It's loaded with essential vitamins and minerals such as zinc and calcium, and plenty of DASH-friendly lean protein … clean, lean, and tasty.

Yield:	Serving size:	Prep time:	Cook time:
4 fish fillets	1 fish fillet	10 minutes	15 minutes

4 sole fillets, 4 oz. each approximately

1 TB. fresh oregano

Dash Celtic or Himalayan salt

Dash cayenne pepper

1 fresh lemon or lime, juiced

3 TB. dry white wine (optional)

4 cups fresh washed spinach, chopped

$\frac{1}{4}$ tsp. nutmeg

Sprig fresh parsley

Lemon wedges

1. Preheat oven to 350°F.

2. Place fish fillets in baking dish and sprinkle with oregano, salt, cayenne pepper, lemon or lime juice, and wine.

3. Bake for 10 minutes. Remove from oven, and add spinach and nutmeg. Return to oven and bake an additional 5 to 10 minutes or until spinach is wilted.

4. Serve with fresh parsley and lemon wedge.

GOOD TO KNOW

Seafood is high in selenium, vitamin B_{12}, niacin, iron, and zinc. The antioxidants in fish are known for reducing inflammation and the risk of cardiovascular disease.

Versatile Vegetable Dinners

In This Chapter

- Blood pressure–lowering delectable dinners
- Blood sugar– and weight-reducing dishes

We now know that it is vegetables and not meat that is the main attraction to any well-rounded meal in the DASH plan. Studies continue to prove that when it comes to the health of your heart, you will want to include as much variety of luscious seasonal vegetables as you possibly can.

The best rule of thumb I can give you is to include some vegetables and a few fruits at every meal, every day. Try filling half of your plate with them at each meal and choosing more vegetarian-style meals. Ideally, aim for ten servings between the two food groups each day.

I've added some delicious and highly nutritious foods to these recipes, such as tempeh made from fermented soybeans, which you'll love. They specifically keep your digestion and metabolism efficient and your energy levels high. Your weight will go down without you even thinking twice about it.

Artichoke Pesto Tempeh

You'll love the taste of this delicious tempeh dish, along with its essential fiber and protein. Tempeh increases your body's ability to absorb minerals such as zinc, iron, and calcium. And it tastes simply scrumptious!

Yield:	Serving size:	Prep time:	Cook time:
4 cups	1 cups	15 minutes	10 minutes

1 package tempeh, sliced into rectangular pieces

½ cup dry white wine

2 (14-oz.) cans artichokes, quartered, in water

4 large cloves garlic, roughly chopped

10 sun-dried tomatoes, hydrated if dried or rinsed of oil

Pinch Celtic or Himalayan salt

Dash fresh ground black pepper

1 cup vegetable stock (optional)

1 TB. capers

2 TB. extra virgin olive oil

Dash cayenne pepper

Fresh parsley to garnish

1. Steam tempeh in a medium saucepan with a steamer basket over medium heat for 5 minutes.

2. In a large, wide pan, add 2 tablespoons grape seed oil and heat over medium heat. Add tempeh and sauté for 4 to 5 minutes on each side until golden brown.

3. Remove tempeh from pan and set aside.

4. Keep heat at medium and add white wine to deglaze. Reduce heat to low and simmer for 2 to 3 minutes.

5. Meanwhile, rinse artichokes and add two thirds to a food processor or blender. Add garlic and sun-dried tomatoes. Pulse to achieve medium texture.

6. Add mixture to reduced wine in pan and sauté for 3 to 4 minutes.

7. Add salt and black pepper to taste. Depending on how much liquid is in the sauce, you can add stock if needed or add remaining chopped artichokes if you prefer a thicker consistency.

8. Add capers.

9. Add tempeh back to the pan and allow to sauté on low heat for 3 to 4 minutes so tempeh can absorb the flavors.

10. Serve with your favorite vegetable dish.

> **HEART-HEALTHY TIP**
>
> Tempeh is a great choice for people who have difficulty digesting beans or soy foods, as its fermentation process makes it easier for your system to enjoy. In addition, tempeh is extremely low in sodium, unlike other fermented soy products.

Thai Tempeh Cakes with Sweet Spicy Dipping Sauce

With its spicy freshness that's delivered with tempeh, there's plenty to enjoy with this delicious dish. Serve these cakes with your favorite vegetables or a mixed green salad. This is also great for breakfast the next day or to eat as a cold snack.

Yield:	Serving size:	Prep time:	Cook time:
8 cakes	2 cakes	20 minutes	8–10 minutes

3 TB. mirin (sweet Asian rice wine)

3 TB. white wine vinegar

2 spring onions, finely chopped and sliced

1 TB. plus 1 tsp. agave nectar

4 chiles, seeded and finely chopped

6 TB. fresh coriander, chopped (plus pinch for garnish)

Celtic or Himalayan salt

1 TB. lemon grass, fresh or dried

2 cloves garlic, chopped

1-inch piece ginger root, peeled and finely chopped

2¼ cups tempeh, sliced

1 TB. fresh lemon or lime juice

3 TB. plain flour

1 large egg, lightly beaten

Freshly ground black pepper

1. In a small bowl, make the dipping sauce by mixing together mirin, white wine vinegar, sliced spring onions, 1 teaspoon agave, two chiles, 4 tablespoons coriander, and pinch salt. Set aside.

2. In a food processor or blender, place lemon grass, garlic, chopped spring onions, two chiles, ginger, and 2 tablespoons fresh coriander. Blend into a coarse paste.

3. Add tempeh, lemon or lime juice, and 1 tablespoon agave. Blend until combined.

4. Add flour, egg, large pinch salt, and black pepper. Blend again until mixture forms a coarse, sticky paste.

5. Divide tempeh mixture into eight equal parts. Form into balls with your hands. Cover hands lightly in flour to avoid sticking.

6. Press balls to form small cakes.

7. Heat 3 tablespoons grape seed oil in large frying pan over medium heat.

8. Fry tempeh cakes for 5 to 6 minutes, turning once, until golden.

9. Drain cakes on paper towel and serve warm with dipping sauce, garnished with chopped coriander.

> **HEART-HEALTHY TIP**
>
> Tempeh is heart food since it is packed with vitamins and minerals, including high amounts of magnesium. Involved in over 300 metabolic reactions, magnesium plays a vital role in heart health.

Simple Stir-Fry with Fresh Herbs

This recipe is low in calories and high in nutrients that nourish your heart. You'll not only find good tastes and flavors in this delicious dish, but you'll also receive a healthy dose of your daily requirements for antioxidants, phytochemicals, and important minerals magnesium and calcium, as well as your daily fiber and folate. What's not to like about that!

Yield:	Serving size:	Prep time:	Cook time:
4 cups	2 cups	15 minutes	10 minutes

2 TB. extra virgin olive oil

2 cloves garlic, chopped

1 medium onion, chopped

1 cup zucchini, sliced

3 large carrots, sliced

1 cup celery, chopped

8 crimini mushrooms, sliced

1 large green bell pepper, chopped

2 TB. Bragg Liquid Aminos

Pinch Celtic or Himalayan salt

Dash cayenne or fresh ground
    black pepper

1. In a skillet over medium-high heat, sauté garlic and onion in 2 tablespoons extra virgin olive oil, until softened.

2. Add zucchini, carrots, celery, mushrooms, green pepper, amino acids, salt, and cayenne or black pepper.

3. Cook, stirring often, until vegetables are crisp-tender.

4. Serve immediately.

HEART-HEALTHY TIP

When buying fresh leafy greens and vegetables, always choose crisp leaves with a fresh look and vibrant green colors to them. Yellowing is a sign of age and this will affect your flavor and nutrient density of that plant.

Veggie-Packed Penne Pasta

This delicious dish is an excellent source of your daily fiber, folate, calcium, and magnesium. It's also packed with all of your heart-healthy nutrients. Toss in your favorite dressing, if desired, but it's all here and tastes great.

Yield:	Serving size:	Prep time:	Cook time:
4 cups	2 cups	15 minutes	15 minutes

$\frac{1}{2}$ lb. whole-wheat penne pasta

$\frac{1}{4}$ red onion, sliced

2 cloves garlic, chopped

1 medium carrot, skin on, cut to matchstick-size pieces

1 celery stalk, medium, chopped

1 small zucchini, sliced to half moons $\frac{1}{4}$-inch thick

Pinch plus $\frac{1}{4}$ tsp. Celtic or Himalayan salt

1 (20-oz.) can fire-roasted tomatoes, organic, diced

$\frac{1}{3}$ cup black olives, pitted and chopped

2 TB. plus 3 TB. fresh basil, chopped

$\frac{1}{8}$ tsp. red pepper flakes

1 (14-oz.) can cannellini beans, rinsed and drained

1 TB. balsamic vinegar

Pinch of ground black pepper

Dash of cayenne pepper (optional)

1. In a large pot over high heat, cook pasta in boiling, salted water. When pasta is almost tender, add kale to pasta water. Drain both pasta and kale when pasta is tender.

2. Meanwhile, heat 1 tablespoon olive oil in a large sauté pan over medium heat. Add red onion and sauté for 3 minutes.

3. Add garlic, carrot, celery, zucchini, and pinch salt, and sauté for approximately 5 more minutes, or until carrot and zucchini start to soften. Stir frequently.

4. Add tomatoes with their juice, olives, 2 tablespoons basil, red pepper flakes, and $\frac{1}{4}$ teaspoon salt to onion mixture.

5. Cook for 3 to 5 more minutes to let tomatoes simmer.

6. Add cannellini beans and cook for 2 more minutes or until beans are heated through.

7. Add pasta, kale, balsamic vinegar, and 3 tablespoons basil to tomato mixture. Add pepper and cayenne. Toss and cook for 2 to 3 more minutes, until pasta is heated through.

8. Serve immediately.

GOOD TO KNOW

Studies continue to show that making half of your diet as vegetables and fruit significantly reduces heart disease risk by as much as 20 to 40 percent.

Grilled Tempeh with Kale and Broccoli

One of the many great things about tempeh is how easily it absorbs the flavors of other foods. A highly nutritious fermented food that's made from soybeans (and sometimes other grains), it originated in Indonesia more than 2,000 years ago, where it is still a staple. Tempeh is a wonderful protein substitute for meat.

Yield:	Serving size:	Prep time:	Cook time:
8 cups	2 cups	2 hours, 15 minutes	15 minutes

1 (8-oz.) package tempeh

$\frac{1}{2}$ cup plus 1 TB. tamari

$\frac{1}{2}$ cup apple cider, pasteurized

$\frac{1}{2}$ cup plus 2 TB. filtered water

1 TB. brown rice vinegar

$\frac{1}{3}$ cup arrowroot

1 TB. fresh basil, or 1 TB. dried basil

$\frac{1}{4}$ tsp. fresh ground black pepper

4 cups broccoli spears

$1\frac{1}{2}$ cups fresh mung bean sprouts

1 TB. umeboshi, or balsamic vinegar

1. Cut tempeh into 1-inch cubes or triangles and place in a large, shallow bowl.

2. In a small bowl, mix together $\frac{1}{2}$ cup tamari, apple cider, $\frac{1}{2}$ cup water, and rice vinegar to make a marinade.

3. Pour over tempeh and marinate for at least 2 hours.

4. In a quart-size, sealable plastic bag, combine the arrowroot, basil, and black pepper.

5. Place half of the tempeh in the bag and shake until well coated. Remove and repeat with remaining tempeh. Set aside.

6. In a large skillet over medium-high heat, heat 3 tablespoons grape seed oil and grill tempeh until brown on each side.

7. Drain on paper towels and set aside.

8. Add broccoli and bean sprouts to the skillet and sauté for 2 minutes.

9. Stir in remaining 2 tablespoons water, 1 tablespoon tamari, and umeboshi vinegar.

10. Cover and cook until broccoli is bright green and tender-crisp.

11. Mix in the reserved tempeh and serve immediately.

GOOD TO KNOW

Tempeh is exceptionally healthy. It is high in fiber plus it provides more than 20 percent of the daily value for magnesium, beneficial in cardiovascular health.

Vegetarian Spaghetti

Vegetables are cleansing and detoxifying to your entire body. They are healthy for your heart, and you would be wise to include them every day—you'll soon enjoy them more than ever. There's simply no better elixir for lowering hypertension.

Yield:	Serving size:	Prep time:	Cook time:
6 cups	2 cups	15 minutes	15 minutes

1 (8-oz.) packet whole-grain or spinach spaghetti

1 tsp. plus dash Celtic or Himalayan salt

½ TB. extra virgin olive oil

1 large onion, chopped

2 garlic cloves, chopped

3 cups fresh tomatoes, peeled and chopped

1 TB. fresh basil, chopped finely

1 cup filtered water

Pinch of ground black pepper

1 TB. fresh parsley, chopped finely

4 oz. tempeh (optional)

1. Cook spaghetti in boiling water with 1 teaspoon salt and ½ tablespoon oil, for 12 to 15 minutes or until al dente. Then drain and set aside; keeping it warm.

2. In a large frying pan, heat ½ tablespoon olive oil. Sauté onion and garlic until onion is transparent.

3. Stir in tomatoes, basil, and water, mix well.

4. If including tempeh, add to pan and cook for 3 to 5 minutes. Add dash salt and black pepper, then cover pan and simmer gently for 7 to 10 minutes or until cooked.

5. Add extra water if mixture becomes too dry. Add fresh parsley and mix in. Serve immediately with spaghetti.

HEART-HEALTHY TIP

Loaded with lycopene and important antioxidants, tomatoes are excellent blood cleansers. They have the ability to eliminate uric acid from the body and so are an excellent food for people with arthritis, gout, and rheumatism.

Crimini and Goat Cheese Burgers

Crimini mushrooms are loaded with important antioxidants and phytonutrients, and are effective as a food that strengthens your heart as well as reduces cholesterol levels. Not only are they a wonderful source of plant-based protein, but they taste simply delicious when served with goat cheese over burgers.

Yield:	Serving size:	Prep time:	Cook time:
6 patties	1 patty	15 minutes	15 minutes

4 cups crimini mushrooms, chopped

1 cup red onion, chopped

1 cup red bell pepper, chopped

2 TB. shallots, chopped

1 TB. fresh thyme, chopped

1 TB. oregano, dried or fresh chopped

2 TB. dry white wine

Dash Celtic or Himalayan salt

Pinch of fresh ground black pepper

Dash of cayenne pepper (optional)

2 cups pecans, roughly chopped, lightly toasted

1 cup pecan meal (made by lightly chopping in food processor)

$\frac{1}{2}$ cup rice flour

$\frac{1}{3}$ cup goat cheese (chevre)

$\frac{1}{3}$ cup fresh parsley, chopped

4 whole-wheat buns, split

1. Preheat oven to 350°F.

2. In a large pan, heat the 2 tablespoons grape seed oil and add the mushrooms, onions, bell pepper, shallots, thyme, and oregano. Cook 5 to 10 minutes or until tender.

3. Add the wine, salt, and black pepper. Remove from heat and let cool.

4. Place toasted pecans in food processor and pulse a few times to break them up. Add the cayenne.

5. Add two thirds of cooled vegetable mixture and pulse until just combined. Transfer to a medium mixing bowl.

6. Blend in the pecan meal and rice flour. Then add vegetable mixture, goat cheese, and parsley.

7. Form into patties and place on an oiled baking tray. Bake for 15 minutes or until warmed through.

8. Transfer on to buns and serve with your favorite green salad or vegetables.

HEART-HEALTHY TIP

Studies have proven that crimini mushrooms have the highest ORAC values. ORAC is a measure used to assess antioxidant content and stands for oxygen radical absorbance capacity. The higher the ORAC number, the better for your health.

White Bean and Tempeh with Pine Nuts

Not only is tempeh very nutritive and healthy for your heart, it contains many health-promoting phytochemicals, such as soy isoflavones. These help strengthen bones and reduce risk of cardiovascular disease and some cancers. This dish is a ten out of ten on its flavor scale also! You'll love it, and so will your heart.

Yield:	Serving size:	Prep time:	Cook time:
6 cups	2 cups	15 minutes	30 minutes

1 (8-oz.) package of tempeh, cut into 1-inch cubes

1 TB. extra virgin olive oil or grape seed oil

2 TB. Bragg Liquid Aminos

1 large onion, chopped

3 garlic cloves, chopped

3 TB. sun-dried tomatoes, sliced

1/2 cup canned artichoke hearts, chopped roughly

2 TB. dry white wine

1/4 cup chopped fresh basil

1 (15-oz.) can cannellini beans, rinsed and drained

Dash Celtic or Himalayan salt

Dash cayenne pepper (optional)

1/4 cup roasted pine nuts

1. Preheat oven to 350°F.

2. Combine tempeh, olive or grape seed oil, and amino acids in a medium bowl.

3. Toss gently and transfer tempeh onto a baking sheet and bake for about 20 minutes. Set aside.

4. In a large pan, heat 1 tablespoon olive oil and sauté onion and garlic until tender.

5. Add the sun-dried tomato, artichoke hearts, wine, basil, beans, and salt. Simmer gently for 15 minutes.

6. Add the roasted tempeh, pine nuts, and cayenne. Stir until mixed and serve hot.

HEART-HEALTHY TIP

It's easy to make tempeh at home at a very low cost. Simply cook dehulled soybeans for about 30 minutes and mix with tempeh starter, then soak overnight. Look online for places to purchase your tempeh starter. It takes between 36 to 48 hours incubation and you'll have delicious tempeh.

Roasted Quinoa with Cumin and Coriander

High in fiber and plant protein, quinoa is as good as it gets for optimum heart-healthy nourishment. It tastes scrumptious and is friendly to your waist line and your blood sugar levels. The addition of cumin and coriander adds exotic flavors that are medicinally potent also.

Yield:	Serving size:	Prep time:	Cook time:
4 cups	1 cup	15 minutes	20 minutes

1 cup quinoa, rinsed well and drained

1½ cups vegetable stock or filtered water

Dash of Celtic or Himalayan salt

1 TB. cumin seeds

1 TB. coriander seeds

Dash of cayenne pepper

½ cup fresh cilantro, chopped

1 TB. fresh lemon or lime juice

1. Preheat oven to 350°F.

2. Place quinoa on a baking sheet and bake about 10 minutes.

3. Transfer quinoa to a pot and add stock or water and salt.

4. Place cumin and coriander seeds in a dry skillet with medium heat. Toast them stirring often, about 1 to 2 minutes.

5. Add the toasted cumin and coriander to the quinoa mixture. Bring to a boil, reduce heat and cover. Simmer about 10 minutes.

6. Transfer into a serving dish and fluff with a fork and stir in cayenne, fresh cilantro, and lemon or lime juice.

GOOD TO KNOW

Quinoa is actually more a seed than a grain, as most people tend to think or classify it under. It is almost a complete protein, making it a healthy choice.

Shiitake and Asparagus Risotto

Your immune system will get a big boost from this nourishing dish, and so will your heart. Shiitake mushrooms are known for their ability to lower cholesterol and blood pressure levels as well as their high levels of selenium, vitamin C, protein, and fiber. The addition of asparagus makes it a powerful duo.

Yield:	Serving size:	Prep time:	Cook time:
6 cups	2 cups	15 minutes	15 minutes

1 tsp. saffron

4 cups vegetable stock

2 TB. extra virgin olive oil

1 small onion, chopped

2 garlic cloves, chopped

1 tsp. dry basil

2 sprigs fresh thyme

Dash Celtic or Himalayan salt

1½ cups arborio rice

¾ cup dry white wine

¾ cup asparagus, cut into 1-inch lengths

1 cup shiitake mushrooms, sliced

¼ cup fresh or frozen peas

1 tsp. lemon rind, grated (zest)

1 TB. fresh basil, chopped

½ cup fresh parsley, chopped

Dash of ground black pepper

1. Warm the saffron in the vegetable stock and set aside.

2. In a large pan, heat the oil and add the onions and garlic until transparent.

3. Add dry basil, thyme sprigs, and salt. Sauté for 1 minute.

4. Add the rice, stirring and cooking for several minutes.

5. Add the wine and stir for 1 minute, then add the asparagus, mushrooms, and frozen peas. Cook for 3 to 5 minutes.

6. Add the saffron and vegetable stock, 1 cup at a time, and stir continuously.

7. Remove the thyme sprigs and cook uncovered, stirring often until most of the water is absorbed and rice is thickened and slightly creamy.

8. Add more stock if rice is dry. Stir in the lemon zest, fresh basil, parsley, and black pepper.

9. Serve immediately.

HEART-HEALTHY TIP

The blood cholesterol–lowering compound in shiitake mushrooms is known as eritadenine.

Beans and Grains on the Side

In This Chapter

- A variety of beans to nourish you on every level
- Grains that go great with any meal or snack

No DASH-healthy diet is complete without a regular serving of beans and grains, which are complex carbohydrates. High in plant-based proteins and low on the glycemic index, beans and grains convert to energy much more slowly than simple carbohydrates. Whole grains are far healthier as they have not gone through the milling process and contain their valuable inner germ and outer bran layers.

Whole grains are an important source of dietary fiber, B-complex vitamins, and essential minerals such as potassium, magnesium, calcium, and zinc. Many of the recipes in this chapter taste just as good at breakfast time as they do at any other meal of the day. Try to enjoy a heart-healthy side dish of beans or grains at least once a day.

Lemony Red Lentil Pâté

Lentils are full of beneficial vitamins and essential minerals also. Enjoy the delicious combinations and flavors of the herbs and spices, and antioxidants galore!

Yield:	Serving size:	Prep time:	Cook time:
1½ quarts	1 cup	50 minutes	35 minutes

4 cups dried red lentils

6 cups filtered water

2 cups vegetable stock

1 tsp. Celtic or Himalayan salt

6 cups onions, chopped

3 TB. garlic, chopped

2 TB. dried basil

2 tsp. dried oregano

2 tsp. dried thyme

2 cups celery, chopped

½ cup plus ½ cup fresh parsley, organic

2 cups rice or almond flour, or 1 cup whole-wheat bread-crumbs

3 TB. fresh lemon or lime juice

1 tsp. ground black pepper

Dash cayenne pepper

1 cup pitted black olives, sliced

½ cup red bell pepper, chopped

1. Preheat the oven to 375°F.

2. Wash lentils.

3. In a large pot, combine lentils, stock, and water and bring to a boil over medium-high heat.

4. Reduce heat to medium-low and cook, stirring occasionally, for about 30 to 40 minutes, or until lentils are soft and the water is absorbed.

5. Add salt and keep warm.

6. Meanwhile, in a large, deep skillet, heat ⅓ cup extra virgin olive oil over medium heat and sauté onions and garlic for 10 to 15 minutes.

7. When onions start to caramelize, stir in basil, oregano, thyme, celery, and half the fresh parsley. Turn off heat.

8. Heavily coat the bottom of an oiled 9- to 12-inch baking pan with 1 cup of flour or the breadcrumbs.

9. Add onion mixture, lemon or lime juice, black pepper, cayenne pepper, and olives to the cooked lentils and mix together well.

10. Pour the mixture into the baking dish and bake for about 15 minutes, or until mixture is set.

11. Let cool for 5 minutes.

12. Turn onto a serving tray and garnish with fresh parsley and bell peppers.

HEART-HEALTHY TIP

Heart-healthy lentils are loaded with magnesium and even higher in potassium, achieving the highest ranking of all the DASH nutrient recommendations. Lentils are most beneficial when used as the main source of protein in any meal.

Home-Style Baked Beans

Enjoy the rich heavenly flavors of everybody's best home-style cooking dish. Navy beans provide virtually fat-free, high-quality, plant-based protein. Keeping blood sugar levels stable for hours, this meal is excellent for individuals with diabetes, insulin resistance, or hypoglycemia. It's a fiber all-star. It doesn't get any better for being nourishing on all levels.

Yield:	Serving size:	Prep time:	Cook time:
4–6 cups	1 cup	9 hours	1½ hours

1¾ cups dried navy beans

4 cups filtered water

½ tsp. Celtic or Himalayan salt

¾ cup sun-dried tomatoes

⅓ cup hot water

⅓ cup barley malt

2 TB. tamari

1 TB. prepared brown mustard

1½ TB. extra virgin olive oil

1 TB. garlic, chopped

½ tsp. chili powder

¼ tsp. onion powder

¼ tsp. crushed dried rosemary or 1 tsp. fresh rosemary, chopped

¼ tsp. dried thyme

1 cup onions, chopped

1. Wash beans. Soak overnight.

2. Preheat the oven to 350°F.

3. In a large saucepan, combine soaked beans and filtered water and bring to a boil over high heat.

4. Reduce heat to medium-low and cook for 45 minutes.

5. Add salt and cook for additional 15 minutes, or until the beans are soft.

6. Meanwhile, in a small bowl, soak tomatoes in the ⅓ cup hot water for 15 minutes to rehydrate and soften them.

7. In a blender or food processor, blend tomatoes and soaking water until pasty.

8. Add barley malt, tamari, mustard, oil, garlic, chili and onion powders, rosemary, and thyme to the blender and blend until well combined.

9. In a lightly oiled 9 inch by 12 inch baking pan, combine soft beans, tomato mixture, and onions.

10. Bake for 20 to 25 minutes. Serve immediately.

HEART-HEALTHY TIP

Navy beans are high in the DASH minerals potassium and magnesium and vitamin B_1. Critical for brain cell and cognitive function, thiamin, as it is also called, is essential for important neurotransmitter function. Thiamin is also critical for people with senility issues and Alzheimer's. Just 1 cup of navy beans provides 25 percent of the daily value for thiamin.

Herbed Brown Pilaf

Brown rice is a rich source of phytochemicals and antioxidants to boost cardio energy and output. This simple pilaf dish is easy to make, yet is mixed with a blend of DASH powerhouses. It offers the richness of heart-healthy B vitamins, magnesium, vitamin E, and more, along with tons of flavor—tasty and delicious!

Yield:	Serving size:	Prep time:	Cook time:
1 quart	1 cup	15 minutes	35 minutes

2 cups uncooked brown basmati rice

3 cups filtered water

1/2 cup vegetable stock (optional)

2 tsp. dried thyme, or 2 TB. fresh thyme, chopped

1 1/2 tsp. dried marjoram, or 1 1/2 TB. fresh marjoram, chopped

1/2 tsp. Celtic or Himalayan salt

2 TB. extra virgin olive oil

1/3 cup pine nuts

1/2 cup fresh parsley, chopped

1/2 cup fresh or frozen peas (optional)

1. Wash and drain the rice.

2. In a medium-size saucepan, combine rice, water, stock, thyme, and marjoram. Bring to a boil. (If using fresh herbs, add after the rice has cooked for 20 minutes.)

3. Add salt.

4. Reduce heat to simmer and cook, covered, for 35 minutes, or until rice is soft and the water is absorbed.

5. Fluff rice with a fork and stir in olive oil, pine nuts, parsley, and peas.

6. Serve immediately.

HEART-HEALTHY TIP

The high content of magnesium in brown rice gives it more horsepower, as it acts as a co-factor for over 300 enzymes. This includes control of blood sugar and insulin levels, especially important in type 2 diabetes and insulin resistance. Lower cholesterol and blood pressure levels are guaranteed with this important mineral.

Adzuki Beans and Kale with Pine Nuts

You'll be pleasantly delighted by the wholesome and delicious flavors blended into this simple, easy vegetarian side dish. Adzuki beans alone are filled with amino acids and protein and are bursting with potassium and magnesium and many more heart-healthy nutrients. Serve with green salad or your favorite mixed greens.

Yield:	Serving size:	Prep time:	Cook time:
1 quart	1 cup	20 minutes	1 hour, 30 minutes

1 cup dried adzuki beans	4 medium to large kale leaves, washed, de-veined, and chopped
1 3-inch strip kombu, cut into $\frac{1}{8}$-inch wide strips	
3 cups filtered water	$\frac{1}{2}$ TB. tamari
1 tsp. ground cumin	2 TB. roasted pine nuts
1 tsp. ground coriander	2 TB. extra virgin olive oil
$\frac{1}{2}$ tsp. Celtic or Himalayan salt	Dash of cayenne pepper (optional)

1. Wash beans. Soak overnight or use the quick-soak method.

2. In a large saucepan, layer kombu strips and soaked beans.

3. Cover with filtered water to barely cover the beans and bring to a boil over medium-high heat.

4. Reduce heat to medium-low heat and cook for approximately 1 hour.

5. Add cumin, coriander, and salt and cook for 20 more minutes, or until the beans are soft, adding more water if needed to prevent burning on the bottom.

6. Stir in kale and tamari, turn heat off and cover with lid to let steam for 3 to 5 minutes. Add olive oil and cayenne. Toss in roasted pine nuts and serve immediately.

GOOD TO KNOW

Soaking adzuki (and most dried beans) in cold water for 2 to 3 hours before cooking them releases the enzyme inhibitors, which allows greater digestion and assimilation. Releasing these nutrients swells the beans, so you should use 3 cups of water for every cup of adzuki beans.

Basmati Almond Rice

Enjoy a taste of the East with this flavorful and fluffy basmati rice dish with its jasmine aromatics. The additional vegetables and roasted almonds combine well to give an unforgettable taste sensation with a dose of DASH-friendly nutrients.

Yield:	Serving size:	Prep time:	Cook time:
1 quart	1 cup	10 minutes	20–30 minutes

1¼ cups uncooked brown basmati rice

2 cups filtered water

½ cup carrots, chopped

½ cup zucchini, chopped

½ cup green beans, cut in ½-inch pieces

½ cup green bell peppers, chopped

½ tsp. Celtic or Himalayan salt

½ TB. cumin seeds

⅛ tsp. ground black pepper

Pinch ground nutmeg

Dash cayenne pepper (optional)

Pinch ground cinnamon

½ cup roasted almonds, chopped

¾ cup fresh parsley, chopped

1. Wash and drain rice.

2. In a medium-size saucepan, combine rice, water, carrots, zucchini, green beans, and bell peppers. Bring to a boil over medium-high heat.

3. Add salt.

4. Reduce heat to simmer over low heat and cook, covered, for 20 minutes, or until rice is soft and water is absorbed.

5. In a small skillet, add 2 tablespoons olive oil over medium heat and sauté cumin seeds for 30 seconds. Stir in black pepper, nutmeg, cayenne pepper, and cinnamon. Set aside.

6. Add reserved spice mixture to the cooked rice and mix together with a fork.

7. Stir in almonds and parsley.

8. Serve immediately.

HEART-HEALTHY TIP

Nutrient-dense brown basmati rice is less processed than white and retains its outermost layer, called the hull. It's heart healthier, also.

Wild Rice Pilaf

Your DASH diet cooking isn't complete until you've included a serving of wild rice pilaf. Laced with minerals and cardiovascular benefits, your cup can easily runneth over with this deliciously sweet side dish.

Yield:	Serving size:	Prep time:	Cook time:
1 quart	1 cup	20 minutes	25 minutes

$\frac{1}{3}$ cup uncooked wild rice

1 cup uncooked long-grain brown rice

2$\frac{1}{4}$ cups filtered water

$\frac{1}{4}$ tsp. Celtic or Himalayan salt

$\frac{1}{2}$ cup carrots, skin on, julienned

1 cup fresh cremini mushrooms, sliced

$\frac{1}{2}$ cup celery, chopped

$\frac{1}{2}$ TB. tamari

1 tsp. sesame oil

$\frac{1}{3}$ cup whole almonds

$\frac{1}{2}$ cup fresh parsley, chopped

1. Wash and drain wild rice and long-grain rice separately.

2. In a medium-size saucepan, combine wild rice and water. Bring to a boil over medium-high heat.

3. Reduce heat to a simmer and cook, covered, for 10 minutes.

4. Add long-grain rice and return to a boil over medium-high heat.

5. Add salt.

6. Reduce heat to a simmer and cook, covered, for 25 minutes, or until rice is soft and water is absorbed.

7. Preheat the oven to 350°F.

8. Meanwhile, in a medium-size skillet, heat 1 tablespoon extra virgin olive oil and sauté the carrots, mushrooms, and celery for 5 minutes.

9. Stir in tamari and sesame oil and set aside.

10. In a small baking pan, roast almonds in oven for 5 minutes, stirring frequently. Let cool.

11. Chop cooled almonds into large pieces and set aside.

12. Add carrot mixture and almonds to the cooked rice and stir together with a fork.

13. Add parsley and serve immediately.

HEART-HEALTHY TIP

Brown rice is high in the mineral manganese and B vitamins, along with selenium and tryptophan. It is energizing while at the same time relaxing and mood enhancing.

Couscous with Chickpeas

High in plant protein, couscous is made from semolina grain. Comparable to pasta or rice in its texture and flavor, it easily retains the herbs and spices you serve with it. Light on your stomach and cleansing to your system, this DASH-healthy dish is two thumbs-up, nutritionally speaking.

Yield:	Serving size:	Prep time:	Cook time:
1 quart	1 cup	20 minutes	2 hours

1 cup dried chickpeas, soaked 1–2 hours in cold water

5 cups filtered water

1 tsp. Celtic or Himalayan salt

2 TB. extra virgin olive oil

2 tsp. Bragg Liquid Aminos

¼ cup fresh lemon or lime juice

1½ cups uncooked couscous

¼ cup fresh parsley, chopped

1. Rinse soaked chickpeas.

2. In a large saucepan, combine chickpeas and 3½ cups water and bring to a boil over medium-high heat.

3. Reduce heat to medium and cook for 1 hour and 20 minutes.

4. Add salt and more water, if needed, and cook for about 20 more minutes, or until the chickpeas are very tender.

5. Drain and set aside.

6. In a separate saucepan, combine remaining 1½ cups water, oil, amino acids, and lemon or lime juice. Bring to a boil.

7. Turn off heat and mix in couscous and fresh parsley.

8. Cover and let stand for 12 to 15 minutes, or until water is absorbed.

9. Mix in chickpeas and parsley. Serve immediately.

HEART-HEALTHY TIP

Couscous first became popular in Morocco. It contains fewer calories compared with a cup of rice or quinoa and is high in potassium and selenium—both important nutrients for your heart.

Best Bean Pie

This recipe's nutrient richness and flavorsome whole foods with fresh herbs and spices will please any palate. This can easily be turned into your main dish and served with a side salad for added antioxidants and heart-healthy plant enzymes.

Yield:	Serving size:	Prep time:	Cook time:
2 quarts	1 cup	15 minutes	50 minutes

2½ cups cooked rice

1½ TB. unsalted butter

4 large eggs, beaten

2 TB. parsley, chopped

1 small onion, chopped

1–2 cloves garlic, chopped

2 cups cooked kidney beans

1½ cups reduced fat cheddar cheese, shredded

¾ cup cooked lean ham, nitrite free, diced

¼ cup black olives, sliced

½ cup light sour cream

½ cup skim milk

Dash cayenne pepper (optional)

1 tsp. Celtic or Himalayan salt

1 tsp. ground black pepper

1 tomato, sliced

1. Preheat the oven to 350°F.

2. In a bowl, combine rice, butter, 1 egg, and parsley. Press firmly against a greased 10-inch pie plate pan to form crust.

3. In a medium-size skillet, heat 1 tablespoon extra virgin olive oil over medium heat and sauté onion and garlic for 3 to 5 minutes, or until onion is translucent. Set aside.

4. Layer as follows in the rice shell: 1 cup beans, ¾ cup cheese, ham, onion and garlic, black olives, 1 cup beans, and ¾ cup cheese.

5. In a separate medium mixing bowl, combine sour cream, 3 beaten eggs, milk, cayenne pepper, salt, and pepper.

6. Pour over layered pie.

7. Bake in oven for 35 minutes.

8. Remove pie from oven. Place tomato slices around edge of pie.

9. Return pie to oven, bake for 5 to 10 more minutes.

HEART-HEALTHY TIP

Kidney beans' contribution to heart health lies not just in their high magnesium and folate content, but in their high fiber and healthy plant protein supply. The magnesium and folate helps muscles to relax and blood to flow freely—a cardiovascular and DASH benefit.

Mighty Mushroom Risotto with Herbs

The combination of delicious flavors, herbs, and nutrients in this dish are a favorite in DASH cooking.

Yield:	Serving size:	Prep time:	Cook time:
2 quarts	1 cup	15 minutes	30 minutes

½ cup wild rice

1 small onion, finely chopped

2½ cups arborio rice

1 cup dry white wine

5 cups vegetable stock, low salt

2 cups shiitake mushrooms, sliced thinly

3 TB. fresh oregano, chopped

3 TB. fresh chives, snipped

4 TB. fresh parsley, chopped

4 TB. fresh basil, chopped

1 cup low-fat Parmesan cheese, grated

Pinch salt

Pinch ground black pepper

Dash cayenne pepper

1. Rinse and drain rice.

2. Cook wild rice in boiling, salted water according to instructions on packet.

3. In a large saucepan, heat 1 tablespoon extra virgin olive oil and 1 tablespoon unsalted butter over medium heat and sauté onions.

4. Add arborio rice and cook for 2 minutes, stirring occasionally.

5. Pour in wine and bring to a boil over medium-high heat.

6. Reduce heat to low and simmer for 10 minutes until wine is absorbed.

7. Add stock, a little at a time, and simmer uncovered, stirring, for 20 to 25 minutes, until liquid is absorbed and rice has a light, creamy texture.

8. Add the mushrooms and continue stirring, for 5 minutes.

9. Add oregano, chives, parsley, basil, and wild rice. Heat for 2 minutes, stirring.

10. Turn heat off and stir in ²/₃ of Parmesan cheese until melted. Add salt, pepper, and cayenne. Serve, sprinkled with remaining cheese.

HEART-HEALTHY TIP

Shiitake mushrooms are known for their immune-boosting properties and have long been favorites of Asians. The Chinese have used these delicious medicinal plants for centuries to increase longevity and promote health. Shiitakes are high in minerals and can be easily substituted with meats as a form of protein.

Kidney Beans with Yams

Feel free to eat this dish on its own or with a tossed salad and you'll be well satisfied.

Yield:	Serving size:	Prep time:	Cook time:
6 cups	1 cup	3 hours, 15 minutes	30 minutes

1½ cups dried kidney beans

3½ cups filtered water

2½ cups yams, chopped into 1 inch pieces

½ tsp. Celtic or Himalayan salt

1 TB. red miso or barley miso diluted in 2 TB. warm water

1 TB. extra virgin olive oil

1. Wash beans. Soak in cold water for 2 to 3 hours.

2. In a large saucepan, combine soaked beans and filtered water. Bring to a boil over medium-high heat.

3. Reduce heat to medium-low and cook for 30 minutes.

4. Add yams and return to boil. Add salt.

5. Reduce heat to medium and cook for 20 minutes, or until beans are soft.

6. Stir in diluted miso, olive oil, and cook for an additional 5 minutes.

7. Serve immediately.

GOOD TO KNOW

Not only high in heart-healthy antioxidants and minerals, yams win the prize when it comes to being lower on the glycemic index yet still sweet, and for keeping blood sugar and insulin levels in check. They are also high in fiber and B vitamins combined with immune-boosting minerals.

Yams are one of the oldest food plants known to man. They were first cultivated in Asia and Africa in 50,000 B.C.E., where they were a diet staple. Natives have very little cardiovascular problems or diabetes—perhaps this is one of the reasons why.

Very Veggie Sides

In This Chapter

- Making vegetables the main meal means a lot
- Vegetables packed with more nutrients for you

Choose vegetables as your mainstay of every meal and you'll be eating an ideal diet that's about as heart healthy as it gets. Many of us have been raised with the idea that meat should be the focal point of the plate, but that's gotten us into trouble health-wise.

Variety is the key when it comes to your diet and your health, and vegetables are no exception. Choose from fresh seasonal fruits and vegetables and always include some green leafy ones for at least one meal a day. Your digestion will thank you and you'll have a lot more energy to get you through your day.

Vegetables and fruits are loaded with antioxidants and important minerals that your body craves and loves getting each day. This will keep your blood pressure low and your blood flowing through your veins more freely.

Zesty Broccoli with Garlic and Ginger

Broccoli is among the superfoods that contains heart-healthy minerals in abundance. Loaded with magnesium, calcium, and potassium to regulate blood pressure, you will enjoy the added flavors of garlic and ginger to enhance this already delicious dish. Include it alongside any cooked grain, meat, fish, or salad.

Yield:	Serving size:	Prep time:	Cook time:
4 cups	1 cup	10 minutes	10 minutes

4 cups broccoli florets, cut into quarters

2 TB. extra virgin olive oil

2 TB. fresh ginger, chopped finely

2 garlic cloves, chopped finely

2 TB. fresh lemon or lime juice

1. Place broccoli into a steamer with 2 inches of water.

2. Let steam for 5 to 10 minutes.

3. In a separate bowl, mix the olive oil, ginger, garlic, and lemon or lime juice.

4. Arrange broccoli in serving dish and pour herb mixture on top.

5. Serve hot.

HEART-HEALTHY TIP

One cup of broccoli contains the recommended daily allowance (RDA) of vitamin C, an antioxidant that reduces inflammation and builds collagen and strong blood vessels.

Green Beans Almondine

Green beans with almonds are deliciously healthy and loaded with heart-healthy minerals such as calcium and potassium. These are lightly steamed to bring out their peak flavor and crunchy texture, especially when you add almonds.

Yield:	Serving size:	Prep time:	Cook time:
4 cups	1 cup	10 minutes	10 minutes

1 tsp. ginger, chopped finely	1 TB. fresh lemon or lime juice
Dash Celtic or Himalayan salt	3 TB. roasted almonds, slivered
4 cups green beans, cut into 1-inch pieces	4 TB. fresh parsley or cilantro, chopped finely

1. Add ginger and salt to green beans and mix lightly.

2. Place green beans in a steamer and steam for 7 to 10 minutes until bright green and still crisp.

3. Remove from heat and place in serving dish.

4. Toss with lemon or lime juice, and sprinkle with almonds and parsley or cilantro.

HEART-HEALTHY TIP

Green beans contain some omega-3 essential fatty acids, making them an important cardiovascular food. They are high in fiber, too!

Brussels Sprouts with Shiitake and Pine Nuts

Enjoy the crisp, dense texture and slightly sweet taste of this delicious brussels sprouts, mushrooms, and pine nuts combo. It also makes a nice addition to cold salads and is one of the most nutritious dishes that will fill you up without filling you out.

Yield:	Serving size:	Prep time:	Cook time:
4 cups	1 cup	15 minutes	10 minutes

4 cups brussels sprouts

4 shiitake mushrooms, sliced

½ cup pine nuts or sunflower seeds

½ tsp. ginger, fresh chopped

1 garlic clove, chopped

1 cup filtered water

Dash Celtic or Himalayan salt

Dash cayenne pepper

1. Place the brussels sprouts in a steamer and cook for 10 minutes, until tender.

2. In a separate sauce pan, cook the mushrooms, pine nuts, ginger, garlic, salt, cayenne, and water until tender.

3. Arrange brussels sprouts on a serving dish and pour mushroom mixture on top.

4. Serve hot.

 HEART-HEALTHY TIP

The combination of brussels sprouts and shiitake mushrooms make this dish a medicinal powerhouse all by themselves. Rich in plant protein, dietary fiber, minerals, and antioxidants that work wonders on your health. You'll love the crunchy texture and creamy combination of the flavors inside this delicious side dish.

Sautéed Vegetable Medley

High in antioxidants, which are great for cleaning out arteries and ensuring good blood flow, there's nothing quite as delicious or more beneficial than lightly cooked fresh vegetables. Adding cruciferous vegetables will ensure that you get tons of fiber and heart-healthy minerals.

Yield:	Serving size:	Prep time:	Cook time:
2 quarts	2 cups	15 minutes	15 minutes

2 cups carrots, julienned

1½ cups onions, sliced

1 TB. ginger, chopped

1 TB. garlic, chopped

2 cups zucchini, diagonally sliced

1 cup celery, diagonally sliced

1 cup cruciferous vegetable, such as cauliflower or broccoli

½ tsp. Celtic or Himalayan salt

1 TB. cilantro, chopped (optional)

1. In a large skillet, heat 2 tablespoons extra virgin olive oil over medium heat and sauté carrots for 7 to 10 minutes.

2. Add onions, ginger, and garlic, and sauté for an additional 5 minutes.

3. Add zucchini and sauté for 2 to 3 minutes.

4. Add celery, cruciferous vegetables, and salt. Cook, stirring occasionally, for 5 to 7 minutes, or until the vegetables are tender-crisp and just beginning to brown. Add cilantro, turn off heat, and cover the skillet with lid for 1 minute.

5. Serve immediately.

WARNING

As with all vegetables, be sure not to overcook cauliflower or broccoli. Healthy sautéing is a great way to retain crispness, vitamins, and important mineral content. Traditional methods of boiling or steaming can often make them water-logged, mushy, and flavorless.

Stuffed Tomatoes with Wild Rice and Cilantro

Deliciously loaded with heart-healthy antioxidants and phytonutrients such as lycopene, this dish contains all of the key minerals necessary to keeping your blood pressure in check.

Yield:	Serving size:	Prep time:	Cook time:
4 tomatoes	1 tomato	15 minutes	25 minutes

4 medium tomatoes

$\frac{1}{3}$ cup corn kernels

2 TB. fresh lemon juice

$\frac{1}{4}$ cup cooked wild rice

1 garlic clove, minced

$\frac{1}{2}$ cup Parmesan cheese

1 TB. fresh coriander, chopped

Dash Celtic or Himalayan salt

Dash freshly ground black pepper

1 TB. extra virgin olive oil

1. Preheat the oven to 350°F.

2. Cut the tops off the tomatoes and remove the seeds using a teaspoon. Scoop out all the flesh and chop finely; also chop the tops.

3. In a medium skillet, add the chopped tomatoes, corn, and lemon juice. Cover with a close-fitting lid and simmer over low heat until tender, approximately 5 minutes. Drain.

4. In a medium bowl, mix together wild rice, garlic, Parmesan, coriander, salt, and black pepper.

5. Spoon the mixture into the hollow tomatoes, piling it higher in the center to prevent overflowing.

6. Sprinkle oil over the tops of tomatoes and arrange in an ovenproof dish.

7. Bake for 15 to 20 minutes until cooked through.

8. Serve immediately.

HEART-HEALTHY TIP

Because of their moderate amount of vitamin K, tomatoes help in preventing hemorrhages and reduce the risk of developing hypertension.

Roasted Mediterranean Vegetables with Pecorino

High in heart-healthy fiber, this dish is an excellent source of potassium and B vitamins, your stress reducers. The addition of pecorino cheese speaks for itself as it will make any dish taste wonderful. You can't go wrong with this delicious Mediterranean specialty.

Yield:	Serving size:	Prep time:	Cook time:
2 quarts	2 cups	20 minutes	20 minutes

1 medium eggplant, sliced

Dash Celtic or Himalayan salt

2 medium zucchinis, sliced

1 medium red bell pepper, seeded and quartered

1 medium yellow pepper, seeded and quartered

1 large onion, thickly sliced

2 large carrots, skin on, cut into slices

4 plum tomatoes, halved

1 clove garlic, chopped (optional)

2 TB. extra virgin olive oil

Freshly ground black pepper

3 TB. fresh parsley, chopped

3 TB. pine nuts, lightly toasted

1 (4-oz.) piece pecorino cheese

1. Preheat the oven to 425°F.

2. In a colander, layer eggplant slices, sprinkling salt on each layer.

3. Leave to drain over sink or plate for about 20 minutes. Rinse thoroughly, drain well and pat dry with paper towel.

4. Spread out eggplant, zucchini, peppers, onion, carrots, tomatoes, and garlic in a large roasting dish.

5. Brush vegetables lightly with olive oil.

6. Roast in oven for about 20 minutes, or until lightly browned and the skins on peppers have begun to blister.

7. Transfer vegetables to a large serving platter. Peel the peppers if prefer.

8. Trickle over any vegetable juices from roasting pan, and drizzle over some more olive oil. Lightly season with salt and freshly ground pepper.

9. Set aside to cool to room temperature.

10. When vegetables have cooled, mix in chopped fresh parsley and toasted pine nuts.

11. Using a vegetable peeler, shave the pecorino cheese and scatter the shavings over the vegetables.

GOOD TO KNOW

The eggplant is considered a delicacy by many. It was first cultivated in China and then quickly became popular with both the Italians and French. It has been cited as a cholesterol-lowering agent by some studies. As part of the National Diabetes Education program, the eggplant is a highly revered food choice for management of type 2 diabetes.

Beets with Basil and Yogurt

High in antioxidants, calcium, iron, and fiber, you won't find a more nutrient-rich, heart-healthy vegetable than beetroot. The addition of fresh basil with yogurt is unsurpassed when it comes to flavor and goodness. Savor every mouthful of this dish.

Yield:	Serving size:	Prep time:	Cook time:
2 cups	1 cup	15 minutes	10–12 minutes

3 raw beets

1 TB. basil, chopped

1 cup yogurt, plain, low fat

1 tsp. coriander seeds

Dash Celtic or Himalayan salt

Pinch ground black pepper

Granulated kelp

1. Wash and roughly scrape the beets under water.

2. Shred or grate beets coarsely.

3. Add beets to Dutch oven or heavy covered pan and steam with a little water over low heat until soft, about 5 minutes.

4. Place beets on serving platter or dish.

5. Mix the basil, salt, pepper, and kelp with yogurt and pour over beets.

6. Sprinkle coriander seeds over to garnish.

7. Serve immediately.

HEART-HEALTHY TIP

Beets contain a nutrient that lowers plasma homocysteine levels, a known risk factor for cardiovascular disease. Juiced beets are excellent to purify blood toxins.

Snow Peas with Sesame Seeds

Enjoy the crispness of snow peas paired with the crunchy texture of sesame seeds in this flavor combination. It's high in antioxidants and is calcium rich to support your healthy metabolism and lower your cholesterol.

Yield:	Serving size:	Prep time:	Cook time:
6 cups	1 cup	35 minutes	50 minutes

½ cup vegetable broth

2 cups snow peas, well rinsed in cold water and drained

2 tsp. Bragg Liquid Aminos

1 tsp. mirin (rice wine)

½ cup white sesame seeds

1. Bring ¼ cup broth to a simmer.

2. Chop off ends of snow peas and add them to the simmering broth for 1 minute.

3. Remove peas with slotted spoon and place in serving dish.

4. Add amino acids, mirin, and remaining broth to the pot. Simmer uncovered for 2 minutes.

5. Use the broth to pour over peas. Add sesame seeds and serve immediately.

HEART-HEALTHY TIP

Succulent snow peas are high in fiber and contain lots of heart-healthy nutrients. Vitamins such as C, K, and A are heart specific for lowering blood pressure and improving the flow of blood around your body. In addition, peas also contain many essential B-complex vitamins that help reduce stress. Peas also contain phytosterols, which are known to reduce cholesterol levels in the body.

Sweet Potato Cheese Casserole

This casserole is a meal all on its own. Just add some mixed vegetables and voilá!

Yield:	Serving size:	Prep time:	Cook time:
6 cups	1 cup	15 minutes	20 minutes

6 medium sweet potatoes, scrubbed, whole, unpeeled

2 cups low-fat cottage cheese, low sodium

2 TB. onion powder

1 tsp. garlic, chopped

¼ tsp. fresh ground black pepper

½ cup nonfat milk

3 shallots, chopped

Dash paprika

1. Preheat the oven to 350°F.

2. In a large pot, boil sweet potatoes until tender.

3. Cool slightly in cold water.

4. Meanwhile, in a blender or food processor, purée cottage cheese, onion powder, garlic, black pepper, and milk until smooth.

5. Slice potatoes in ¼-inch slices.

6. In a 9-inch nonstick baking pan, arrange potato slices and pour cottage cheese mixture over potatoes.

7. Sprinkle with shallots and paprika.

8. Bake for 20 minutes, then place casserole under broiler for 3 to 5 minutes until golden brown and bubbly.

9. Serve immediately.

HEART-HEALTHY TIP

Deliciously high in two powerful antioxidants, vitamins A and C, sweet potatoes are loaded with health benefits. They are rich in carotenoids, which are known for their blood sugar–balancing effects as well as lowering insulin levels—excellent for diabetics and heart patients. Sweet potatoes are also known for their beneficial blood pressure–lowering abilities.

Ratatouille with Pine Nuts

This popular dish from the French Mediterranean that mingles tomatoes, onions, eggplant, bell peppers, zucchini, and herbs. It's easy to prepare and easier to eat, all in one delightful dish.

Yield:	Serving size:	Prep time:	Cook time:
6 cups	1 cup	15 minutes	15–20 minutes

2 medium onions, sliced

3 cloves garlic, chopped

1 tsp. oregano

2 tsp. thyme

1 medium eggplant, unpeeled, cubed

1 medium bell pepper, sliced

2 large zucchini, sliced

4 medium tomatoes, diced

2 carrots, thinly sliced

2 celery stalks, sliced

2 TB. apple cider vinegar

¼ cup pine nuts, or sunflower seeds

1. In a large nonstick frying pan, fry sliced onions and chopped garlic in 1 table-spoon extra virgin olive oil, uncovered, over medium heat until lightly browned.

2. Add oregano and thyme to hot pan and stir for 30 seconds to release flavor from herbs.

3. Stir in eggplant, bell pepper, zucchini, tomatoes, carrots, celery, and vinegar. Cover tightly with lid.

4. Simmer vegetables over medium-low heat for 15 to 20 minutes.

5. Remove from heat.

6. Sprinkle pine nuts or sunflower seeds on top of each serving.

7. Serve immediately.

HEART-HEALTHY TIP

Eggplant is a healthy choice for management of type 2 diabetes. Apart from its low glycemic levels, it is high in fiber and low in soluble carbohydrates.

Sweet Potato Oven-Baked French Fries

Sweet potatoes are high in fiber and taste delicious with cilantro and onion powder. Enjoy this as a snack or accompaniment with any salad or vegetable dish.

Yield:	Serving size:	Prep time:	Cook time:
4 cups	1 cup	10 minutes	30 minutes

4 medium sweet potatoes, scrubbed, unpeeled

2 tsp. onion powder
2 TB. cilantro, chopped

1. Preheat the oven to 450°F.
2. Cut potatoes lengthwise into $\frac{1}{2}$ inch fries and place in large bowl.
3. Sprinkle onion powder over fries and toss until mixed.
4. Spread fries onto a nonstick jelly roll pan and bake in oven for 15 minutes.
5. Turn potatoes after they are brown on one side. Bake for an additional 10 to 15 minutes, or until potatoes are tender and brown.
6. Top with chopped cilantro. Serve immediately.

HEART-HEALTHY TIP

Sweet potatoes get their orange color from their high beta-carotene content. Carotenoids are also known for their anti-inflammatory health benefits. High in antioxidants, vitamins C and A, sweet potatoes are known for their blood sugar–friendly low glycemic levels.

Baked Cauliflower with Miso

This crunchy, hearty vegetable, cauliflower is rich in nutrients and flavor. Combined with the delicious and amazing benefits of miso make it a noteworthy pair when it comes to increasing your heart health.

Yield:	Serving size:	Prep time:	Cook time:
3 cups	1 cup	10 minutes	20 minutes

1 medium head cauliflower, washed and cut into large florets

¼ cup barley miso or red miso diluted in ¾ cup warm water

½ cup filtered water

2 TB. fresh parsley, chopped

1. Preheat the oven to 425°F.

2. Place cauliflower in a baking dish.

3. Spread the diluted miso over cauliflower with a pastry brush.

4. Add water to bottom of pan.

5. Cover and bake for 25 minutes.

6. Uncover and bake an additional 5 to 10 minutes.

7. Sprinkle parsley over top and serve immediately.

HEART-HEALTHY TIP

The amazing benefits of miso are noteworthy when it comes to increasing heart health. Miso is a fermented soy product that originated in Japan and is known for its health and anti-aging benefits. Miso contains phytonutrients called isoflavones, which have been shown in numerous studies to reduce menopausal complaints—especially hot flashes.

Roasted Rosemary Red Potatoes

High in heart-healthy antioxidants, red potatoes are not only delicious, but they offer many benefits to the digestive system and colon. The combination of rosemary and parsley enhances the already tasty flavors of this delicious dish.

Yield:	Serving size:	Prep time:	Cook time:
2 cups	1 cup	10 minutes	40 minutes

12 small red potatoes, washed and unpeeled

2 TB. extra virgin olive oil

1 tsp. dried rosemary, or 1½ TB. fresh rosemary, chopped

½ tsp. Celtic or Himalayan salt

⅛ tsp. ground black pepper

1 TB. fresh parsley, chopped

1. Preheat the oven to 425°F.

2. In a large bowl, mix together potatoes, oil, rosemary, salt, and black pepper.

3. Place mixture in a rimmed baking sheet.

4. Bake for 40 minutes, or until the potatoes are soft on the inside.

5. Check the potatoes occasionally for browning.

6. Serve immediately with chopped parsley mixed in.

GOOD TO KNOW

Red potatoes are high in fiber and rank high in foods containing heart-specific vitamin C. One medium red potato contains 45 percent of the daily recommended value of vitamin C and 37 percent more potassium than bananas, spinach, or broccoli.

Scalloped Sweet Potatoes

High in heart-healthy magnesium and very rich in beta-carotene, this sweet potato dish is more than beneficial. The high fiber coupled with the extraordinary high amounts of antioxidants and nutrients lower your blood pressure, and are only surpassed by the flavors that excite your taste buds.

Yield:	Serving size:	Prep time:	Cook time:
4 cups	1 cup	30 minutes	45 minutes

4–5 medium sweet potatoes, sliced

2 cups Parmesan cheese, grated

1 medium onion, chopped or sliced

¼ cup butter, unsalted

1 garlic clove, chopped

1 cup skim milk

1 tsp. Celtic or Himalayan salt

1 TB. fresh parsley, chopped

1. Preheat the oven to 350°F.

2. Grease a 12-inch baking dish with butter.

3. Layer the sliced potatoes and add a sprinkling of cheese, onion, butter, and garlic over each layer of potatoes.

4. Finish with a sprinkle of salt and cheese over the top, then add the milk, cover, and bake for 30 minutes.

5. Uncover and bake for 15 to 20 minutes more.

6. Sprinkle with parsley. Serve immediately.

HEART-HEALTHY TIP

Sweet potatoes contain high amounts of vitamins C, B_5, and B_6, which all contribute to general health and reduction of stress.

Garlic Kale with Pine Nuts

Not only do kale's antioxidant and anti-inflammatory properties work together to slow aging, they taste delish with garlic or any fresh herb you choose to add. Simple, easy, and light!

Yield:	Serving size:	Prep time:	Cook time:
7 cups	1 cup	15 minutes	20 minutes

6 cups fresh kale, washed, dried, and chopped

¾ cup corn kernels

½ cup red bell pepper, chopped

2 garlic cloves, chopped

½ tsp. Celtic or Himalayan salt

½ tsp. ground black pepper

1. In a large skillet, heat 2 tablespoons extra virgin olive oil over medium heat and sauté kale for 10 minutes, stirring constantly.

2. Mix in corn, bell pepper, garlic, salt, and black pepper.

3. Cook for 10 minutes.

4. Serve immediately.

HEART-HEALTHY TIP

One cup of kale provides over 88 percent of our RDA and is shown to lower blood pressure, strengthen immunity, and protect against diabetes and macular degeneration. In addition, kale is a superstar in the arena of bioflavonoids and carotenoids, two powerful antioxidants that protect your heart.

Collards with Brown Rice and Tamari

Heartily rich in minerals such as calcium, copper, and iron, collards are packed with nutrition. Collards are part of the brassica family, nutritional superstars and tasty to boot. The brown rice and tamari gives this a distinctly Asian flavor that will have you coming back for more. You'll enjoy this tasty and light dish.

Yield:	Serving size:	Prep time:	Cook time:
6 cups	1 cup	10 minutes	20 minutes

1 cup filtered water

8 cups fresh collard greens, washed, dried, and sliced

1 TB. garlic, chopped

1 TB. tamari

2¼ tsp. brown rice vinegar

⅓ cup roasted sunflower seeds

1. In a large, deep skillet, heat water over medium heat and sauté collard greens for about 20 minutes or until tender.

2. Turn off heat.

3. Add garlic, tamari, vinegar, and seeds and mix together well.

4. Serve either hot or cold.

GOOD TO KNOW

To roast sunflower seeds, preheat oven to 275°F. Place the seeds in a small baking pan and bake for 4 to 6 minutes or until golden, stirring frequently.

Oriental Vegetables

This low-calorie dish is a great choice if you want to shed a few pounds. Bok choy or Chinese cabbage are both prime candidates for a nutrient-dense, low-carb meal.

Yield:	Serving size:	Prep time:	Cook time:
4 cups	2 cups	15 minutes	10 minutes

1 carrot, sliced diagonal and thin	½ cup bean sprouts
1 parsnip, sliced diagonal and thin	1 garlic clove, chopped
2 cups filtered water	1 TB. fresh ginger, chopped
1 cup broccoli, cut slender	1 TB. kuzu
2 stalks celery, sliced thin	2–3 tsp. tamari or Bragg Liquid Aminos
3 cups bok choy or Chinese cabbage, chopped	1 tsp. sesame seeds

1. In a large skillet, warm 2 teaspoons sesame oil over medium heat and sauté carrots and parsnips until they start to absorb the oil.

2. Add 1 cup water, quickly cover, and simmer for 5 minutes.

3. Add broccoli, celery, bok choy or cabbage, bean sprouts, garlic, and ginger. Cover and simmer for 3 to 5 minutes.

4. Dissolve kuzu in cold water and stir into vegetables until the sauce thickens.

5. Flavor with tamari or amino acids to taste and sprinkle with sesame seeds.

6. Serve with steamed rice or quinoa.

HEART-HEALTHY TIP

Bok choy is low in sodium and a great source of potassium and calcium, two of the important minerals on which the DASH diet is based.

Crustless Zucchini Quiche with Fresh Herbs and Spices

Enjoy the creamy crunchiness of this tasty zucchini quiche that's low calorie and high nourishment. Each mouthful will not only provide sensational flavor, it will serve the body well with all its powerful antioxidants. It's loaded with goodness.

Yield:	Serving size:	Prep time:	Cook time:
6 cups	1 cup	15 minutes	40 minutes

1 small onion, diced

2 cloves garlic, minced

4 green onions, stems and roots, chopped

$\frac{1}{4}$ cup red or green bell pepper, chopped

1–2 TB. filtered water

4 cups zucchini, sliced very thin

2 cups low-fat cottage cheese, low sodium, whipped

$\frac{1}{2}$ tsp. garlic powder

$1\frac{1}{2}$ tsp. onion powder

$\frac{1}{8}$ tsp. red pepper

2 tsp. dill weed

Dash of nutmeg

6 large egg whites

1 TB. whole-wheat flour

1. Preheat the oven to 325°F.

2. In a nonstick frying pan, sauté onion, garlic, green onions, and bell pepper over medium heat until brown and softened. Add water as needed to keep onions from sticking and burning.

3. Stir in zucchini slices until zucchini is slightly softened. Remove from heat.

4. In a blender or food processor, whip cottage cheese until smooth.

5. In a large mixing bowl, whisk garlic powder, onion powder, red pepper, dill weed, nutmeg, egg whites, and flour.

6. Stir in cottage cheese mixture, zucchini, and onion mixture.

7. Pour into a 12-inch nonstick or glass oven-proof baking dish.

8. Bake quiche for 30 to 35 minutes or until set.

9. Allow quiche to cool for 10 more minutes before serving.

HEART-HEALTHY TIP

One cup of zucchini contains over 10 percent of the RDA of magnesium, a DASH-specific nutrient. It's also high in folate, which helps to reduce homocysteine levels.

Spinach and Swiss Chard with Pine Nuts

A staple of the healthy Mediterranean cuisine, Swiss chard is about as good as it gets when it comes to DASH-friendly nutrients. It tastes great with quiche, or any poultry or meat dish.

Yield:	Serving size:	Prep time:	Cook time:
6 cups	1 cup	10 minutes	10 minutes

2 small shallots or 3 cloves garlic, minced

4 cups Swiss chard, washed and chopped

8 cups baby spinach, washed

$\frac{1}{4}$ cup toasted pine nuts

Dash cayenne pepper

Dash Celtic or Himalayan salt

1. In a large sauté pan, heat 2 tablespoons extra virgin olive oil over medium heat. Add shallots or garlic and sauté until translucent.

2. Add Swiss chard and sauté for 2 more minutes.

3. Add spinach and stir until wilted.

4. Stir in toasted pine nuts, cayenne pepper, and salt.

5. Serve hot.

HEART-HEALTHY TIP

Swiss chard is loaded with antioxidants for strengthening your heart and reversing aging. It will nourish your cells—and you'll enjoy every last bite. In addition, the leaves and stems are both edible with Swiss chard. It has a sweeter flavor than kale. Toss some in the blender when you're making green smoothies, too!

Ginger Sesame Carrots

Enjoy this dish any season, as carrots are readily available year-round. This recipe is nutrient dense with DASH-specific minerals and antioxidants, starting with beta-carotene and vitamin C. The ginger and sesame flavors gives it more bang for each bite.

Yield:	Serving size:	Prep time:	Cook time:
2 cups	1 cup	10 minutes	20 minutes

4 carrots, skin on, diagonally sliced

1 TB. fresh ginger, chopped finely

Dash of Celtic or Himalayan salt

Dash of cayenne pepper

1. In a medium skillet heat 1 teaspoon sesame oil, and sauté carrots for 3 minutes.

2. Add ginger, salt, and cayenne pepper.

3. Stir lightly and cover pan with lid.

4. Cook for 20 minutes on low heat until tender.

5. Serve hot.

HEART-HEALTHY TIP

Carrots are the second-most-popular type of vegetable after potatoes. They are high in calcium, fiber, and vitamins A and C.

Sesame Stir-Fried Asparagus

With its high folate content, asparagus is a must for any heart-healthy diet. Shown to reduce heart disease and control hypertension, asparagus is also known for reducing inflammation and arthritis. This recipe is deliciously flavored with sesame and crunchiness. Enjoy!

Yield:	Serving size:	Prep time:	Cook time:
4 cups	1 cup	10 minutes	5 minutes

1 TB. filtered water

1 tsp. sesame oil

4 cups fresh asparagus, cut into 2-inch lengths

1 tsp. Bragg Liquid Aminos

1 tsp. sesame seeds

1. In a medium sauté pan, add water and heat.

2. Add oil. Add asparagus, amino acids, and sauté 1 minute.

3. Cover and cook 2 to 4 minutes until crisp and bright green.

4. Sprinkle with sesame seeds and serve immediately.

GOOD TO KNOW

Asparagus dates back centuries ago when it was used as an aphrodisiac and potent system detoxifier. It is the folate content that has been shown to reduce the risk of heart disease.

The Best of Breads

In This Chapter

- Sweet breads for sweet occasions
- Savory breads for all others

When it comes to breads, who can resist—we all love them. The trick is to choose whole grains and experiment with making your own by substituting out some of the not-so-healthy ingredients, like sugar. You'll find plenty of ways to sweeten your breads without using sugar in these recipes.

Grains form an essential part of your healthy diet—they are loaded with fiber and minerals, and reduce the risk of heart disease and high blood pressure. Feel free to experiment by adding some of your favorite grains to the recipes in this chapter, such as ground sunflower or pumpkin seeds.

I've kept these recipes as low on the glycemic index as possible, and you can do more of that simply by adding more nuts and less fruit. Add some of your own delicious and nourishing spreads to a slice of fresh bread, or have a mashed banana with peanut butter, which is my favorite treat. Have fun with making these recipes, as I'm sure you will enjoy the end result of cooking them.

High-Fiber Carrot Bread

This delicious carrot bread can be made sweeter by adding raisins or dates. The addition of nuts gives it added nourishment and delectability. Feel free to experiment and enjoy your creation.

Yield:	Serving size:	Prep time:	Cook time:
9-inch loaf	1-inch slice	20 minutes	45 minutes

1½ cups whole-wheat flour, or almond or rice flour

1½ tsp. xanthan gum

¾ tsp. baking soda

2 tsp. baking powder

2 TB. almond meal (ground almonds)

1 tsp. cinnamon

½ tsp. Celtic or Himalayan salt

1 tsp. grated ginger

1 tsp. orange peel, finely grated (zest)

2 TB. agave nectar or molasses

2 eggs, lightly beaten

2 TB. unsalted butter, melted

½ cup yogurt or skim milk

1 cup grated carrots, squeezed and patted dry

1. Preheat oven to 350°F.

2. Grease a 9×4×3-inch loaf pan.

3. In a mixing bowl, combine the flour, xanthan gum, baking soda, baking powder, almond meal, cinnamon, salt, ginger, and zest.

4. In a medium bowl, combine the nectar or molasses, eggs, butter, and yogurt, and blend. Add the carrots and combine into mixture.

5. Spoon into the prepared loaf pan and bake for 60 minutes.

6. Remove to cool completely before slicing.

GOOD TO KNOW

Carrots are loaded with beta-carotene, an antioxidant that converts to vitamin A in the body. The soluble fiber in carrots can help lower blood cholesterol levels by binding with and removing bile acids.

Zesty Date Nut Loaf

When it comes to eating bread that goes beyond tasty, this has to be it. Walnuts are packed with brain- and heart-healthy omega-3s, and dates are full of minerals, such as iron, B and C vitamins, your body loves and are a good source of fiber. This bread is good as an anytime snack, or serve it with a dollop of whipped cream or yogurt for dessert.

Yield:	Serving size:	Prep time:	Cook time:
9-inch loaf	1-inch slice	20 minutes	45 minutes

1 cup dates, pitted, chopped

1 tsp. baking soda

¾ cup boiling filtered water

1½ cups whole-wheat flour or almond flour

¾ tsp. Celtic or Himalayan salt

¾ tsp. xanthan gum

1 TB. baking powder

2 eggs, lightly beaten

¾ cup molasses

1 tsp. vanilla extract

2 TB. olive or grape seed oil

1 TB. orange peel, finely grated (zest)

1 cup walnuts, chopped

1. Preheat the oven to 325°F.

2. Grease a 9×5-inch loaf pan with 1 tablespoon unsalted, organic butter.

3. In a large mixing bowl, place dates and baking soda. Cover with boiling water. Let cool.

4. Meanwhile, in a medium bowl, combine flour, salt, xanthan gum, and baking powder. Set aside.

5. In a small bowl, beat eggs well. Add molasses, vanilla, and oil.

6. Add egg mixture to the cooled date mixture.

7. Add dry flour mixture, and beat until smooth.

8. Fold in orange zest and nuts.

9. Pour into the prepared pan and bake for approximately 45 minutes.

10. Remove from pan while still hot.

11. Cool before cutting. Store in refrigerator.

HEART-HEALTHY TIP

Walnuts are high in heart-healthy antioxidants and vitamin E. Walnuts also positively affect your blood cholesterol levels due to their high fiber content that helps remove bile acids from the body.

Banana Raisin Nut Muffins

These muffins are not only highly nourishing as a meal all on their own, they come packed with DASH-friendly minerals. You'll love the flavor combinations that leave you feeling satisfied and ready to go.

Yield:	Serving size:	Prep time:	Cook time:
12 muffins	1 muffin	10 minutes	12–15 minutes

¾ cup sorghum flour

½ cup tapioca flour

¼ cup cornstarch

¼ tsp. Celtic or Himalayan salt

1 tsp. baking powder

½ tsp. baking soda

1 tsp. orange peel, finely grated (zest)

2 TB. molasses unsulphured, (optional)

1 egg, lightly beaten

½ cup yogurt

2 TB. unsalted melted butter or 2 TB. extra virgin olive oil

Juice from 1 medium orange

1 banana, mashed

1 cup raisins

½ cup walnuts or pecans, chopped

1. Preheat oven to 375°F.

2. Grease the muffin tins with vegetable oil or butter.

3. In a mixing bowl, combine sorghum and tapioca flours, cornstarch, salt, baking powder, baking soda, orange zest, and molasses. Set aside.

4. In a small bowl, beat the egg, yogurt, and butter or oil. Mix in the juice and mashed banana.

5. Pour this into the flour mix and stir in the raisins and nuts until just blended.

6. Spoon into the prepared pans. Bake for 15 minutes. Serve warm or cool.

HEART-HEALTHY TIP

Walnuts are high in these three heart-healthy minerals: potassium, magnesium, and calcium.

Banana Berry Nut Bread

It doesn't get any sweeter than this! You'll also love that there's no sugar inside this delicious bread. It's simply scrumptious as a snack, treat, or even dessert. Just add your favorite topping!

Yield:	Serving size:	Prep time:	Cook time:
10 slices	1 slice	15 minutes	1 hour

¼ cup unsalted butter, softened

⅛ cup coconut oil, warm to liquid consistency

2 large eggs, lightly beaten

½ cup molasses, unsulphured

2 medium ripe bananas

1 tsp. baking soda

1 cup walnuts, chopped

1⅓ cups whole-wheat flour

1 cup fresh or frozen raspberries

1. Preheat the oven to 375°F.

2. Grease a 9×4×3-inch loaf pan.

3. In a medium bowl, mix butter, coconut oil, eggs, and molasses.

4. In a blender or by hand, purée bananas and add butter mixture.

5. Gradually add baking soda, walnuts, and flour. Mix until smooth.

6. Blend in the raspberries.

7. Pour mixture into greased loaf pan.

8. Bake for 15 minutes; reduce the oven to 350°F and bake for 40 to 45 more minutes.

HEART-HEALTHY TIP

Bananas are loaded with vitamin B_6 and potassium, which are both calming to the central nervous system. Potassium is an essential mineral for helping to maintain normal blood pressure and heart function.

Chocolate Cherry Nut Loaf

The nutritional benefits of cherries are huge, especially in comparison to their size. Their bold and bright color comes from their high antioxidant content. Combine them with the chocolate and the nuts in this delicious loaf, and you'll think you're in heaven.

Yield:	Serving size:	Prep time:	Cook time:
10 slices	1 slice	20 minutes	50–60 minutes

1½ cups whole-wheat flour or almond flour

1½ tsp. xanthan gum

⅓ cup molasses

1 tsp. baking soda

1 tsp. baking powder

¼ tsp. Celtic or Himalayan salt

1 cup walnuts, chopped

¾ cup semisweet chocolate chips

2 TB. unsalted butter

2 eggs, lightly beaten

¾ cup skim milk or yogurt

½ cup cherry fruit spread (no sugar) or 1 cup frozen cherries

1 tsp. cherry or vanilla extract

1. Preheat the oven to 350°F.

2. Grease a 9×5-inch loaf pan.

3. In a medium mixing bowl, whisk together flour, xanthan gum, molasses, baking soda, baking powder, salt, and walnuts. Set aside.

4. In a small saucepan over low heat, melt chocolate chips and butter.

5. In a medium bowl, whisk eggs lightly. Add milk, fruit spread or frozen cherries, and flavoring. Beat until well blended.

6. Add fruit mixture and chocolate to flour mixture and beat until moistened.

7. Spoon into the prepared pan and bake for 50 to 60 minutes or until a tester inserted in the center comes out clean.

8. Cool approximately 5 minutes before turning out from the pan.

9. Cool completely before slicing.

HEART-HEALTHY TIP

Cherries contain a phytonutrient called anthocyanin. This is a natural pain reliever and anti-inflammatory, which inhibits the production of COX-2 enzymes and helps prevent cardiovascular disease.

Savory Breads

Cheesy Corn Bread

Who doesn't love cheese and corn with bread? The addition of onions and fresh herbs with the creamy texture of cheese makes this a favorite for all occasions.

Yield:	Serving size:	Prep time:	Cook time:
10 slices	1 slice	20 minutes	45 minutes

1½ cups whole-wheat flour or almond flour

1 cup cornmeal

½ tsp. xanthan gum

¼ cup molasses or agave nectar

1 tsp. baking soda

1 tsp. baking powder

¾ tsp. Celtic or Himalayan salt

1 cup plain yogurt, low fat

2 eggs, lightly beaten

2 TB. unsalted butter, melted

¼ cup orange juice or filtered water

1 cup corn kernels, canned or frozen, drained

1 cup low-sodium cream cheese, light

½ cup carrots, skin on, grated

½ cup onion, finely chopped

2 TB. fresh parsley, chopped

1. Preheat the oven to 375°F.

2. Grease the 9×13-inch baking pan.

3. In a large mixing bowl, whisk together flour, cornmeal, xanthan gum, molasses or nectar, baking soda, baking powder, and salt.

4. In a smaller bowl, blend yogurt, beaten eggs, butter, and orange juice or water.

5. Add to dry mix and stir until blended.

6. Stir in corn, cheese, carrots, onion, and parsley.

7. Spoon batter into the prepared pan and bake 45 minutes, or until the bread springs back when gently pressed.

8. Cut into squares and serve warm or at room temperature.

HEART-HEALTHY TIP

In addition to being sweet and satisfying, this corn bread is high in heart-healthy nutrients. It is loaded with fiber to help lower cholesterol levels and blood sugar levels also. It's well balanced with the protein and healthy fats inside, too.

Cheese, Chives, and Dill Soufflés

Since the ages, cheese is considered a comfort food as much as a nourishing food. These delicious soufflés are high in calcium and B vitamins. They taste delicious.

Yield:	Serving size:	Prep time:	Cook time:
6 soufflés	1 soufflé	15 minutes	20 minutes

6 ramekins

4 TB. unsalted butter

⅓ cup plain whole meal flour or gluten-free flour

1¼ cups milk

1 cup cheddar cheese, low fat, grated

3 eggs, with yolks separated

2 TB. fresh dill, chopped

Pinch Celtic or Himalayan salt

Dash cayenne pepper

Freshly ground black pepper

2 TB. Parmesan cheese, grated

1 TB. fresh chives, chopped

1. Preheat the oven to 400°F.

2. In a large saucepan, gently melt butter and add flour.

3. Cook for 2 minutes, stirring continuously, then gradually add milk, stirring. Simmer until thickened, then allow to cool.

4. Stir in cheese, egg yolks, dill, salt, cayenne pepper, and black pepper into the sauce.

5. In a small bowl, beat egg whites with a pinch of salt until stiff.

6. Fold the egg whites into cheese sauce, and fold in the remainder.

7. Butter six small ramekins and dust with Parmesan cheese.

8. Divide mixture among the ramekins.

9. Bake for 15 to 20 minutes until the soufflés are puffed and golden brown.

10. Garnish with chives and serve immediately.

GOOD TO KNOW

If you're lactose intolerant, feel free to substitute the cow's milk cheese with goat's or sheep's milk cheese, or use a lactose reduced yogurt instead of milk.

Yeast-Free Zucchini Cheese Bread

Enjoy all flavor and cholesterol-lowering effects from this delicious cheesy, yeast-free bread dish. It's higher in fiber than the recommended daily amount, plus contains the antioxidants, as well as vitamins A and C, to prevent oxidation and promote cardio-vascular health. You'll love it!

Yield:	Serving size:	Prep time:	Cook time:
8–10 slices	1 slice	15 minutes	50–60 minutes

1½ cups whole-wheat flour or almond flour

1½ tsp. xanthan gum

⅓ cup molasses or agave nectar

2 TB. Parmesan cheese, grated

1 tsp. baking powder

½ tsp. Celtic or Himalayan salt

1 tsp. baking soda

⅔ cup zucchini, shredded

2 large eggs, lightly beaten

3 TB. unsalted butter, melted

⅔ cup buttermilk, low fat

Dash cayenne pepper (optional)

1¼ TB. fresh onion, grated

2 TB. fresh parsley, chopped

1. Preheat the oven to 350°F.

2. Grease 9×13-inch pan.

3. In a mixing bowl, whisk together flour, xanthan gum, molasses, Parmesan cheese, baking powder, salt, and baking soda.

4. Add shredded zucchini and blend well.

5. In a small bowl, combine eggs, butter, buttermilk, cayenne pepper, onion, and parsley. Beat until well combined using a whisk or eggbeater.

6. Pour liquids into dry ingredients and mix thoroughly.

7. Spoon into the pan and bake for 50 to 60 minutes.

8. Leave in the pan to cool for 15 minutes and then remove to cool completely before slicing.

HEART-HEALTHY TIP

Zucchini is high in heart-healthy magnesium, an essential mineral to lower your risk of heart disease. It's also high in folate, which helps break down homocyste-ine, an amino acid that contributes to cardiovascular disease.

Sesame Chive Crackers

You'll love the crunchy, nutty-flavored sesame seeds throughout these delicious crackers, which are loaded with calcium, copper, and tryptophan that keep your heart healthy and your taste buds happy.

Yield:	Serving size:	Prep time:	Cook time:
60 crackers	4 crackers	15 minutes	30 minutes

3 cups almond flour

1 tsp. Celtic or Himalayan salt

1 dash cayenne pepper

1 cup sesame seeds

2 TB. grape seed oil

2 large eggs

$\frac{1}{4}$ cup fresh chives, chopped

1. Preheat the oven to 350°F.

2. Set aside two large baking sheets. Cut three pieces of parchment paper to the size of the baking sheets.

3. In a large bowl, combine almond flour, salt, cayenne pepper, and sesame seeds.

4. In a medium bowl, whisk together grape seed oil and eggs. Add the chives.

5. Stir the wet ingredients into almond flour mixture until thoroughly combined.

6. Divide dough into two pieces.

7. Place one piece of dough between two sheets of parchment paper and flatten with a rolling pin to $\frac{1}{16}$-inch thickness.

8. Remove the top piece of parchment and transfer the bottom piece with rolled-out dough onto a baking sheet.

9. Repeat with the remaining piece of dough.

10. Cut dough into 2-inch squares with a knife or pizza cutter.

11. Bake for 12 to 15 minutes, until lightly golden.

12. Let crackers cool on the baking sheets for 30 minutes, then serve.

HEART-HEALTHY TIP

Sesame seeds contain lignans, which have been shown to have a cholesterol-lowering effect and to prevent high blood pressure. They are also high in calcium.

Herbed Yogurt Bread

Moist, tender, and delicious, this bread adapts well to variations in flavor with the addition of nuts, seeds, dried fruits, or herbs. Yogurt makes a great choice for lactose-intolerant celiac sufferers, and it also adds precious protein.

Yield:	Serving size:	Prep time:	Cook time:
10 slices	1–2 slices	20 minutes	1 hour

$1\frac{1}{2}$ cups almond flour

1 tsp. xanthan gum

$\frac{1}{2}$ tsp. Celtic or Himalayan salt

$\frac{1}{2}$ tsp. baking soda

1 tsp. cinnamon

1 tsp. orange peel, grated (zest)

1 TB. dry yeast

1 egg, plus 1 egg white

2 TB. unsalted butter

1 tsp. unflavored gelatin

$\frac{1}{2}$ tsp. dough enhancer

2 TB. agave nectar or molasses

$\frac{3}{4}$ cup yogurt, warmed to 110°F

$\frac{1}{2}$ cup filtered water, warmed to 110°F

1. Preheat oven to 110°F. Place yogurt in oven for approximately 10 minutes.

2. Grease a 9×9-inch baking pan.

3. In a large bowl, combine the flour, xanthan gum, salt, baking soda, cinnamon, orange rind, and yeast. Set aside.

4. In separate bowl, whisk the egg and egg white, butter, gelatin, dough enhancer, and nectar or molasses. Add the warm yogurt and most of the warm water. Add the remaining water as needed after mixing.

5. Using a mixer that's turned to low, add the dry ingredients including the yeast, a little at a time. Dough should be like a cake batter in consistency.

6. Turn oven temperature up to 400°F.

7. After adding the water turn the mixer to high and beat for $3\frac{1}{2}$ minutes.

8. Spoon the dough into the prepared pan, cover.

9. Bake for 50 to 60 minutes, covering after 10 minutes with aluminum foil.

HEART-HEALTHY TIP

Almond flour is not only a good choice for those with gluten intolerance, but it is highly nourishing and nutritious. It is high in protein and low in carbohydrates and sugars, making it a healthy choice for your heart by lowering cholesterol and blood sugar levels.

Delectable Desserts

Desserts and sweet treats aren't entirely off limits if you're aiming for a heart-healthy diet; you just have to choose carefully and know what's available to you. I have made that relatively simple by providing you with a selection of low-fat, healthy recipes that allow you to have your cake and eat it, too.

You'll find all-natural ingredients in these desserts, and feel free to add more or less honey, fruit, or molasses should you want your deserts a little more or less sweet.

Cookies and Cakes

In This Chapter

- Cookies that never tasted so good
- Cakes to suit any occasion or celebrate yourself

No diet is complete without irresistible treats—but with the DASH diet, desserts are made from fresh wholesome ingredients and not an ounce of sugar is added to them. You will be pleasantly delighted and inspired by how healthy you can make cookies and cakes without the high calories of sugar.

In these delicious treat recipes you will find an array of flavors and goodness that keep your blood sugar balanced and your appetite in check. I've used natural sweeteners such as honey, maple syrup, molasses, and fruit. If this is a new experience for you, then you'll be pleasantly surprised.

I have tried to pack in as many heart-healthy minerals and vitamins as possible, along with high fiber, to help make your cooking and eating experience a pleasurable one.

No-Bake Almond Chocolate Oatmeal Cookies

Simple, easy, and delicious is the best way to describe these nutritious no-bake treats. Almonds are abundant in vitamin E, a heart-healthy nutrient, along with magnesium, fiber, and tryptophan. The combination of rolled oats and natural sweeteners will keep you in the heart-health zone for hours.

Yield:	Serving size:	Prep time:	Cook time:
24 cookies	2 cookies	20 minutes	None

¼ cup raw honey or molasses

½ cup brown rice syrup

3 cups rolled oats

6 fresh dates, pitted and chopped

3 tsp. carob or cocoa powder

2 tsp. vanilla extract

¼ cup unsalted butter, melted

1 cup almond butter

1 tsp. cinnamon

1. In a large bowl, mix honey or molasses, syrup, oats, dates, carob or cocoa powder, vanilla, butter, almond butter, and cinnamon together.

2. Form into cookie rounds and place on a large cookie sheet covered with waxed paper.

3. Place in the refrigerator to cool.

4. Serve cold or at room temperature.

GOOD TO KNOW

Almonds are high in heart-healthy monounsaturated fats. Studies show that almonds' ability to reduce heart-disease risk may also be partly due to their high levels of vitamin E, an antioxidant with known cardio-strengthening properties.

Heart-Healthy Cookies

These melt-in-your-mouth cookies not only taste scrumptious, they are a perfect heart-healthy treat. Packed with goodness for keeping your cholesterol levels low and your blood sugar stable, they are high in fiber and DASH-friendly minerals and vitamins.

Yield:	Serving size:	Prep time:	Cook time:
25–30 cookies	1–2 cookies	15 minutes	10 minutes

1 large egg, beaten

¼ cup almond or rice milk

½ cup unsalted butter, softened

½ cup coconut oil, warmed to liquid consistency

½ cup raw honey

1 tsp. vanilla extract

1½ cups oat flour

1 tsp. baking soda

1 tsp. cinnamon

½ tsp. Celtic or Himalayan salt

3 cups rolled oats

½ cup walnut, chopped into pieces

¼ cup sunflower seeds, shelled

½ cup apple, peeled and diced

1. Preheat the oven to 375°F.

2. In a large bowl, mix together egg, almond or rice milk, butter, coconut oil, honey, and vanilla.

3. In a separate, smaller bowl, mix together flour, baking soda, cinnamon, and salt.

4. Slowly add dry ingredients to wet ingredients, stirring constantly, until you have a smooth batter.

5. Add oats, walnuts, seeds, and apple, stirring gently until mixture is uniform.

6. Drop with a spoon onto a greased cookie sheet.

7. Bake for 9 to 12 minutes until lightly browned.

GOOD TO KNOW

Oats are high in soluble dietary fiber, along with heart-healthy minerals selenium, magnesium, and tryptophan. A 19-year health study on the effects of cereal consumption on heart-failure risk found that men who ate whole-grain cereal at breakfast had a 29 percent reduced risk.

Healthy Banana Cake

Moist, luscious, and naturally sweetened with banana and honey, you'll be coming back for seconds with this one. Bananas contain heart-healthy potassium, and vitamins B$_6$ and C. This cake is high in fiber and definitely passes the taste test.

Yield:	Serving size:	Prep time:	Cook time:
12 slices	1 slice	10 minutes	25 minutes

1½ cups mashed bananas, fully ripened

⅔ cup honey or molasses

1 TB. extra virgin olive oil

6 large eggs, organic

1 tsp. plus sprinkle cinnamon

½ tsp. coriander

½ tsp. nutmeg

2 TB. skim milk or nonfat yogurt

1½ tsp. vanilla extract

½ cup raisins

½ cup walnuts, chopped

2¼ cups whole-wheat or rice flour

1 TB. baking soda

1 tsp. baking powder

1. Preheat the oven to 350°F.

2. In a large mixing bowl, whisk together bananas, honey, oil, eggs, 1 teaspoon cinnamon, coriander, nutmeg, skim milk or yogurt, vanilla, raisins, and nuts.

3. In a medium bowl, mix together flour, baking soda, and baking powder.

4. Add to dry mix to banana mixture, whisking just until blended. Do not overmix.

5. In a 9×13-inch nonstick baking pan, spread batter evenly.

6. Sprinkle cinnamon on top and bake for 25 minutes, or until a cake tester, inserted in center, comes out clean. Do not overbake.

GOOD TO KNOW

Rice flour is higher in protein than wheat flour and contains vitamins and minerals. Since rice flour contains no gluten, it is a good alternative for people who cannot tolerate gluten in their diets due to allergic reaction (or celiac).

Cashew Coconut Lime Cheesecake

This tangy, no-bake cheesecake has all the taste and texture sensations of a real cheesecake but contains no dairy. With cashew butter and coconut cream, it is higher in fats so you'll want to save this delicious dessert for special occasions only.

Yield:	Serving size:	Prep time:	Cook time:
10 slices	1 slice	8 hours, 30 minutes	None

3 cups cashew pieces

4 cups water, filtered

$1\frac{1}{2}$ cups raw almonds

$\frac{1}{2}$ cup unsweetened, shredded coconut

$\frac{3}{4}$ cup dates, pitted and chopped

1 tsp. fresh ginger, chopped finely

$\frac{1}{4}$ tsp. plus 2 tsp. vanilla

Pinch Celtic or Himalayan salt

$1\frac{1}{2}$ cups coconut milk

1 cup fresh lime juice

$\frac{1}{2}$ cup maple syrup

$\frac{1}{2}$ cup coconut oil

3 TB. lecithin

Fresh berries for garnish (optional)

Lime zest for garnish (optional)

1. In a medium bowl, place cashews and cover with filtered water. Soak overnight in the refrigerator.

2. In a food processor or blender, place almonds, coconut, dates, ginger, $\frac{1}{4}$ teaspoon vanilla, and salt. Pulse until mixture becomes crushed enough that it stays together when pinched.

3. Oil a 9-inch round pie pan and press filling into the bottom.

4. In a small bowl, combine coconut milk, lime juice, maple syrup, and 2 teaspoons vanilla. Set aside.

5. Drain and rinse soaked cashews. Place in a food processor or blender.

6. Purée until cashews start to become smooth. With the motor running, slowly add coconut milk mixture and blend until smooth.

7. With the motor running, slowly add coconut oil and lecithin, and blend until smooth.

8. Pour over crust and chill overnight.

9. Serve slices of the chilled cheesecake with fresh berries, or lime zest if desired.

GOOD TO KNOW

Coconut is low in sodium and high in fiber. The fatty acids in coconut oil, in biochemistry terms, are primarily medium chain, which are shorter than long chain, typically found in other fats and oils. These medium-chain fatty acids are more easily metabolized by the body. Remember that with all fats, a little bit goes a long way.

Oatmeal Raisin Chews

Not your average cookie, these chewy raisin delights are your go-to choice for comfort food that's close to your heart. They're full of fiber and goodness.

Yield:	Serving size:	Prep time:	Cook time:
36–48 cookies	1–2 cookies	10 minutes	20 minutes

2 cups rolled oats

2 tsp. cinnamon

2 tsp. nutmeg

1 tsp. coriander

¼ cup shredded coconut

¼ cup raisins

¼ cup walnuts or pecans, chopped

Dash cayenne pepper (optional)

½ cup frozen concentrated apple juice

4 large egg whites

2 tsp. molasses

1. Preheat the oven to 375°F.

2. Place 2 cups rolled oats on a baking sheet. Toast in the oven for 8 to 10 minutes.

3. Remove from oven and place in a large mixing bowl.

4. Add cinnamon, nutmeg, coriander, coconut, raisins, nuts, cayenne pepper, and apple juice and mix together.

5. With an electric mixer, beat egg whites until foamy.

6. Beat in molasses until stiff but not dry, then gently fold eggs into oats mixture.

7. Immediately drop mixture by teaspoon onto two nonstick cookie sheets and bake for 20 minutes, or until they are dark brown.

HEART-HEALTHY TIP

Coriander has numerous heart-healthy benefits. Some of the acids present in coriander are very effective in lowering cholesterol in the blood as well as plaque build-up in the arteries.

Divine Desserts

In This Chapter

- Delicious natural desserts for your health
- New-to-you ingredients that make dessert fun

You will want to leave room for the nutritious and healthy desserts that satisfy any sweet tooth. There is no sugar in any of these recipes, only wholesome and healthy natural sweeteners such as fruits, honeys, and syrups.

I have chosen ingredients that increase the nutritional value of the dessert by using natural ingredients and delicious combinations. Healthy desserts do exist, and there are thousands more to be discovered. Experiment with the flavors and ingredients here and add your own favorites that are light on the calories and heavy on the DASH support.

Feel free to refrigerate most of these divine desserts and spread them out over several days for maximum enjoyment. Some of them are even great for breakfast or snacks. Enjoy every luscious bite.

Zesty Strawberry-Rhubarb Pudding

Rhubarb is a perfect fruit for your DASH diet or those who are diet conscious; you could not do better with this plant that is high in calcium, as well as heart-healthy antioxidants. Combined with delicious strawberries and a nice zest of lime, your taste buds and palate will have you feeling like you're in seventh heaven.

Yield:	Serving size:	Prep time:	Cook time:
1 quart	1 cup	15 minutes	10 minutes

5 cups strawberries (organic) plus slices for garnish

2 cups rhubarb, chopped

3 TB. pure maple syrup

1 tsp. grated lemon rind (zest)

2 TB. agar-agar flakes, (vegetable gelatin made of sea vegetables and available in supermarkets)

1 TB. kuzu

3 TB. filtered cold water

1 TB. fresh mint, chopped

1. In a medium saucepan, bring strawberries, rhubarb, maple syrup, and lemon zest to a boil and sprinkle with agar-agar flakes. Simmer until all flakes are dissolved (about 10 minutes).

2. In a separate bowl, dissolve kuzu in water. Add it to the saucepan and stir until it thickens.

3. Transfer to a bowl or individual cups and refrigerate until set.

4. Garnish with strawberry slices and a sprig of fresh mint.

GOOD TO KNOW

Rhubarb is high in several notable vitamins and compounds such as lutein, which keeps your skin and eyes healthy. Lutein helps neutralize free radicals, which are dangerous compounds that can lead to cancer.

Baked Apples with Cherries and Walnuts

Enjoy this antioxidant-laden dessert that's as healthy as it delicious. The combination of wholesome apples with cherries mixed with the crunch texture of brain-friendly walnuts will leave you satisfied and nourished.

Yield:	Serving size:	Prep time:	Cook time:
6 apples	1 apple	15 minutes	45 minutes

6 large apples, cored, organic

4 TB. unsalted butter, softened

$\frac{1}{3}$ cup molasses

2 TB. fresh lemon or lime juice

3 TB. walnuts, chopped

$\frac{1}{3}$ cup cherries, fresh or dried, depitted, chopped

1 TB. grated lemon zest

1 tsp. fresh ginger, finely chopped

$\frac{1}{4}$ tsp. ground cloves

1. Preheat oven to 350°F.

2. Core the apples from stem side through the center (but not entirely through) and peel from top to about $\frac{1}{3}$ the way down.

3. In a bowl, cream the butter and molasses. Stir in lemon juice, walnuts, cherries, lemon zest, ginger, and cloves.

4. Place a spoonful of stuffing into each apple.

5. Place in an oiled baking pan with a little water.

6. Bake about 45 minutes or until apples are tender.

GOOD TO KNOW

Walnuts have a favorable impact on blood vessels and cardiovascular health. They contain an ample presence of antioxidant and anti-inflammatory nutrients that supports blood vessel walls. They are high in brain-boosting omega-3 essential fatty acids.

Banana Crème Brûlée

A banana (with milk) constitutes almost a complete balanced diet with potassium, vitamin B_6, and fiber, and eggs are a complete meal on their own with their protein content—with this delicious combo you'll be nourished and satisfied for hours. It's a wonderful treat to have as a breakfast dish or a dessert … sweet enough and no sugar required.

Yield:	Serving size:	Prep time:	Cook time:
4 cups	1 cup	20 minutes	1 hour

1 large or 2 small bananas

1 cup whole milk, or almond milk

1 cup heavy cream, plus 1 cup half and half milk, organic

5 egg yolks

1 tsp. vanilla extract

1 cup raisins (optional)

1 cup fresh berries

1. Preheat oven to 325°F.

2. Peel and mash bananas and line the bottom of a large 9- or 10-inch oven dish with them.

3. Warm milk and cream gently over a low flame.

4. Beat egg yolks together. Blend milk mixture with eggs, stirring gently constantly.

5. Blend in vanilla and raisins and slowly pour the mixture over the top of bananas.

6. Place the dish into another larger baking dish and pour hot water into that dish. Cover the brûlée with foil and bake for 1 hour, or until a knife inserted into the center comes out clean.

7. Chill before serving. Serve with fresh berries or fruit of your choice.

GOOD TO KNOW

One banana contains your daily supply of potassium. This mineral is key to help prevent high blood pressure and protect against atherosclerosis.

Luscious Brown Rice Pudding

This high-fiber, delicious pudding is especially helpful in reducing cholesterol levels and managing heart disease. The eggs and cream combine well to give a fluffy texture, and the nuts provide crunch and essential omega-3 fatty acids.

Yield:	Serving size:	Prep time:	Cook time:
4 cups	1 cup	20 minutes	45–50 minutes

3 eggs

1 cup heavy cream, organic

⅓ cup maple syrup

1 tsp. vanilla

1 tsp. cinnamon

½ tsp. nutmeg

1½ cups whole-grain brown rice, cooked

1 cup pecans or walnuts, chopped

1 cup raisins

1–2 bananas (optional)

1. Preheat oven to 325°F.

2. Beat the eggs with cream, maple syrup, vanilla, cinnamon, and nutmeg.

3. Stir in rice, nuts, raisins, and bananas if adding.

4. Pour into a buttered 9×12-inch size oven-safe dish or soufflé dish.

5. Bake covered for approximately 45 to 50 minutes.

GOOD TO KNOW

Brown rice is one of the healthiest foods and is a staple in many cultures around the world. It's high in fiber and heart-healthy minerals, magnesium, manganese, selenium, and tryptophan.

DASH'n'Berry Heart-Felt Smoothie

Blueberries and raspberries—or let's just say all berries—contain amazing health and cardio-supportive properties. With their bright blue, red, and purple colors from their high levels of antioxidants, they are packed full with many heart-protective vitamins and minerals, not to mention incredible flavor and high fiber. It's truly berries to the rescue, and you simply must indulge in them. Try often and your heart will reward you.

Yield:	Serving size:	Prep time:	Cook time:
1 quart	2 cups	10 minutes	None

¾ cup raspberries, fresh or frozen

½ cup blueberries, strawberries, or cranberries

1 scoop or 2 heaping tablespoons whey protein powder

2 cups filtered water, or 1 cup filtered water and 1 cup coconut milk, light

1 TB. flax seed oil

½ cup tofu, silken or soft, with 1 cup more water

1 banana (optional)

1 TB. hazelnut butter, or almond, peanut, or sesame seed

1. Place in a blender the berries, protein powder, water, coconut milk if using, flax seed oil, tofu, banana, and nut butter. Blend for 3 to 5 minutes on high speed.

2. Chill or serve immediately over ice.

GOOD TO KNOW

As protein is such an important nutrient that's essential for regulating metabolism, whey protein powder is an easy and great way to take care of your body's daily needs. Protein repairs body cells, provides a source of much-needed energy, and builds strong, healthy bones and muscles, including your heart.

Chocolate-Date Indulgence Pudding

Save this divine dessert for one of those extra-special occasions when your spirit needs to soar. Chocolate is heavenly and stimulates secretion of endorphins, which produce pleasurable sensations. It contains medicinal qualities that go layers deep, not to mention its anti-depressant properties.

Yield:	Serving size:	Prep time:	Cook time:
1 quart	1 cup	15 minutes	10 minutes

3 cups milk (organic dairy, almond, or rice)

1 TB. agar-agar powder, or 2 TB. agar-agar flakes

1 tsp. cinnamon

¼ tsp. cardamom

⅓ cup cocoa, unsweetened

⅓ cup pure maple syrup

1 TB. molasses, unsulphured

⅓ cup prepared coffee

1 TB. kuzu dissolved in ½ cup cold milk, almond milk, or rice milk

4 fresh dates, chopped

¼ cup coconut flakes, toasted or shredded

1. Place in a blender the milk, agar-agar, cinnamon, cardamom, cocoa, maple syrup, molasses, coffee, dates, and coconut, and blend together for 5 minutes.

2. In a large saucepan, combine dissolved kuzu mixture and milk mixture and cook on medium-high heat for 12 to 15 minutes, stirring constantly or until mixture begins to thicken. Remove from heat and add dates.

3. Combine both mixtures and serve hot or cold.

GOOD TO KNOW

Agar-agar comes from several species of seaweed, and has been used for centuries as a setting agent for desserts, jams, jellies, and more. It is high in calcium and iron and is well known for its ability to aid digestion and weight loss. It's a healthy vegetarian substitute for gelatin.

Glossary

A

agar-agar   Comes from several species of seaweed, and has been used for centuries as a setting agent for desserts, jams, jellies, and more.

antioxidants   Phytochemicals, vitamins, minerals, and other nutrients that protect our cells from damage caused by free radicals.

barley malt powder   Sometimes called flour, it is made from grain that is fermented, then dried and ground.

body mass index (BMI)   A calculation that uses your height and weight to estimate how much body fat you have.

Celtic or Himalayan salt   All natural unrefined salts that are full of natural minerals that make it healthy and delicious.

DASH   Dietary Approaches to Stop Hypertension named after the landmark study that proved it lowered blood pressure to a much healthier level within 14 days.

farina   Flax seed.

free radicals   Any atom or molecule that has a single unpaired electron in an outer shell. Free radicals cause oxidation of cells. Oxidation is defined as the interaction between oxygen molecules and all the different substances they may contact, from metal to living tissue. Oxidation creates a process also known as rusting, which equals rapid aging when applied to your cells.

glycemic index (GI)   A measure of the effects of carbohydrates on blood sugar levels. It is based on a scale from 0 to 100.

homeostasis   An ideal state of internal balance, in which all body systems are working and interacting in an appropriate way to sustain life.

hydrogenated fats   Unsaturated fats with hydrogen added. These are also called trans fats and are considered unhealthy.

hypertension   Also known as high blood pressure, a condition in which the blood pressure in the arteries is chronically elevated.

kuzu   Kuzu is a thickener made from the kudzu plant. The plant root is dried and flaked.

lycopene   A red pigment found in plants and is part of a large class of plant compounds called carotenoids.

macronutrients   The three main macronutrients are protein, fat, and carbohydrates.

metabolism   The chemical processes that occur within a living organism in order to maintain life.

micronutrients   As opposed to macronutrients (protein, carbohydrates, and fat), micronutrients are comprised of vitamins and minerals, which are required in small quantities throughout the body to sustain metabolism.

mirin   A kind of rice wine that has a low alcohol content. It is commonly used in Japanese or Asian foods.

miso   miso is a term used for fermented soybean paste. It originated in Japan and is considered a staple in their diet.

nutrient dense   The amount of nutrients you get from a food, given the number of calories.

omega-3 fatty acids   Are considered essential unsaturated fatty acids. They are necessary for human health but the body can't make them so you have to get them through food. They are found mostly in fish, such as salmon, mackerel, halibut, sardines, and tuna, and seafood such as krill and algae, and some plants and nuts.

phytonutrients   Nutrients derived from plant material that have been shown to be necessary for sustaining human life.

tahini   A vegan sesame seed paste used in many ethnic cuisines.

tamari   Tamari is made with more soybeans than ordinary soy sauce, resulting in a smoother, more complex flavor. It originated in Japan.

trans fats   The common name for unsaturated fat with trans-isomer (E-isomer) fatty acid. In other words, it has hydrogen added to it.

triglyceride   A type of fat found in your blood that is a major source of energy and an important measure of heart health.

vagar   A vagar is a type of sauté in which spices are cooked in oil or butter. This technique helps release the flavor of the spices before other ingredients are added.

whole foods   Foods that are unprocessed and unrefined, or processed and refined as little as possible, before being consumed.

Glycemic Index Values of Food

The Glycemic Index or GI index is a ranking of carbohydrates on a scale from 0 to 100 according to the extent to which they raise blood sugar levels. It measures how much your blood glucose increases after eating. The glycemic index range is as follows:

Low GI = 55 or less

Medium GI = 56 – 69

High GI = 70 or more

Glycemic Index Table

Category	Name	GI Score
Vegetables and Beans		
	Baked beans, 4 oz.	48
	Black beans, 4 oz.	30
	Kidney beans, 3 oz.	27
	Lima beans, 3 oz.	32
	Navy beans, 3 oz.	38
	Pinto beans, 4 oz.	45
	Soybeans, 3 oz.	18
	Beets, 3 oz.	64
	Tomato sauce, 1 oz.	49
	Peas, 3 oz.	48
	Sweet corn, 3 oz.	48
	Broccoli, celery, mushrooms, cauliflower, 3 oz.	10–25

continues

Glycemic Index Table   (continued)

Category	Name	GI Score
Breads		
	Banana bread, 3 oz.	47
	Dark rye, 1.7 oz.	51
	French baguette, 1 oz.	95
	Hamburger bun	61
	Pita bread, whole wheat, 1 slice	57
	Sourdough, 1 slice	52
	White bread, 1 slice	70
	Wheat bread, stone ground, 1 slice	53
	Whole wheat, 1 slice	69
	Raisin bread, 1 slice	53
	Bagel, plain, 2 oz.	72
	Whole-grain bread	40
	Multigrain breads	45
Cereals		
	Bran flakes, ⅔ cup	75
	Cheerios, 1 cup	75
	All-Bran Kellogg's, ½ cup	43
	Cocoa Krispies, 1 cup	78
	Corn flakes, 1 cup	84
	Corn Chex, 1 cup	83
	Cream of Wheat, 1 oz.	74
	Frosted Flakes, 1 oz.	65
	Frosted Mini-Wheats, 1 cup	58
	Grapenuts Flakes, ¾ cup	80
	Multi Bran Chex, 1 cup	58
	Muesli, ⅔ cup	43
	Oatmeal, old fashioned, 1 cup	48
	Raisin Bran, ¾ cup	73
	Rice Chex, 1¼ cup	89
	Shredded Wheat, ½ cup	83
	Smacks, ¾ cup	56
	Special K, 1 cup	54
	Total, ¾ cup	76

Category	Name	GI Score
Rice		
	Long grain, white, 1 cup	56
	Short grain, white, 1 cup	72
	Basmati rice, 1 cup	58
	Barley, pearled, ½ cup	25
	Instant, 1 cup, cooked	87
	Uncle Ben's, converted, 1 cup	44
	Couscous, ½ cup	25
	Quinoa, 1 cup	35
Cookies		
	Oatmeal cookie, 1 cookie	55
	Vanilla wafers, 7 cookies	77
	Chocolate chip cookies, 1 cookie	64
Crackers		
	Rice cakes, plain, 3 cakes	82
	Stoned Wheat Thins, 3 crackers	67
	Water cracker, 3 crackers	78
Meats		
	Deli meat, 6 oz.	40
	Beef casserole, 6 oz.	55
	Chicken with noodles, 6 oz.	44
Dairy		
	Ice cream, vanilla, 10 percent fat	61
	Low-fat ice cream	35
	Milk, almond, 1 cup	25
	Milk, whole, 1 cup	27
	Milk, skim, 1 cup	32
	Milk, 1 percent, chocolate, 1 cup	34
	Milk, soy, 1 cup	31
	Tofu frozen dessert, low fat, ½ cup	98
	Yogurt, nonfat, fruit, 8 oz.	33
	Custard, ¾ cup	43

continues

Glycemic Index Table (continued)

Category	Name	GI Score
Fruits		
	Apple, 1 medium, 5 oz.	38
	Apple juice, unsweetened, 1 cup	40
	Apricots, 3 medium, 3 oz.	57
	Banana, 5 oz.	55
	Cherries, 10 large, 3 oz.	22
	Cranberry juice, 8 oz.	52
	Grapefruit, raw, $\frac{1}{2}$ medium	25
	Grapes, green, 1 cup	46
	Kiwi, 1 medium	44
	Mango, 1 small	55
	Orange, 1 medium	44
	Orange juice, 1 cup	48
	Peach, 1 medium	30
	Pear, 1 medium	69
	Pineapple, 2 slices	66
	Plums, 1 medium	69
	Prunes, 6	29
	Raisins, $\frac{1}{4}$ cup	64
	Tomatoes, 1 small	15
	Watermelon, 1 cup	72
Pasta		
	Fettuccine, 6 oz.	45
	Linguine, 6 oz.	46
	Ravioli, meat, 4 large	39
	Macaroni, 5 oz.	45
	Spaghetti, wheat, 6 oz.	41
	Spaghetti, white, 6 oz.	44
	Tortellini, cheese, 8 oz.	50
	Vermicelli, 6 oz.	35
	Lasagna, beef, 6 oz.	47

Category	Name	GI Score
Snacks and Chips		
	Pretzels, 1 oz.	83
	Potato chips, 14 pieces	54
	French fries, 4 oz.	75
	Popcorn, light, microwave, 3 oz.	55
	Sponge cake, plain, 1 slice	46
	Snickers, 2 oz.	41
	Vanilla wafers, 7 cookies	77
	Pop Tarts, chocolate, 1 tart	70
	M&M's chocolate candy, peanut, 1 oz.	33
	Granola bar, chewy, 1 oz.	61
	Corn chips, 1 oz.	72
	Graham crackers, 4 squares	74
Drinks		
	Coca-cola, 12 oz.	77
	Gatorade, 8 oz.	78
	Flavored soft drink, 12 oz.	63

Body Mass Index (BMI) Chart

The Body Mass Index (BMI) is a number based on both your height and weight. It is used to help determine the degree to which a person is overweight and assesses their total body fat. The normal BMI is 20 to 25.

Table of Body Mass Index (BMI) *

Your BMI>	19	20	21	22	23	24	25	26	27	28	29	30	31	32	33	34	35	36	37	38	39	40
Your Height		Good Weights									Increasing Risks											
4'10"	91	96	100	105	110	115	119	124	129	134	138	143	148	153	158	162	167	172	177	181	186	191
4'11"	94	99	104	109	114	119	124	128	133	138	143	148	153	158	163	168	173	178	183	188	193	198
5'	97	102	107	112	118	123	128	133	138	143	148	153	158	163	168	174	179	184	189	194	199	204
5'1"	100	106	111	116	122	127	132	137	143	148	153	158	164	169	174	180	185	190	195	201	206	211
5'2"	104	109	115	120	126	131	136	142	147	153	158	164	169	175	180	186	191	196	202	207	213	218
5'3"	107	113	118	124	130	135	141	146	152	158	163	169	175	180	186	191	197	203	208	214	220	225
5'4"	110	116	122	128	134	140	145	151	157	163	169	174	180	186	192	197	204	209	215	221	227	232
5'5"	114	120	126	132	138	144	150	156	162	168	174	180	186	192	198	204	210	216	222	228	234	240
5'6"	118	124	130	136	142	148	155	161	167	173	179	186	192	198	204	210	216	223	229	235	241	247
5'7"	121	127	134	140	146	153	159	166	172	178	185	191	198	204	211	217	223	230	236	242	249	255
5'8"	125	131	138	144	151	158	164	171	177	184	190	197	203	210	216	223	230	236	243	249	256	262
5'9"	128	135	142	149	155	162	169	176	182	189	196	203	209	216	223	230	236	243	250	257	263	270
5'10"	132	139	146	153	160	167	174	181	188	195	202	209	216	222	229	236	243	250	257	264	271	278
5'11"	136	143	150	157	165	172	179	186	193	200	208	215	222	229	236	243	250	257	265	272	279	286
6'	140	147	154	162	169	177	184	191	199	206	213	221	228	235	242	250	258	265	272	279	287	294
6'1"	144	151	159	166	174	182	189	197	204	212	219	227	235	242	250	257	265	272	280	288	295	302
6'2"	148	155	163	171	179	186	194	202	210	218	225	233	241	249	256	264	272	280	287	295	303	311
6'3"	152	160	168	176	184	192	200	208	216	224	232	240	248	256	264	272	279	287	295	303	311	319
6'4"	156	164	172	180	189	197	205	213	221	230	238	246	254	263	271	279	287	295	304	312	320	328

BMI Under 19 Underweight
BMI 19–25 Healthy Weight
BMI 26–30 Overweight
BMI 31–39 Obesity
BMI 40 and Above Extreme Obesity

Note: This table is the industry/gold standard for BMI. I do not have permission directly but it is widely used and published freely.

*Table is referenced from: Contemporary Diagnosis and Management of Obesity. George A. Bray, Copyright ©1998, Handbooks in Health Care Co.

DASH Diet Shopping List

Following is a list of food items that serve as the foundation for your healthy DASH pantry. These items supply many of the ingredients you'll need to prepare the recipes, so stock up for those dishes and any number of nutritious variations.

Grain Products

Barley

Brown rice

Flours (whole and unbleached)

Millet

Oatmeal

Popcorn

Quinoa

Whole-grain bread

Whole-wheat flour

Whole-wheat pasta

Whole-wheat crackers

Herbs and Spices

Chile powder or other chile

Cinnamon, nutmeg, cumin, turmeric, curry, allspice

Ginger, fresh

Fresh and dried oregano, sage, savory, thyme, paprika, rosemary, onion powder, marjoram, garlic powder, etc.

Mustard, prepared and powdered

Parsley, fresh; cilantro, fresh; basil, fresh

Salt substitutes, including lemon-pepper, Bragg Liquid Aminos, tamari seasoning, reduced sodium soy sauce, celery salt

Beans and Lentils

Dried legumes (navy beans, chickpeas, pinto beans, kidney beans, lentils, split peas)

Tempeh

Tofu, soft and firm

Dairy Products

Butter (unsalted, organic)

Cream (organic)

Eggs (omega-3 rich, farm raised, organic)

Milk (low fat, skim, or raw)

Yogurt (plain, low fat)

Nuts, Seeds, and Butters

Nuts (walnuts, almonds, pecans, cashews, filberts)

Nut butters (almonds, cashew)

Seeds (flax, pumpkin, sunflower)

Seed butters (tahini), sunflower

Vegetables and Fruits

Dried fruit (raisins, figs, apricots, dates, prunes)

Fresh greens (kale, collards, cabbage, broccoli)

Frozen vegetables (peas, beans, broccoli, cauliflower, etc.)

Frozen fruits

Garlic and onions

Seasonal vegetables

Seasonal fruits

Tomato sauce, paste, and canned vegetables, no salt added

Fats and Oils

Coconut oil

Extra virgin olive oil

Flax seed oil

Grape seed oil

Nut oils (sesame, walnut)

Vegetable or lecithin spray

Meats

Canned tuna (packed in spring water) and salmon

Fresh fish (deep sea, wild caught)

Lean beef, poultry

Sweeteners

Barley malt, rice syrup, maple syrup

Blackstrap molasses, unsulphured (high in magnesium)

Honey (locally grown and raw)

Beverages

Cereal-grain beverages, such as dandelion or chicory

Coconut milk

100 percent fruit and vegetable juices

Leaf and herbal teas

Nut milks (almond, cashew)

Seasonings, Condiments, and Other

Bragg Liquid Aminos

Chicken or vegetable stock (preferably homemade)

Curry paste

Miso

Seaweed (hiziki, dulse, wakame, nori, agar)

Tamari or soy sauce (low sodium only)

Vinegar (apple cider, rice, wine, balsamic)

DASH Resources

In case you may be interested in reading scientific articles about the DASH diet, following is a list you may find interesting. More articles are being written all the time, so if you wish to find more recent selections you may search online by visiting Medline (www.nlm.nih.gov/medlineplus/highbloodpressure.html).

DASH Menu Plans

Here are a couple of resources for help with simple meal planning.

From **Meals Matter**:
www.mealsmatter.org

From the **Mayo Clinic**:
www.mayoclinic.com/health/dash-diet/HI00046

From the **U.S. Department of Health and Human Services**:

www.nhlbi.nih.gov/health/public/heart/hbp/dash/new_dash.pdf

www.iom.edu

www.heart.org

Information for Consumers

Here are some resources for help with understanding and using the nutritional facts label on products.

From the **U.S. Food and Drug Administration**:
www.fda.gov/Food/LabelingNutrition/ConsumerInformation/

From **Mrs. Dash**:
www.mrsdash.com/downloads/GetSmartAboutSalt.pdf

From registered dietitians who work at the **USDA's National Agricultural Library** as nutrition information specialists:
www.nutrition.gov

From the **United States Department of Agriculture**:
www.choosemyplate.gov

From **Fruits and Veggies More Matters**:
www.fruitsandveggiesmorematters.org

DASH Studies and Research

- Appel, L. J., M. W. Brands, S. R. Daniels, N. Karanja, P. J. Elmer, and F. M. Sacks. "Dietary Approaches to Prevent and Treat Hypertension: A Scientific Statement from the American Heart Association." *Hypertension* 47, 2 (2006 February): 296–308.

- Appel, L. J., T. J. Moore, E. Obarzanek, et al. "A Clinical Trial of the Effects of Dietary Patterns on Blood Pressure." *New England Journal of Medicine* 336 (1997 April 17): 1,117–124.

- Elmer, P. J., E. Obarzanek, W. M. Vollmer, et al. "Effects of Comprehensive Lifestyle Modification on Diet, Weight, Physical Fitness, and Blood Pressure Control: 18-Month Results of a Randomized Trial." *Annals of Internal Medicine* 144, 7 (2006 April 4): 485–495.

- Karanja, N., T. P. Erlinger, L. Pao-Hwa, E. R. Miller III, and G. A. Bray. "DASH Diet for High Blood Pressure: From Clinical Trial to Dinner Table." *Cleveland Clinic Journal of Medicine* 71, 9 (2004 September): 745–753.

- Levitan, E. B., A. Wolk, and M. A. Mittleman. "Consistency with the DASH Diet and Incidence of Heart Failure." *Archives of Internal Medicine* 169, 9 (2009): 851–857.

Index

Y–Z

Yeast-Free Zucchini Cheese Bread recipe, 263
yogurt, Herbed Yogurt Bread recipe, 265-266

Zesty Broccoli with Garlic and Ginger recipe, 230
Zesty Date Nut Loaf recipe, 255-256
Zesty Strawberry-Rhubarb Pudding, 278-279
zucchini
    Crustless Zucchini Quiche with Fresh Herbs and Spices recipe, 248-249
    nutrient benefits, 249
    Yeast-Free Zucchini Cheese Bread recipe, 263